Experience

JEROME
AND THE VERDE VALLEY

Legends and Legacies

THORNE
ENTERPRISES

P.O. Box 2371
Sedona Arizona 86336

(Dedication)

To the Miners, Lawmen, Pioneers,
Pony Soldiers and People of the Sun,
and to my fellow authors
who wrote so eloquently about them.

Editor Aliza Caillou
Historic Maps Reed Thorne
Cover and Interior Design Ron Henry Design
Printed by: Northland Printing

ISBN: 09628329-IX   paperback

Library of Congress Catalog Number 90-071606

Copyright 1990 Thorne Enterprises Publications

II

TABLE OF CONTENTS

THE LAND OF THE ETERNAL SUMMER

What was the Verde Valley like eons and eons ago? Who were its first inhabitants? How have waves of civilization and geological turbulence affected its environment? What was the character of the people who carved their niche into its history? And perhaps most compelling of all, what does the future hold for the valley the Spanish referred to as "The Land of the Eternal Summer?"

Eight authors combined their talents to answer those questions. Each brought to the task an individual approach by virtue of their diverse backgrounds and interests. Through their original research and personal interviews, they have gathered detailed information which is being presented for the first time in this book. Unquestionably, a single author would have needed many years to achieve a similar result.

What were the greatest impressions stamped upon the minds and hearts of these authors once their task was finished? For one, all agree that this valley is as intriguing today as it was when first formed over two billion years ago.

The Verde River - This river remains a valuable lifeline for the People of the Verde Valley. Photo by Alan Caillou.

One has only to hike into the valley's canyons to witness the geological mystery of its "mountain islands and desert seas." Or, look for the "bathtub" rings in its rocky layers and realize that they are mute testimony to at least four, and possibly seven different oceans whose waves splashed against the "shores" of present day Jerome. Eons ago, the Verde Valley was the western-most point of the continental United States.

For perhaps 10 million years, an enormous lake dominated its landscape, and giant animals fed along its shores. Small, nomadic people raced through grasses taller than their heads in pursuit of these animals, some of which stood more than two stories high.

The legends of these ancient people tell of a time when the mountains reached the sky, and how First Woman emerged from a place now called Montezuma Well. She was the grandmother of First Man, who heroically fought these giant monsters, and made the land safe for all the people.

Centuries would pass before another kind of monster imposed its two-headed self upon the Verde Valley, one that ravaged the land and nearly exterminated the ancestors of its ancient folk. That two-faced monster was Greed and Hate. He plundered the region in search of its vast mineral riches, caring nothing about the en-vironmental and human devastation he left in his wake. One of the worst examples of his environmental destruction occurred during the copper mining era of Jerome.

When gold was discovered near present day Prescott, soldiers were sent to protect the mining interests from the Indian people whose lands and way of life were threatened. Settlers who arrived in the Verde Valley would not have survived without the protec-tion of these soldiers. All endured unbelievable hardships and horrors as the blood of thousands of men, women and children - red and white - soaked the soil of this verdant valley during the turbulent years following the Civil War.

After the Indian Wars ended, more settlers arrived and another episode began. Some were miners, many of whom had spilled over the mountains and hills from the Prescott area following the Arizona gold rush. Most were cattlemen and farmers. Almost all were poor. The majority had left the East in hopes of providing a more promising future for their children in a place where the land was free, and a lack of education or money was of little consequence.

With few exceptions, life on this frontier proved lonely and dangerous. Doctors were rare. Infants and mothers died regularly during childbirth, and entire families could be wiped out in days during one of the numerous epidemics which swept the area.

This was a time too, when individuality was at a zenith. Arizonans have always been a 'stand on your own feet' kind of people, a characteristic which prevails today. This individuality took many forms, but it was best exemplified by the mining moguls of Jerome who epitomized the American dream. They started with little and through ingenuity and hard work, amassed some of the greatest fortunes of the nineteenth century.

The outlaws, the lawmen, cowboys, miners and prostitutes were individuals as well. So was most of the population of the Verde Valley. Their legends and legacies remain, and from them we have much to learn and much to preserve.

The geological and human history of this valley is alive and ever changing. The wind still sculpts the canyon walls, the river still erodes the land. Until recently, nature has been the dominant force. Is it possible that man will take over her power?

If so, it is the responsibility of all who live here to see that this power is never abused. If we become watchful caretakers over this land, it will continue to be "The Land of the Eternal Summer."

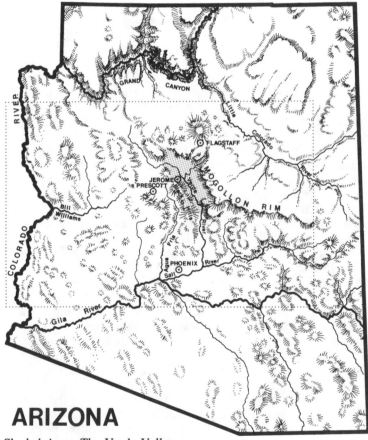

ARIZONA

Shaded Area: The Verde Valley
Dotted Box: Enlarged on page 100

Chapter One
THE VALLEY
How Nature Created It
By James Bishop Jr.

n that clear air each angle and crack cast a shadow
as harsh, clean, sharp, real as the rock itself -- so
that though they endured for tens of millions of
years, the rocks and cliffs hold the illusion of a
terrible violence suddenly arrested, paralyzed in time,
latent with power.
                                                    Edward Abbey

Think of the Verde Valley as a great book or a marvelous symphony. It asks us to fathom it on many different levels from all directions. Yet despite the dedicated efforts of legions of artists, cowboy poets, explorers, scientists and writers to capture its essence, the haunting beauty of the place remains beyond reach, now as then a place of myth, lore and great imaginings.

To be understood even in flashes it must be smelled, felt, tasted and seen. Even then this mysterious region, at once lush and arid, barren and beautiful, harbors rocks, rills and templed hills which mask answers to questions modern Man has yet to learn to ask.

A stream-blessed no man's land, strange, spooky and full of wonders, the valley sprawls between the rugged, faulted mountains to the south and the jagged pine-topped escarpment of the soaring Colorado Plateau to the north. And it's been here for a long, long time.

Witness the fact that the Verde Valley's oldest rocks near Jerome, the onetime copper boomtown, are estimated to be 1,900 million, that is 1.9 billion years old. What a startling statistic in an era when political and telecommunication events are measured in miniseconds and instant gratification for millions of citizens, takes too long.

Think of it! As Flagstaff-based geologist Wayne Ranney has observed, a billion tiny sand grains side by side would stretch over 615 miles -- all the way from Flagstaff to San Francisco, California. Viewed another way, a billion minutes would take one back to the time of Jesus, while a billion years summons up a distant epoch when blue-green algae was planet Earth's most advanced form of life.

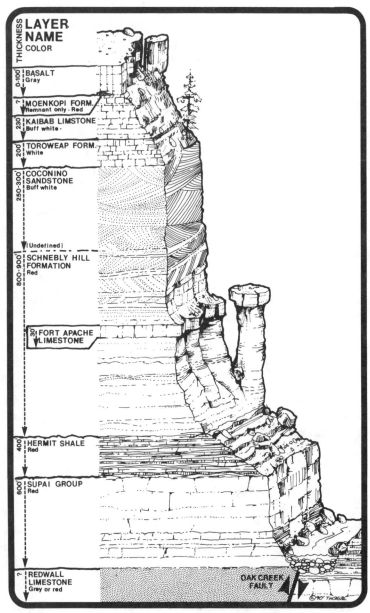

LAYER
NAME
COLOR

THICKNESS

0-100'	BASALT	Gray
?	MOENKOPI FORM.	Remnant only - Red
230'	KAIBAB LIMSTONE	Buff white -
200'	TOROWEAP FORM.	White
250-300'	COCONINO SANDSTONE	Buff white
	Undefined	
800-900'	SCHNEBLY HILL FORMATION	Red
30'	FORT APACHE LIMESTONE	
400'	HERMIT SHALE	Red
800'	SUPAI GROUP	Red
?	REDWALL LIMESTONE	Grey or red

OAK CREEK FAULT

©'90' THORNE

Stratigraphic Column of Oak Creek Canyon Area Near Sedona.

An amazingly turbulent geologic legacy, the Verde Valley is today a high desert grassland which measures some 30 miles long and up to 20 miles wide, veritably teeming with flora, fauna and Homo Sapiens.

And as new visitors are invariably surprised to discover, this region of Arizona is nourished by hundreds of fresh springs and by the Verde River, called El Rio de Los Reyes, (The River of the Kings) on the first Spanish maps beginning in 1610. But it wasn't always thus; about 1.8 billion years ago, the valley, reports Ranney, "was unrecognizable as we know it now."

Imagine a land perched along the vast coast of the ancient North American continent some 325 million years ago. Visualize a white sandy beach, long and wide, awash with the foaming waters of rolling ocean combers.

Imagine volcanoes erupting on the ocean floor, spewing red hot lava in all directions. Picture 300-foot-high sand dunes shaped by hurricanes and fierce blowing winds. Envision slices of the earth's crust colliding together here, breaking apart there and sliding past one another somewhere else nearby and imagine a range of mountains 25,000 feet high.

Then as now, water played a powerful role. Over hundreds of millions of years, the story the valley tells today in the layers of the rocks is one of a succession of sub-tropical seas that were in deadly competition with the unforgiving desert climate, neither force ceasing its herculean effort in the eternal struggle to dominate the other.

No wonder geologists journey to this valley from all over the world to study its turbulent history and that of the vast, haunting Colorado Plateau. "A geologic wonderland," writer-geologist Halka Chronic calls the region, "an open textbook of geology."

These scientists travel here to marvel at the mountain islands and the desert seas and at the Verde River itself that enters the valley from the north at Paulden through a narrow, deep canyon, then wanders southward out of the valley toward Phoenix. And no wonder they exult at discovering the cold canyon waterways which feed the river -- Sycamore, Oak Creek, Beaver Creek and West Clear Creek and are stunned to learn that the Verde watershed drains 6,646 square miles and collects an average 464,253 acre feet of water per year.

Although one need not be a trained geologist to appreciate this wonderland, some academic structure can be helpful [see chart]. To geologists, the formative years almost 2 billion years ago is known as the Pre-Cambrian era, a tumultuous period of mountain building, faulting and uplift characterized by oceans flowing through and departing, depositing sediments that are still clearly visible in the red rocks of Sedona and in many nearby canyons, the ones known and those still unexplored.

The Paleozoic era came next, beginning about 500 million years ago, and lasting for about 260 million years. To students, this period is known as the Age of the Fishes whose fossil traces can be seen today in the rocky nooks and crannies where hikers wander in the valley and among the red rocks.

The Mesozoic period or the Age of the Reptiles followed, a time when giant dinosaurs wandered hungrily on layers -- now eroded away -- of the Mogollon Rim to the north and east of the Verde Valley, there to feed on lush grasses and down on the banks of great lakes between where Sedona and Cottonwood lie today. Thus the stage was set 63 million years ago for the the Cenozoic period, the Age of Mammals which has lasted until today.

See through the eyes of Spanish explorer, Antonio Espejo, in 1583, the first documented European to pass through the Verde Valley. From where Clarkdale is today, he gazed out across vast sea of high green grass as far as his eye could see.

Jerome historian, Dr. James W. Byrkit, suggests that the adventurous Spaniard, who'd ridden down from the Hopi Mesas guided by marathon runners, likely observed a remnant of a giant lake reduced to riverine marsh and bog cut through by rivulets digging sharp and winding incisions in the valley floor near present day Clarkdale. The river murmered through canopies of ash, sycamore, walnut and cottonwood trees as it does today, although now merely a sliver of its former self.

Espejo gazed upon the same sandstone mesa escarpments to the north and east where Sedona and the Village of Oak Creek are today, then as now intriguingly layered with the weathered deposits of yesteryear.

Likely, he was struck by the whitish-grey limestone formations left by as few as four and as many as seven rising and receding seas, all still visible to the curious in the remote recesses of Sycamore Canyon, on the West Fork of Oak Creek, in the Clear Creek Wilderness area and through the bathtub rings up and down the red rocks.

Although Espejo and his men lacked any scientific basis for their speculations, their curiosity must have been aroused by the sweep and majesty of the valley, and by the remains of networks of pit houses and pueblos constructed by the First Americans, beginning with wandering Nomads some 10,000 to 15,000 years ago. Out of these people grew the Cochise Culture, which dominated until a few hundred years before Christ.

In turn, they were followed by the ancient ones, the Anasazi, around the time of Christ; then the Sinagua arrived early in the first century. Soon they learned to grow beans, corn and squash, to spin cotton, then for reasons which remain mysterious, vanished. Soon thereafter, the Yavapai and Apache dwelt in the valley during the time of the middle ages in Europe. Their descendents still reside there today.

Indeed, a tourist driving up I-17 toward the Verde Valley from the Prescott exit at Cherry Road can share Espejo's experience and those of the non-anglo visitors earlier. The runaway truck ramp five miles to the north of that exit marks the highwater mark of the last great lake, or playa, that filled the valley.

Picture large mastadons grazing on the mesas that were then many thousands of feet higher, with giant condors soaring above them. Imagine, too, hundreds perhaps thousands of great beasts feeding on the banks of a vast lake -- camels, bears, giant mammoths and elephant-like creatures, three-toed horses together with carnivores such as the jaguar, American lion and ring-tailed cat.

This is no Hollywood fantasy. Scientists have catalogued the tracks of some of these creatures cast in stone near Montezuma castle. Though rarely observed, the fossil evidence provides us with an extraordinary glimpse of life in the Verde Valley before the great ice ages.

It was a tapestry reminiscent of the grassy savannahs of east Africa with large animals roaming everywhere at will. Solid confirmation of that past came with the discovery in 1981 of the huge tusks and jaws of a stegomastadon, unearthed at the Phoenix Cement Plant at Clarkdale in 1981.

Elsewhere, the footprints of large elephants were uncovered in shallow water limestone. As John Parsons, Verde Valley eco-historian observes, "Those prints recall a day probably five million years ago when those huge creatures were searching for food along the shoreline."

Scientific speculation about the creation of the great lake around which those great creatures wandered centers on a massive and violent upthrust which occurred perhaps 8 million years ago and created mountains surrounding the valley which were many thousands of feet higher than they are today.

This explosive event had the effect of damming the ancestral Verde River which had been flowing north for perhaps 30 million years. Today one can use real scenes to imagine what the valley looked like seven or eight million years ago. "Travel to Hawaii to watch the eruptions of Mount Killawea pouring hot, molten lava into the sea, destroying every growing thing in its path. That's what was happening in the Verde Valley in those days," Parsons declares.

How long did the giant lake, or series of lakes, last? Some two million years ago, according to a consensus of geologists, relentless wind and water erosion finally crumpled the large natural dam at the southern juncture of the valley, somewhere between where Camp Verde and Childs are today.

Summarizes Ranney: "The lakes slowly emptied, leaving only the river itself and such small streams as Beaver Creek, later to be the lifelines for the residents of Montezuma Castle and Tuzigoot. The Verde River surged into its modern course, heading southward."

By the time the first nomads arrived, having armed themselves with stone-tipped sticks to slay game for food, the legacy of the

Feeding time five million years ago on the shores of the Verde Lake.

giant oceans and lakes was clearly visible. They found deep beds of salt which would later provide the Sinagua in the 16th and 17th century with a commodity for trade.

These first nomads also saw huge beds of limestone, the last remains of the lakes and oceans. This limestone, known as the 3,000 foot thick Verde Formation, can be seen by sharp-eyed observers in the rocks around the Verde Valley today. Visitors are advised to look for the bathtub rings on the rocks for signs of the departed oceans.

The Nomads, the very first visitors, likely encountered a valley of high grass and marsh. Imagine them as smallish people running through grass over their heads, in pursuit of elephants and camels as tall as two-story buildings.

To first maim and then slay the wild creatures, the bravest nomads would chase them into box canyons. Their companions would climb to the canyon rim to roll huge rocks down on their heads.

Then even braver young warriors would creep into the canyon and try to slice the tendons of their intended prey with sharp chunks of that hardest of hard rocks, obsidian. Moments later other warriors would move in to slice the arteries of their prey.

Indeed, so powerful was the volcanic activity in the valley that as they feasted on their slain prey, these nomads's eyes burned with volcanic ash, their noses flared by the pungent smell.

About 11,000 years ago, the hunting days of these nomads ended: Mammoths and most other large animals became extinct. Were they hunted into oblivion? Was there a severe climatic change? Was there a cosmic event such as meteorite bombardment which darkened the skies and destroyed their food and habitat? Despite the efforts of science, this mystery has never been solved. The fossil legacy may be enough. It is for generations to come to decipher that past, and for future generations to analyze their findings.

Take studies of the Kaibab Formation, which is the whitish grey layer visible around Sedona - and up at the Grand Canyon rim. They suggest, several geologists conclude, that the chert layers in the formation originated from sponges that grew on the ocean floor about 265 million years ago.

These sponges had spicules in their bodies, needlelike strands or rods of silica. When the sponges died millions of these spicules fell to the ocean floor, and over time formed sheets of silica which hardened and solidified into a dense chert which proved to be resistant to erosion. "Believe it or not," Ranney asserts, "it's those ancient blooms of sponges that have preserved the ancient scenery of the Mogollon Rim in Arizona."

Down through the centuries nature continued as the most powerful force shaping the contours of the valley, whittling away with her great chisel, her flowing waters and high winds shaping the buttes and mesas to her liking.

Then came Modern Man in the early 1860s -- and cattle. Before long overgrazing of the tall grass, the bogs and marshes became commonplace and degradation of the land began, a process that continues until today.

Next came the pothunters beginning in the late 19th century. They pillaged the ancient ruins for bones and artifacts, a shameful sacriledge which also continues to this day, although now it has become illegal.

Still the Verde River runs, but as more and more people come to the valley, seeking a piece of "old Arizona" the demands placed on the water and the land threaten its existence.

Oldtimers recall that the lush growth of sycamore and cotton-wood, which still flourishes on the floor of the valley, once grew and thrived in the Salt River Valley where the City of Phoenix is today.

Fortunately for the future prospects of the valley's air, land and water, the day of the "frontier ethic" is fading. As theologian Thomas Merton put it three decades ago, "the pioneer, the frontier culture here, is a product of the wilderness, but at the same time it's destroyer. His success as a pioneer has depended on the ability to fight wilderness and win, victory being reducing wilderness to something else - a farm, a village, a road, a mine, a railway, a city -- and finally an urban nation."

Modern threats feared by current valley dwellers include toxic chemical waste dumps, gravel mining operations in the Verde River bed and projected residential and commercial building developments atop underground water reservoirs.

By any measure, the valley is under siege as rarely before from powerful interests that would drain water tables, plow under the remaining marshes, build on hillsides and natural washes.

But also as never before, citizens are calling for more responsible resource management to prevent further environmental damage to the valley, damage which reached its peak during the copper mining boom in the late 19th and early 20th century. Then the air was filled with acrid, yellow smoke, killing off all vegetation, including pines and oaks. Even after all these years, little grows on Jerome's Cleopatra Hill, the scene of decades of copper mining.

Nowadays there's an invisible but perceptible current among the populace regarding the future of the valley; the land has survived incredible natural tumult and will again.

Along with the bison of the Great Plains and the spotted owl in the forests of the northwest, it will be Man that is endangered if his definition of progress is total development of the Verde Valley. In future, Man has no choice but to live in harmony with the land.

At first, it was the economic rewards contained within the rocks of the Verde Valley that drew attention. Tomorrow it could be the spiritual and educational rewards rocks give which will satisfy the needs of the majority.

It is Ranney's hope, shared by increasing numbers of others, professional scientists, historians and local people alike, that as people discover the rich diversity of the Verde Valley's past, as they begin to understand the agents of change, they can limit the way the hand of man will fall on this place.

Meantime, nature's hand is everywhere and the pulsing heart of the Valley, "the El Rio de Los Reyes," still runs free over rocks from the basement of time.

BIOGRAPHY

James Bishop, Jr. is a Sedona-based freelance writer who is at work on a book about the late Edward Abbey. A Newsweek correspondent for 19 years, he also held posts at the White House and at the Rand Corp, Santa Monica, Ca.

Chapter Two
YAVAPAI - THE PEOPLE OF THE SUN
Before and After White Contact
By Kate Ruland-Thorne

HE YAVAPAI LEGEND OF WHEN EVERYTHING BEGAN - Ahagaskiaywa (Montezuma Well) is where the people came out first. This lake has no bottom and underneath, the water spreads out wide. When a baby is born, it is given its first bath in this sacred water.

Long ago, there was no water in this lake. People were living down there. They lived in the inner earth with their gods, and it was a good life. But, as the anglos know, there is always a 'bad apple' in the box. They had a chief, who was a bad man and did evil things to his daughter (incest?). His daughter got mad and made him very sick. Then she made a flood and tried to kill all the people.

The chief knew he would die soon and that a great flood might come. He told the people to burn his body when he died and not let coyote get his heart. He told them to put dirt over his heart and something would grow from it.

When the chief died, the people did as they were told and corn grew up from the place where the dirt was on the chief's heart. This corn grew real big. It grew up along side of the well. When the flood came all the people including the quail, rabbits and other "people" climbed up the roots of the corn. This flood stayed level with the well.

All the ones who climbed out of the well spoke Yavapai (the Apache say they spoke Apache). But the animals wanted to exterminate the people. When the Creator heard this, he fixed it so they could no longer speak Yavapai.

After some time there was another flood, (there is only one flood in the Apache version). This happened because the people did something wrong. This flood was made of rain water. Only two people were saved in this flood...a girl and a woodpecker.

When this flood started, the people put this girl in a hollow cottonwood log. They put food in the log with her and put a small hole in it. The woodpecker made the hole in the log so she could breath.

The people told the girl to not eat all the food right away. They told her the flood would raise her up and she would hit the sky. "You will hear the noise when the log hits the sky," they said. "Just lay still, and you will get out in the end."

The girl stayed in the log 40 days and 40 nights. The girl stayed in there all the time. When the water was gone, she was in a high place people today call Sedona.

The girl came out of the log. Her name was Komwidapakwia which means, 'Old Lady White Stone.' She brought a white stone with her which protected her. She was First Woman, and the Yavapai people all come from her. She came out at Sedona where all Indians come from. It is said that her footprints were left in the wet earth (in Boynton Canyon) and those foot marks were proof that this story is so. (Present day Yavapai recall seeing these footprints, which they say were dug up and removed, possibly by archaeologists some time ago.)

Woodpecker led Komwidapokwia to a cave in a place now called Boynton Canyon. There he left her all alone. One morning she ran over to Mingus Mountain and lay down before the sun came up. When the sun came up, it hit her inside. She went to a cave where the water drips down and lay down again. The water hit her inside too. This self-insemination (virgin birth?) from the sun and purified spring water made her a baby, a little girl. (The Apache say Changing Woman had a daughter by the water, and later her daughter had a son by Father Sun.)

When the little girl came of age, her mother told her to go to the mountain and to the cave and do what she had done so they could have more people. The girl did as she was told, but the sun in the sky and the water in the cave recognized her as their daughter, so they would not go inside of her.

The girl went home and told this to her mother. Her mother said she would fix it. The mother tried many different ways to fix it, but had many problems. As a last resort, she decided to trick the sun and the water. She took her daughter back to the mountain and lay on top of her. When sun came out, he started to hit her inside, but the old lady moved over and the sun hit her daughter inside instead. She took her daughter to the cave and tricked the dripping water in the same way. This way, the girl got pregnant and had a little boy. He was called Sakarakaamche (Skara-ga-umja). The lesson in this is what women will do to get what they want. (The Apache version does not involve doing anything to "trick deities.")

When the boy was still a baby, a bad (pre-historic) eagle killed his mother. This eagle lived high on a mountain and ate anybody under him. He saw Sakarakaamche's mother gathering wild spinach one day. He grabbed her and took her to the top of his mountain and fed her to his two eaglets. So the little boy was raised by his grandmother.

In those days, there were all kinds of giant (pre-historic?) animals and they were bad. Grandmother worried that one of them would eat Sakarakaamche, just as the giant eagle had eaten his mother. Grandmother did not realize that Sakarakaamche had special medicine man power and ways given to him by the spirits. He also had great courage given to him by Father Sky, ruler of the rain, the clouds and the lightning. (The Apaches say he was sent by Grandmother to Father Sun to learn things and be tested. When he proved himself, he was given special powers to use to conquer the enemies.)

Many times, Sakarakaamche ventured out despite his grandmother's warnings and each time he would meet one of these dangerous animals. Every adventure ended with Sakarakaamche tricking then killing one of these enormous and terrible monsters. After awhile, he had killed almost

Montezuma Well - place of origin for the Yavapai and Tonto Apache. (photo by Kate Ruland-Thorne)

Montezuma Castle - ancient Sinagua dwelling, believed to be inhabited by the sacred spirits of the Gaan and the Kakaka. (photo by Kate Ruland-Thorne)

everything that was mean, cut it into pieces and scattered the pieces around. Finally all that was left was the monster eagle.

One day, Sakarakaamche asked his grandmother why he didn't have a mother. At first his grandmother would not answer and walked away. He asked all the different animals to tell him, too. But like grandmother, they were afraid that if he knew, he would be killed just like his mother was. It was a quail who finally told him the truth about his mother after Sakarakaamche had fixed his broken bones.

The quail said, "you want to know why you do not have a mother? You had a mother, but there is a bad one around...an eagle up there on that high mountain. He killed your mother."

Sakarakaamche was mad when he heard this. He went back to his grandmother and asked why she hadn't told him about his mother, and said he was going to kill that eagle. His grandmother began to cry. She told him she was afraid to tell him about the eagle because she didn't want him to be killed, too.

The young hero set out to kill the evil eagle, who soared through the heavens like a jet airplane. He knew that this monster would be the hardest of all to kill. All the little people like the dove, the mouse and the hummingbird decided to help him with this difficult task.

The dove told Sakarakaamche he must first kill the giant bull (prehistoric buffalo?) so he could use the bull's blood to trick the monster eagle. This giant bull lay on a hill between Cottonwood and Sedona, (the Apaches say they know where the exact location is even today), and every time this bull saw smoke from a campfire, he would run to it and eat everyone in sight.

Dove told Sakarakaamche to go to the river and get four weeds called okadya. He was to use them as arrows and shoot them into the four directions. These sacred arrows contained prayers that requested protection from the Four Directions. This Sakarakaamche did. The first arrow hit a pine tree and it burned. When the bull saw the fire, he ran towards it. Then the giant bull saw another pine tree burning and ran there...then another and another. Four times. Each time the bull ran away, the animals were digging a tunnel to the place where the giant bull liked to lay. All of the digger animals helped - squirrels, badgers, rats, gophers and mice. The badger was the last to make the tunnel bigger. (In Apache legend, only the gopher gets credit.)

When the bull came back, he was very tired and lay down. Mouse went into the tunnel and started to take the hair off the bull where the bull's heart was.

"What are you doing that for?" asked the bull.

"My kids are going to be cold and I want to make a bed for them with your warm fur," answered the mouse.

"All right," answered the bull, and he rolled over so the mouse could get all the fur away from where his heart was. When this was done, hummingbird hurried to get Sakarakaamche to tell him the bull was ready.

Sakarakaamche was given a red hot spear and told to go into the tunnel. All the creature people ran away because they knew what was going to happen. The young hero found the giant bull's heart right under his shoulder. He plunged the hot iron into the bull's heart, then ran back through the tunnel.

The bull had long horns and tried to kill Sakarakaamche by pushing

his long horns into the tunnel. *But Sakarakaamche escaped unharmed just before the giant bull fell down dead.*
Sakarakaamche cut the bull into many pieces and made a vest of his blood. He dipped grape leaves into the bull's blood and tied them to the vest. Then he put a handle on the vest and laid down to wait for the giant eagle to find him. (The Apaches say he crawled into the bull's stomach and covered himself with guts to cushion the eagle's drop.)
Soon the eagle came. Three times the eagle tried to get Sakarakaamche, but the boy saw to it that the eagle missed. On the fourth try, the boy turned so the eagle could grab the handle on his vest. The boy wanted to make sure that the eagle was very tired by the fourth time.
The eagle carried him up to his nest and told his two children that he had brought them something to eat. Then he flew away to find other meat. When the baby eagles tried to eat the blood vest, Sakarakaamche whispered shhhh...this frightened them because the vest sounded rotten, so they wouldn't eat it.
Soon the giant eagle returned and asked why they hadn't eaten the food he had brought them. They said, because the food made a shhhh noise and they didn't know why. "Oh, that's because it is rotten," answered the giant eagle. The giant eagle picked Sakarakaamche up and shook him around, then threw him back on the rocks. "It's all right to eat him now," he told his children. Once again the eagle flew away.
When the children approached Sakarakaamche, he whispered shhh once more, and the children backed away. Then the boy asked the eagle children to tell him where their father sat when he came to the nest. They told him their father sat on the rim and looked around and around, then put his head under his wing and went to sleep.
"All right," said Sakarakaamche, "don't say a word when he comes back or I will kill you."
When the giant eagle returned, he sat on the rim and looked around and around, then put his head under his wing and fell asleep. As soon as he was asleep, Sakarakaamche cut the eagle's head off and threw it down the cliffs. These cliffs were so high they were half-way to the sky. Then he waited for the mother eagle to return and did the same to her. After that, he chopped off the heads of the children and threw them down the cliffs as well. It is said that you could hear the sound (thunder) for miles as each of the eagles hit the sides of the cliff.
Now with all the evil monsters dead, the young hero must find a way to get down the high, high cliffs. He sang the sacred Blackroot song, taught to him by his father, the sky. Slowly, slowly the high cliff began to go down. He saw an old woman bat gathering food below, and he called to her for help. She came to help him, but told him not to open his eyes. About 3/4's of the way down, he opened one eye, and they crashed to the ground. This broke the old bat-woman in pieces. Sakarakaamche gathered her up, and using his medicine-man power, put her back together again. She danced away, singing her gathering song. In the Apache version, "Killer of Enemies" then sets out to find his wife, who was kidnapped by Coyote.
The high, high cliffs where Sakarakaamche killed the monster eagles is now called Bell Rock, and the red mountains around Sedona are all that is left of the many monsters slain by this hero boy. It is the blood of these monsters that has caused the rocks to be red. The Apaches say

*that the beads from necklaces worn by all the people who were killed
by this giant eagle, can still be found scattered throughout this sacred
place called Bell Rock.*

A similar verson of this Yavapai origin legend is shared by the
Apache. Legends such as these could only be told on autumn and
winter nights by the grandfather of the family. The origin story
took four nights to tell, and the preferred place to tell the story
was in a cave with a good fire burning.

Grandfather sat on one side of the fire while his audience completed the circle. Just before daylight, all the children and young
men and women listening to the story were told to run to a stream
and wash their face in the icy water.

"You must do this because this is a great story," said grandfather,
"and if you do not, you will get crippled feet (arthritis)." This also
helped create a diversion for the children.

It was dangerous to tell stories on summer nights, because spiders,
bears and snakes would listen and bite the listeners. (The Apache
say they are messengers who should not hear because they tell the
forces who might come back to haunt you). In the winter, these
creatures were hibernating, so it was a much safer time.

The Yavapai divided time into the four cycles of creation. Cycle
One was when the people emerged from the underground at
Montezuma Well. It terminated when a great flood welled up and
covered the land.

Cycle Two was the time of the goddess Komwidapokwia
(K-weden-buk-wea), "White Shell Woman" who survived the
second flood and the story of her grandson, Sakarakaamche
(Skara-ga-umja), the heroic monster slayer who made the world
safe for all the people.

The Apache version refers to First Woman as "Changing Woman"
(Echa-na-glese) and First Man, Naa-ye-nes-yane, or "Killer of
Enemies".

Cycle Three was terminated by a great world fire, when Coyote
stole the sun and burned up all the vegetation around the world.
It was also the time when both men and animals spoke the same
language, according to the Apache.

Both Apache and Yavapai consider their fourth cycle to be the
present one.

"Our legends are teaching tools for the children," explains Mabel
Dogka, oldest living member of the Yavapai-Apache Tribe of
Clarkdale, Arizona. "They teach right and wrong, to be proud,
to be strong. . .things that apply to life. When you think about these
legends, you look at yourself and decide whether you are bad, good
or a damn fool."

Coyote figures prominently in numerous Yavapai tales as a
trickster, a wise person, or more often - a fool. The Apaches say
Coyote is not wise, he only wishes he could be. Although the

Yavapai Raider - before white contact. Illustration by David Sine.

Apache and the Yavapai originate from two different language groups, they share not only a similar origin legend, but through the centuries their close proximity caused them to borrow a great deal from one another's lifeways, customs, and culture.

THE YAVAPAI - PEOPLE OF THE SUN

by Kate Ruland-Thorne

Nicha stood on a rocky ledge outside his gwa'bun-yav (round house) and looked eastward into the valley below. He watched the first rays of dawn reach like crimson fingers across the horizon. In ten more dawns, his people would go on the warpath - a dream that night confirmed this.

For hours, Nicha had been awake thinking about this dream. Long after his camp had gone to sleep, he was alerted by owl that the Kakakas (ga GA gas) would pay him a visit. These dwarf-like, supernatural beings, who traveled through the air from mountain to mountain, only visited Wipukapaya's (Red rock people) who had 'medicine-power.' Nicha was one of those people. Nicha was the bamulva padje of his clan, a high man who had killed enemies with his bare hands.

Nicha fingered his medicine necklace. Necklaces such as this one were sacred, ordained by Sakarakaamche (Skara-ga-umja), First Man, in the long, long ago. Each stone on the buckskin string represented a natural power - wind, hail and rain. Nicha's fingers lingered over the most sacred stone of all - the turquoise. He loved this stone best. Because Nicha was a great warrior, a turquoise bead threaded on buckskin, also was suspended from a perforation in his nose. This symbol of honor was granted only to warriors who had performed heroic deeds and had lived at least 30 winters. Nicha was well-respected by his people.

A medicine man, now past mid-life, Nicha stood tall and lean against the rising sun. His strong, sinewy arms raised heavenward as he greeted Father Sun. Like the other men in his tribe, he wore his long hair bundled at the back of his head. All of his people wore bangs. Two eagle feathers stood upright in the back of his hair.

At the first stirring sounds of his camp awakening, Nicha directed his attention toward his hut. His stomach rumbled. He hoped his wives would start the cooking fires soon. One of them would have to help the other women tend the mescal roasting in a pit nearby. The sweet smell of its steam had permeated the air for three days and nights. Nicha's mouth watered as he thought of tasting this delicious, fibrous staple later that day. Its sweet juices always added flavor to all other food.

Suddenly a wind whipped Nicha's breech clout and raised a dust funnel. His eyes narrowed at this important omen. A whirlwind, no matter how small, signaled the passing of a ghost. Was this the spirit of a slain warrior, he wondered, one who had been killed recently by the 'Red-earth people'? These traditional enemies had raided Nicha's camp several weeks before. The Kakakas told Nicha in his dream that revenge was in order, and this time the Wipukapaya would taste great victory.

Nicha thought about which young warriors he would send as a war messenger to gather other Abaya - People of the Sun - for the dance of incitement. Without this important ceremony, the raid would not be blessed. He knew he must choose warriors who could run for days without stopping, ones who knew how to find the camps of the Tolkepaya (Tolk-a-baya), 'Scrub-oak-people,' and the Kwevikopaya (Kwev-ka-paya) 'Elsewhere people.' These warriors must be capable of not dropping the cane crosses they would carry as they ran, crosses adorned with sacred eagle feathers. Only young warriors with the ability to speak eloquently could be chosen, ones the other clans recognized and respected because of their heroic deeds.

Nicha walked to the gwa-bun-yav of Ma'wa'tha (Bear) and told him to prepare for a long run. He must alert the Kwevikopaya who were gathering mescal in the Mazatzal Mountains. Then he awakened Gwa-gor'rda (Wolf) and told him to prepare to run to the camp of the Tolkapaya who were hunting qwa-qa (deer) in the mountains of the Four Peaks. Wolf and Bear were honored to have been chosen for this important journey.

After the young warriors left, Nicha announced to his people that they must prepare for visitors. Extra gwa-bunyavs must be built and more mescal gathered and cooked in the deep pit fires. Young children were sent off with sticks to find rabbit and wood rat holes. The children were well-trained in how to route out these delicacies, and hit them with their sticks before they could get away.

Young women were sent into the woods with burden baskets strapped to their foreheads. Some would gather wild food plants and berries, others the fruit of the saguaro which was made into a refreshing drink. Still others must find more mescal, uproot it, and clean off its spiny leaves before bringing it back to bake in the fire pits.

Menstruating women, and new mothers were forbidden to scratch themselves with their fingers while the mescal was cooking, and no sexual intercourse was permitted during this important time. Otherwise the mescal might become bitter, or not be properly cooked. Only certain people, or special animals such as Nicha's dog, were permitted to light the cooking fires for the mescal.

Old warriors set to work preparing extra poison for the arrowheads to be used in the raid. Ingredients such as rattlesnake venom, spiders, centipedes, the abdominal parts of 'long-winged bees' and walnut leaves were brought forth in buckskin pouches. It took several days after these were pulverized and mixed to achieve their proper potency. After the mixture was placed in a cleaned-out deer gut, it was buried in hot ashes. A day later, it would be removed and allowed to dry. Warriors carried the poison in the bottom of their quivers. When poison was needed, they simply spread the dry mix on a flat stone, moistened it slightly, and rubbed the arrow head into the deadly concoction. A wound from such an arrowhead caused a lingering and painful death.

Grandmothers, skilled in building shelters, moved out into the lower hillsides of their mountain retreat to search for ocotilla branches. They took their granddaughters with them to help scrape the branches of spines and brace them against a circle of stones embedded in holes. Each hut was given at least three layers of thatch. The girls helped gather the grasses and sticks needed for the thatching. In this way, they learned how to build a proper hut by helping their grandmothers.

Within a few days, Bear and Wolf returned with other People of the Sun. The feasting and dancing began immediately. Warriors painted their faces black, then dipped their fingers in red pigment mixed with deer fat and marked their cheeks with red zig zags. Each painted his bangs red as well. These were the colors of war, which also served as a camouflage at night. Within days, they would attack their enemy, the 'Red-earth people,' sometime before dawn.

Nicha decided they would use war clubs on this raid, and save their poison arrows in case of actual combat. If skillful enough, combat would not be necessary. A surprise attack usually rendered their enemy helpless.

Some warriors asked permission to bring back women and children as prisoners. Nicha agreed. He knew they would be of use to the elderly ones who needed them for slaves. Booty would not to be taken. There were stringent taboos against keeping anything that belonged to the dead.

Nicha was determined to kill the mighty leader of the Red earth people. This leader's scalp could only be taken by Nicha, or another medicine man. They alone were sanctified and immune from the poison of the dead.

As Nicha's dream foretold, the People of the Sun did return victorious. Nicha carried the scalp of the enemy leader on the end of a stick, and paraded it during the victory dance. When the dance was over, Nicha threw it away.

Following the dance, the warriors joined in four days and four nights of purifying themselves in a sweat bath. During this important ceremony, none touched meat or salt. Several times each day, they washed their mouths out with soap root and yucca. By the time the purification ceremony ended, each was relieved to have been cleansed in mind, body and soul of all evil incurred during their successful raid.

Once purified, The People of the Sun returned to their designated boundaries and once gain resumed their daily routine. Mothers and wives gathered foods and medicinal plants, fathers hunted, grandfathers told the stories of the people since the time of First

Man and First Woman, grandmothers trained the children in their daily tasks, and watched over them while their parents went about their centuries-old activities.

Who are these People of the Sun? Where did they come from, and where are they today? The answers to these questions are both surprising and shocking.

WIPUKAPAYA

The People of the Red Rocks

Since ancient times, they called themselves Wipukapaya (wee-buk-abaya), 'the people of the red rock country.' The region they roamed on their hunting and plant gathering forays remains among the most lush and magnificent in the Southwest. Before white contact, the Wipukapaya were a wealthy people in terms of their environment. Unfortunately, the land that sustained them for centuries would be coveted by a more powerful and war-like tribe from the East...the English-speaking Americans.

But Americans were not the first white people the Yavapai encountered. Two hundred years before American contact, Spanish white men from Mexico entered the Verde Valley in search of fabled 'lakes of gold,' and a route to the South Seas. From 1583 until 1604, there were four separate Spanish expeditions, Espejo (1583), Farfan (1598), and Onate (1598 & 1604). Each noticed the Yavapai wearing turquoise crosses symbolizing the Four Directions, a symbol that was also tatooed on their foreheads. Although these Yavapai crosses had double, horizontal bars, the Spanish assumed they were Christian crosses. They also noted in their diaries that turquoise meant gold and silver was probably nearby. Of course, this was true. A mother lode of these precious metals would eventually be discovered deep in the mountains around present-day Jerome.

The Spanish had no difficulty in recognizing the differences in language between the Yavapai and Western Apache, whom they also encountered. The Spanish referred to the Yavapai as "Niojoras," or "old - a people who have been here a long time." They also described them as 'friendly,' and the land they lived in 'full of abounding game, fertile valleys and tall pines.' The Yavapai looked upon the Spanish as 'gods' and for this reason decided it was wise to be on friendly terms with them.

The Spanish viewed the Apaches of Central Arizona in a different light. They named them 'Tonto,' which means 'crazy.' These, the Spanish decided, were a people to be feared, because they gave no quarter, and were ferocious and courageous fighters. The 'Tonto' called themselves *Inde*, the people, and this particular sub-tribe was known as Dil-ze'e. Their two Verde Valley clans were called Chein-chii-ii (Red Rock Clan) and Yaa-go-gain (White Land Clan, named for the limestone formations of their Verde Valley home.)

Neither the Yavapai nor the Tonto Apache took kindly to the next white intrusion into their territory, the mountain men.

Ewing Young, accompanied by his protege, Kit Carson, was the first to trap beaver along the Salt and Verde Rivers in 1828. Although Young and his party of 75 men would gather over $20,000 worth of beaver pelts, they paid a dear price for their gain when 24 of their party were ambushed and killed by 'hostile Indians, who were either Apache or Yavapai. The mountain men didn't bother to make distinctions.

But, the Spanish explorers and the mountain men never posed unalterable threats to the lifeways of the Yavapai or Tonto Apache people. White encroachment would not became life-threatening until 1863.

Prior to that date, the Wipukapaya, (Northeastern Yavapai), roamed freely within their designated boundaries from Bill Williams Mountain to the San Francisco Peaks in Flagstaff, through Oak Creek Canyon and Sedona to the Black Hills near Jerome. They are related to two other regional Yavapai groups; the Tolkepaya, (Western Yavapai), who roamed the Bradshaw Mountains southward to the Yuma area; and the Kwevikopaya, (Southeastern Yavapai), whose area encompassed the Mazatzal, Four Peaks and Superstition Mountain region, possibly all the way to the Catalinas near Tucson. Until 1860, the combined boundaries of these three regional groups and their Tonto Apache neighbors, encompassed over 10 million square miles of territory. If any "A-baya" dared cross his boundary into the land of one of his enemies, ie: the 'Blue-green water people' (Havasupai), or the 'Red earth people' (Walapai), it was considered an open declaration of war.

Anthropologists and archaeologists do not agree on where the People of the Sun's ancestors came from. Many believe their prehistoric ancestors arrived in Central Arizona approximately 12,500 years ago during the first migration of people from Asia across the Bering Strait. They refer to these early ancestors as the Patayan, a hunting and gathering people related to the Iroquois. Others contend they are from the Hakataya cultural tradition with traits basic to all cultures with a "Yuman" root. These people come from the lower Colorado River and Lower California areas.

A variation of this concept presently being discussed suggests the Yavapai are descendants of the Southern Sinagua. This theory is supported by Yavapai oral history and legends, which contend their people lived here during the time of the huge mammoths and mastodons, giant beavers, grizzly bears, camels, horses and large bisons, animals that began to die off by 6,000 B.C.

If the A-baya were not related to the Sinagua culture, they at least co-existed peacefully alongside them. By the 1400's, however, following a 23 - year drought, archaeologists suggest they began to violently displace their pueblo neighbors after joining forces with their Apache neighbors, who had arrived in the valley in approx-

Sun Shield - Symbol of the "People of the Sun" a petroglyph commonly found at ruin sites in the Verde Valley. (photo by Hardy Quaid)

Pre-historic dwelling site near Sedona believed to be Southern Sinagua, possible ancestors to the Yavapai. (Sharlot Hall Museum [SHM]).

21

imately 800 A.D.

The Apache referred to the Cliff-Dwellers as Naa-it-kede (old, or ancient people). Apache and Yavapai legends say that they lived peacefully alongside these prehistoric neighbors, but trouble arose after the Cliff-Dwellers stole their property. This resulted in warfare which forced the Cliff-Dwellers to move to the Salt River Valley. Eventually these people became known as the Pima and Papago, and forever afterwards were considered the traditional enemies of the Yavapai and Apache tribes.

Both the Yavapai and Apache share the origin story which pinpoints exactly where their people came from - Montezuma Well near Sedona. It was here, they say, that First Woman emerged after the Great flood. Following a virgin birth, her grandson, First Man was born and grew up to battle huge, pre-historic monsters (mammoths?) in order to make the land safe for all The People who followed.

Modern ethnologists document the Yavapai as a Yuman-speaking group whose ancestral cousins are the Mojave, Yuma, Cocopa, Walapai, Havasupai, and Maricopa people. The Yavapai beriended and sometimes intermingled with their later-arriving Western Apache neighbors, in particular the Yaa-go-gain Clan. After both tribes were forced to move to the San Carlos Reservation in the 1870s, intermarriage was even more frequent. As a result, it was mistakenly assumed the Yavapai belonged to this linguistically Athabascan group.

"The Apache came here to this land after we did," explained 86 year-old Mabel Dogka, the oldest living member of the Yavapai and Apache tribe. "We mixed with them. That's how we became known as Yavapai-Apache." Mabel's own mother was a Tonto Apache and her father was a Yavapai.

The reservation where Mabel grew up includes portions of Camp Verde (established in 1904) and Clarkdale (1969) in the Verde Valley. In the early days, her people wintered in caves, but switched to brush-covered wikiups...or "teepee houses" as Mabel Dogka calls them, during warmer months. She remembers living in a wikiup as a child.

"When I was a little girl, I remember white people saying, 'why do those people have haystacks everywhere'?" They thought our houses were haystacks.

Prior to the arrival of the white people, the Yavapai and Tonto Apaches easily roamed within the boundaries of their territory in search of ripening plant products and game. There were cordial relations, and on rare occasions, intermarriage between the Wipukapaya and the Ah-why-gas (Yavapai word for Tontos). Not only did these Yavapai and Apache groups sometimes intermarry, but they hunted and gathered freely across one another's boundaries, and often cooperated in war.

In the Sedona and the Verde Valley, the two bands which were

Ancient Yavapai Petroglyphs near Sedona. Photos by Kate Ruland-Thorne.

made up entirely of Apache and Yavapai were the Red Rock Clan (Che'in chii ii) and the White Land Clan (Yaa go gain). These people intermarried over several generations. The Yaa go gain were located along the Mogollon Rim, and Red Rock Clan boundries were Oak Creek, Dry Beaver Creek and Wet Beaver Creek and southward to the west side of the Verde River.

It is interesting to note that the Yavapai and the Apache in these two bands maintained their own distinctive language and identity. The children from these mixed-marriages simply became bilingual, and identified their descent through their mother. Therefore, the child of a Yavapai mother and Apache father was considered a Yavapai.

Among the Apache and Yavapai, war was a well planned affair, usually precipitated by a dream. The warrior's medicine man predicted the happenings to come through his dreams. Very few activities were initiated without 'dream power.'

Rarely did the Yavapai or Apache kill a blood relative or clan member. Such an act was looked upon with horror. It would be like taking vengence upon one's self, they believed. Only if a relative or clan member committed the most heinous crime of all - incest, was such a killing excusable.

The topic of incest was avoided entirely in the belief that it, and all irregular sex practices between members of the opposite sex were linked to witchcraft, which made it all the more repulsive. Anyone caught in such acts was marked for life and ostracized. Families remained very tight-knit in cases like this. The most repugnant of all incestuous relationships were between a father and daughter, or brother and sister, and considered much worse than between blood or clan relatives. In these cases, the culprits were put to death.

It was everyone's duty to look after one another's children. Killing or abusing one's child was the ultimate act of brutality and another inexplicable abnormality. Considering modern day anglo news stories that are rife with such practices, it seems our highly touted 'civilized' society could gain greatly by studying the historical mores of these 'primitive' folk.

The usual purpose behind raiding and warfare was to avenge the death of a kinsman. The Yavapai did not take booty after a raid as the Apache customarily did, because they believed they might be haunted by the dead person's personal effects. The taking of booty in the Apache mind, was all part of the revenge. After white contact, booty, in particular guns and livestock, became the primary reason behind raids by both the Yavapai and Apache. By the mid 1800s, these items signified wealth. Revenge took on greater meaning by then as well.

The other hated enemies of the Tonto and all three Yavapai groups were the Pima and Maricopa tribes. Together, (or separately), the Yavapais and Apaches often made vicious raids upon the Pima,

Maricopa, Havasupai and Walapai...and visa-versa. All of this warring and raiding accelerated their eventual downfall when in the 1870's, General George Crook took clever advantage of these old animosities and employed peaceful Indians as Scouts to help him hunt down and subdue those he considered "hostiles.".

There are no known oral histories of war taking place between the Yavapai and their neighbors, the Navajo and Hopi. With these tribes, the Yavapai were cordial, and carried on a lucrative and beneficial trading activity. The Hopi and Navajo people particularly valued the finely tanned deer and antelope hides of the Yavapai, which they readily traded for their own highly prized blankets. Three Navajo or Hopi blankets was a common price for one tanned Yavapai buckskin.

The Apache, however, had periodic run-ins with the Navajo, their Athabascan-speaking cousins. Whenever the Apache went to Hopi to trade, they crossed the high desert at night in order to avoid any conflict with them.

Traditionally, the Yavapai hunted qwa-qa (deer) before daylight. Hunters were barred from sexual intercourse for two days prior to the hunt in order to conserve strength for the long distances they had to run. Runners with the greatest endurance were sent out to track the deer. Often this took all day. Eventually, the deer were driven into a line of men who surrounded them in a narrow canyon and killed them with bows and arrows.

Other times, runners decoyed the deer by blowing on a piece of grass in their mouth. This whistling sound imitated the cry of a fawn. A lone hunter might wear a stuffed deer head while he stalked the deer. When the stalker came upon a buck, he angered it by striking the horns of his mask against a bush or tree. When the buck charged, the hunter shot him with a bow and arrow. After rifles were introduced, the deer-head mask was seldom used.

The hunter skinned his deer from chin to anal opening, then down the inside of each leg. Once removed, the hide was waved toward the east for good luck. No part of the deer was thrown away. Its brains were preserved by cooking it in ashes, and spread over grass where it dried into a cake-like substance. Brains were essential for tanning the hide. Every portion of the animal's body had a particular use and purpose. All buckskin clothing was made by the men of the tribe, and their skill in tanning hides was widely acclaimed. Many rolls of buckskin showed that a man was a good hunter and that his family was wealthy.

Most of the garments worn by the Yavapai and Apache people were made from these supple hides, fashioned by the men with deer-bone awls and sinew thread. In warm weather, a buckskin breechcloth and knee or hip-high moccasins were the only attire worn by the men. The Apache's knee-length moccasins were distinctive because they had flap that went up over their big toes, which protected them on long runs.

Yavapai and Apache women were required to be more modest. They wore two pieces of buckskin. The piece in front was worn like a butcher's apron, suspended by "spaghetti string" type straps that hung from shoulders to ankles. The back piece hung from the waist down and was tied with a belt. These sleeveless dresses were fringed along the sides, and worn both winter and summer. A Navajo or Hopi blanket served as a warm cape when the weather turned cold. Moccasins for both men and women usually reached to their knees. Children wore nothing at all in the summer months until they turned nine or ten years old.

After her first menses, a young woman was tattooed on her arm, chin and forehead with cactus needles and charcoal pigment. Her mother was never allowed to perform this delicate operation. Meat eating was forbidden until the tattoo healed. Men were tattooed as well.

Mabel Dogka's face and arm were tattooed in this manner when she was a young girl. "This is a clan design, and if you are Apache, it shows which clan you belong to," explained Mabel. All Wipukapaya used tattoo marks to identify themselves.

Eyelids of both sexes were painted black with a stick. Women painted their faces with white earth for certain sacred dances. During the hottest part of the summer, both sexes painted their faces red to prevent sunburn.

The Yavapai and Apache used red mineral pigments (from hemetite, or iron ore) on their faces for social dances as well. The whole face was painted red and decorated with zig-zagging lines scraped by three fingers down the cheeks.

Warriors sometimes painted their hair white before war. Red paint mixed with deer fat, or the bone marrow of the deer, kept the faces of all ages warm and free of chapping in winter. It served as an excellent, primitive 'cold cream.'

Boys 10 to 12 were required to run in winter mornings with a snowball under their armpits in order to prevent the growth of axillar hair. This helped them become 'strong men.' Boys were instructed to drink water only in the morning and evening in order to train them to go without water while hunting or on the warpath. Another endurance lesson required young boys to run to the top of a mountain or hill without stopping. Growing boys were not fed much in order to toughen them for abstinence on long journeys. Most of the young boy's training was done by grandparents or the elders of the clan who tried to prepare him for the harshness of life. A boy was not considered a man until he was at least 25 to 30 years old. A 'man' was one who could shoulder responsibilities. If he was particularly wise, or had reached an 'age of wisdom,' he was automatically referred to as a Ba-yan. This was a term he could not convey upon himself. Only others who admired his wisdom could decide to refer to him in this way.

Mabel Dogka's gwa-bun-ya-v (Apaches say ko-wa), or "teepee

house," was not carried from place to place as the people traveled, but freshly built at each new camp. At traditional campsites, to which the people returned each season, the old homes simply required a new cover. Otherwise, it took one person a full day to build a new hut. The openings to the hut always faced East. When someone died, the hut and all the belongings were burned to the ground. This was done to keep the dead person's spirit from staying around, and to free it to go on to the next world. The dead person's name was not mentioned again thereafter.

The people cooked their food by either boiling it in pots, or in pitched baskets buried in a rock hole. Often they roasted it on hot coals and ashes, or cooked it in 'earth ovens'(bar-b-que pits). Baked mescal, gathered in April and May, was frequently eaten at each meal. Meat was dipped in its hot, sweet juice.

In order to uproot the mescal, (agave or Century plant), the women and children used a digging stick which was driven beneath the mescal with a stone. Once the plant was turned upside down, its thick spiny leaves were cut off with a hunting knife. Each family would dig and trim about a dozen plants and carry them to camp in their burden baskets. Not just any plant was dug out, much trial and error was involved in finding the sweetest ones. Also, the people knew not to clear-cut an area. Always some plants were left, so that they might grow and feed them again.

The agave heads were cooked in a fire (or bar-b-que) pit dug four feet deep in the ground. Placed on top of hot stones, the agave was then covered with a thick coating of grass and earth. Cooking of the mescal began at noon and lasted until dawn of the second or third day. It was pounded into cakes and wrapped in wet buckskin.

Mabel Dogka remembers eating mescal as a child and enjoying it. "When it's first removed from the fire-pit, it is sweet like candy," she recalls. "After you peel it, you have to chew it, because it has lots of fiber. It's like eating sugar cane. After it dries and hardens, it can make your tongue raw if you chew it too long. My people don't even know what mescal is anymore," she adds.

"I remember, as a child, getting rabbits out of a hole," she continued. "We'd all stand around (these were usually group hunts) with sticks. When the rabbit tried to run, we were supposed to hit it with our sticks. I remember I would just holler and couldn't hit it. My parents got after me for that. We did the same with wood rats. We stole from them, too. They packed a lot of pinions in their burrow, and we would take these nuts from them. Sometimes we ran into rattlesnakes doing that."

Snakes were not eaten by either the Yavapai or Apache people, nor were frogs, turtles, fish, ducks or geese. . .or anything that smelled fish-like. These taboos were given to them by the ancients. Large black and yellow caterpillars, and wasp nests were considered a delicacy, however.

Although primarily a hunting and gathering people, the Yavapai and Apache did cultivate corn, squash and beans. Tobacco, which grew wild, was gathered as well. Men were not allowed to smoke tobacco until they were over 40 years old. The legend the Yavapai tell about tobacco is that it was once a very beautiful woman, jilted by a young man. In order to spite him, she turned into tobacco so that all men would desire her forever.

The Gaan (Ga-han), a class of supernatural beings, are the sacred people who possess the power of the Great Spirit Himself. They are equivalent to the Hopi Katchina, and the Navajo Yei, and revered as a significant religious figure by both Yavapai and Apache people.

It is believed that the Gaan were builders of certain prehistoric ruins, and still are the inhabitants of specific mountains and cave sites. Presently, these sacred sites include the Four Peaks area and Montezuma Castle, among others. They share the San Francisco Peaks with the spirits of the Hopi Kachinas and the Navajo Yei. Like the Hopi and Navajo mythological tales, the Gaan are believed to still live on earth as spirits. They are called upon to help during times of war, sickness and death, or special ceremonies. They once were a people who left because of disrespect and went in search of places where eternal life could be lived without evil things.

Because a Gaan is a spirit, he has no known face. When the Crown Dancers imitate him, they wear masks with eyes only. This is because these spirits might be a relative from the past - or now. The Apaches do not share this belief, but consider the Gaan deities.

Yavapai legends claim that their people learned about the Gaan from the Kakaka, or 'little Indians.' (The Apache learned about the Gaan from the Almighty, they say). The Kakaka are known to have dwelled in all sacred ruin sites throughout the Verde Valley. The doors of the ruins were designed for a very 'small' Indian. It was the Kakaka who taught the Yavapai all their dances and songs, had the power to foretell the future, and to heal the sick. They often left important messages on the stones (petroglyphs). These little Indians were like the wind - one minute you see them - one minute you don't. They only communicated with the medicine men. When times were difficult, or someone was terribly ill, it was common for the medicine man to gather all the people together to pray for help from the Kakaka.

Even today, these little Indians are never spoken about by the traditional believers among the Yavapai or Apache. To speak of them with non-believers is bad luck. If anyone ever sees a Kakaka, they can be assured they will soon experience their own, or someone elses - death. An exceptionally good, modern day medicine man is still capable of summoning the spirits of these little Indians for help during sacred healing sings.

We know the most significant legend shared by all three Yavapai groups, as well as the Apache, is the legend of their origin from the depths of Montezuma Well. All land surrounding this ancient limestone sink, which extends throughout present-day Sedona to Boynton Canyon, is considered very holy ground, not only by the Yavapai and Apache, but by the Navajo and Hopi people as well.

CIVILIZATION'S INSATIABLE MONSTERS - HATE AND GREED

Almost two centuries would pass between the last Spanish 'entrada' into the Verde Valley and the arrival of the gold-seeking Americans. It was the Americans who first labeled the Yavapai - 'Mohave-Apache.' Perhaps it was because the Yavapai introduced themselves as A-baya, which sounds somewhat like 'Apache,' or because the language spoken by both the Yavapai and their 'cousins' the Mohave was very similar. Whatever the reason, this misunderstanding, deliberate or otherwise, became the root cause of unspeakable hardships and suffering for the People of the Sun from that time forward.

Following on the heels of the gold-hungry prospectors were the settlers. Together, they insisted on protection from the 'Apache.' By 1864, the U.S. Army was building forts throughout Yavapai and Apache ancestral lands.

Initially the Yavapai made every effort to remain on friendly terms with these new interlopers. The chiefs among the Yavapai sent messengers to all their people telling them, "don't fight the white people. If you fight them, more and more will come. They are like water, like ants. They have an ant hill back where the sun comes up. You can't stop them." The chiefs promised the whites they would not fight, but would rather live among them peacefully. But Yavapai land was too rich to share with such a 'primitive people.' In less than 10 years, white efforts to destroy the well-ordered lifeways of the Yavapai and the Apache, and exterminate them as a people, very nearly succeeded.

The end of the war between the states marked the beginning of drastic changes for the Yavapai people, who lived in the heart of what was to become 'gold-rush country.' For the first time they faced a foe more deadly than any imagined, even in their most frightening legends.

In 1864, new recruits, together with hundreds of seasoned veterans, enlisted to fight new foes - the American Indians of the West. Government policy at that time was to subdue, and if necessary exterminate, all tribes who impeded Western settlement and industry.

Soldiers knew that fighting the fierce Apaches of Arizona and New Mexico, required particular skill and heroic fearlessness. For many, the challenge was irresistible. Unfortunately, the peace-seeking Yavapai of Arizona were mistaken for Apaches...or, as the Yavapai tell it...there was no mistake.

"Calling the Yavapai 'Apache' was a very convenient excuse for the

English speaking Americans to kill the Yavapai and take over our land. The Apache fought with guns when the white people wanted to push them out of their lands. So the white people considered them their worst enemies. 'Apache' meant the same as enemies to them. Anyone called Apache could be killed, they said. And the Yavapai were also 'Apache' to them. We Yavapai had no guns. We had only bow and arrow and club. We knew we could not fight army guns with a bow and arrow and club. So our chiefs promised the white people we would not fight with them. But the Yavapai land contained lots of gold and copper and other valuable metals. The land was good for cattle ranching. Along the rivers and springs, there was good land for farming. The white people wanted that land for themselves alone, and the Indians out. By calling the Yavapai 'Apache' they felt it was only all right to kill us and push us off our land." (THE YAVAPAI OF FORT MCDOWELL - No.701 History Grant of U.S Dept. of Housing and Urban Development).

Well respected Arizona historians support this contention. *"The Yavapais were not immediately hostile to the Americans entering their country, but in the early 1860's with the discovery of gold in the region, large numbers of miners and settlers began to move into the valleys prized by the Yavapai as hunting grounds, and after 1865, the white population grew rapidly. When the first clash occurred between the Indians and the aggressive Americans is not certain, but it appears that attacks against the Yavapai were begun by American miners as early as 1860.*" (SMOKE SIGNAL, 1964 by Sidney" Brinkerhoff - author and Assistant Director for Museums at the Arizona Pioneer's Historical Society).

"The recent discovery of gold near the San Francisco Mountains within the District of Northern Arizona, and the flocking thither of many citizens of the United States, renders it necessary that a small military force should be sent to these new gold fields to protect miners from the Indians." (SMOKE SIGNALS," 1972 - Quoted from General James Carlton, commander of the Department of New Mexico in his 1863 General Order −27 by author and historian, Andrew Wallace of N.A.U. who added, "Nothing was said about protecting the Indians from the miners.") It is also worth noting that no gold has ever been found in the San Francisco Mountains. Carlton probably meant Granite Mountain near Prescott.

Between 1865 and 1875, the population of Arizona's 6,000 Yavapai people was reduced to less than 1,000. What follows is a description of signifcant events beginning in 1860 and ending in 1875 which unveils a pattern that strongly supports the premise that hate and greed provoked vicious wars between the Yavapai, Apaches and the Americans, wars which inflicted untold misery and death upon both sides and very nearly exterminated the Western Apache, and the People of the Sun - forever.

THE INDIAN WARS OF NORTH CENTRAL ARIZONA

Told from the Indian's point of view

"Just now our red brethren are awful thick hearabouts. They are seen in the woods, close to town, in the rocks below town, on Granite Creek. . .in fact everywhere. So keep your powder dry and whenever you see an Indian that says, 'Americano mucho bueno. . .' kill him; he don't mean it." (Arizona Miner, July 27," 1867)

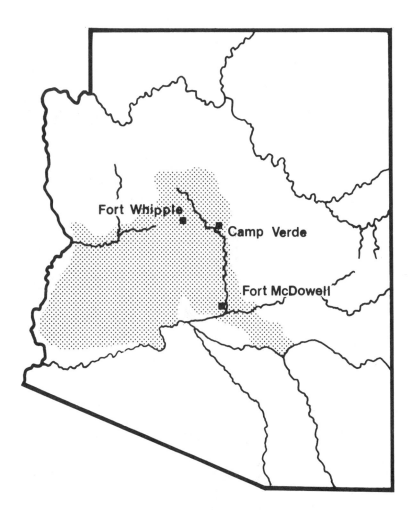

Yavapai Indian Tribe Ancestral Territory (shaded) and Present Day
Reservations (black boxes)

Yavapai warrior with owl feather head dress, 1800s. (Fort Verde State Park [FVSP])

King Woolsey, Rancher, miner and early day Indian fighter. [SHM]

How The West Was Won - Gattling gun at Fort McDowell, c 1890s. [SHM]

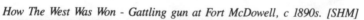

Gold fever! Like a seductive femme fatale, it enticed sane, hard working men into the realm of debauchery and madness. Many abandoned their farms, businesses - their whole way of life - just for the sight of this yellow harlot. Her lure caused men to either abandon, or worse, drag their entire families across mountains and deserts, into the unknown where unspeakable dangers, hardship, and often death was their only reward.

With each new discovery, another 'rush' was on. Beginning in 1849, the rush was first to 'Californey', then to 'Colorady' and by 1863, it was off to 'Arizoney' with a wash pan on my knee.

"If ya stumble on a rock, don't kick it - cash it," was one popular phrase of the time. And, "If ya wash yer face in the Hassayampa River, you kin pan four ounces of gold dust from yer whiskers," claimed others.

Ironically the ones who built the greatest fortunes during this incredible era of greed, were rarely the prospectors. It was the prostitutes, the gamblers, the outlaws, the merchants who supplied goods to the gold and silver camps, and the financiers who sat safely in their plush offices and grubstaked any prospector with a good ore sample in his poke.

The little guy who faced all the dangers, did all the digging and made the discoveries and sacrifices, was lucky if he ended up with the shirt on his back and his scalp still in tact. But even when it was obvious that this 'fever' could be fatal, it was no deterrent to the next rush of prospectors who followed.

In the beginning, only one factor blunted the plundering of the gold fields of North-Central Arizona. This was known as "Apache Land," a dreaded place where death lurked behind every rock, cactus and tree. Of the few who attempted to settle in its vast realm prior to 1860, none succeeded and few returned. The Apache and the Yavapai were its complete masters until the beginning of the 1860s. After the first serious intrusions into their heartland, the Indians discovered they shared only one common purpose with these white intruders - a desire to completely exterminate the other. . .and the war was on.

The Indian people of North Central Arizona had their initial warning of a possible white invasion following the Mexican War and the Treaty of Guadalupe Hidalgo in 1848. Until then, only a handful of mountain men knew anything about their lands, which were acquired from Mexico following this treaty.

Desirous to learn possible routes for wagons, railroads and steamboats through this unknown region, the U.S. Government carefully selected a group of West Point engineers, whom they called the Army Corps of Topographical Engineers, to explore, survey and map this territory. Sitgraeves, Beal and Whipple, all members of this elite corps, would be among those who left an indelible stamp upon the face of Northern Arizona and the Verde Valley. . .an area marked by a line known as the 35th Parallel. This 35th Parallel ran like a dagger through the heart of Yavapai and Apache country.

Based on an interview with mountain man Joseph Walker (who would play a significant role later in North Central Arizona), Capt. Lorenzo Sitgreaves was the first of these scientist-explorers to set out from the Zuni Villages in New Mexico in 1851 and cross through Indian country. During his 650 mile trek, Sitgreaves and his expedition of 20 men, an escort of soldiers, and his guide, mountain man Antoine Leroux, suffered from two savage attacks, one by the Yavapais and the other by Yuma Indians. They finally arrived at Fort Yuma on the Colorado River, starving and barely alive. Despite their harrowing escapes, Sitgreaves and his crew managed to map an area that had previously been considered Terra Incognita.

By 1853, Lt. Amiel W. Whipple was sent on a similar expedition which traversed approximately the same area. Before he left, Whipple interviewed a French-Canadian explorer, Francois X. Aubrey, who claimed to have led a wagon train along the 35th Parallel a few months before. Aubrey told a tale of encountering Indians who used rifle balls made of gold, and who traded large quantities of gold for an old mule and some clothes. His story spread like the desert wind across the Southwest to the eager ears of gold-hungry prospectors in California and Colorado.

Despite several shoot-outs with the Yavapais, Aubrey convinced Whipple that the 35th Parallel was the best route for a future railroad, and the Indians along the way were not in sufficient numbers, and could be subdued. By Christmas of 1853, Whipple, his assistant Lt. Joseph Ives, and their crew were camped at the foot of the San Francisco Peaks in the middle of a severe snowstorm.

At the head waters of the Verde River's West Fork, the Whipple expedition turned south and headed toward the Bill Williams Fork on the Colorado, then northwest to the coast of California. Whipple's meticulous survey confirmed that a railroad could be built through Northern Arizona to California, and his maps and reports provided invaluable information for the future developers of the Santa Fe Railroad and eventually, Interstate 40.

Edward Fitzgerald Beal would be the first to build an actual wagon road across Northern Arizona in 1859. His expedition was perhaps the most unique of all. Beal imported camels as his beasts of burden. But due to the outbreak of the Civil War in 1860, Beal's famous road would not be used until several years later.

Despite Whipple's well-marked map and Beal's first wagon road, the whisperings of fortunes in gold in northern Arizona was still not enough to inspire the hoards of prospectors who usually stopped at nothing. "Them injuns is jest too fearsome in Arizony," most concluded. It would take mountain men like Joseph Walker and Pauline Weaver, men who were more Indian than white, to confirm that there was plenty of gold to be found in 'Arizony,' enough to make the dangers pale by comparison.

Unfortunately for the Yavapai and the Tonto Apaches, the first

HISTORIC SITE

PAULINE WEAVER
1800 · 1867

KNOWN AS PRESCOTT'S FIRST
CITIZEN, WEAVER WAS A TRAP-
PER, MINER, ARMY SCOUT AND
FRIEND OF THE INDIANS.
HE WAS CAMPED NEAR THIS
SPOT IN 1863 AND 1864 WHEN
GOLD MINERS AND GOVERN-
MENT OFFICIALS FIRST ENTER-
ED THE AREA.

SPONSORED BY
THE ARIZONA BANK
and
THE ARIZONA HISTORICAL SOCIETY

great bonanzas of this precious metal would be discovered throughout their ancestral lands by these very same mountain men.

In 1861, one of America's great pathfinders, Joseph Walker, led an expedition of 18 prospectors into northern Arizona with the hopes of finding gold around the San Francisco Peaks. Having no luck, and with cold weather setting in, the Walker party continued on to Santa Fe to sit out the winter. There he met Gen. James Carleton, military commander of New Mexico.

Carleton, who had led the successful California Volunteers during the early stage of the Civil War against Southern intrusions into the Southwest, was obviously well acquainted with the reports of the potential gold fields in North-Central Arizona. He very likely had also heard the tales of Indians using golden bullets and wearing ornaments made of gold. Surely he too had been affected by 'the fever' because by the time he met the Walker party, he was ready to share some vital information.

To Walker's great advantage, Carleton directed him to return to Arizona and head straight to an area later known as the Bradshaw Mountains near present day Prescott. Carleton sent along his friend, Albert Benedict, also a member of his California Volunteers, to insure his own interests in any possible mining claims. We know that by 1864, following the Walker Party's great discoveries in the Bradshaws, Benedict was 'overseeing Carlton's mining claims in the area.'

The Walker Party began placer mining near Granite Mountain, Lynx, Turkey and Big Bug Creeks in February of 1863. By May 10, they hit the first of the major 'Mother Lodes' and established the Pioneer Mining District. The gold rush was on to 'Arizony.'

By June 25 of that same year, the Weaver Mining District was established in traditional Yavapai land. Immediately, General Carleton saw to it that the capital of Arizona Territory was moved from Tucson to Prescott, making it the only wilderness capital in United States history.

In his report on the strike at the Walker Mining District, Capt. N. Pishon, First Regiment, Cavalry, California Volunteers, reported to his commanding officer, Brig. Gen. James Carlton: "The new government of Arizona, if it ever will come, will be at the new gold fields, not at the insignificant village of Tucson." As a result, Carlton was motivated to establish Fort Whipple, from which the town of Prescott sprang, on October 23, 1863. "By General Order –27, I hereby establish the Military District of Northern Arizona," wrote Carleton. One can only suspect that his motivation was just a little self-serving.

The Weaver Mining District came next. It was named after the famous mountain man, Indian scout and explorer, Pauline Weaver. Weaver claimed to be half Cherokee. He was a member of the Ewing Young trapping party, which included Kit Carson, when they trapped along the Salt and Verde Rivers in 1831.

Weaver was the first to hit a bonanza of gold on the Colorado River, which initiated the western boom towns of La Paz and Ehrenberg. Concerned about what was happening to his Indian friends during the Arizona gold rush, Weaver taught them the password, "Pauline Tobacco." Early settlers knew that when an Indian used that password, they were friendly Indians. This saved many lives on both sides at first. But, newcomers ignored the password. Their attitude was: "Injuns is injuns, and the only good 'uns is dead 'uns." Eventually Weaver was accidentally attacked by a Yavapai war party in 1867, and wounded. He managed to crawl to Fort Lincoln (later renamed Fort Verde) where he died, some say of malaria and others of the wounds. When the Yavapai learned what they had done, they were deeply sorry and for months afterwards inquired daily about their friend 'Paulino.' The final words written on his tombstone were: "His greatest achievement was as peacemaker between races."

Another man who played a prominent role in gold seeking and the Indian wars was King Woolsey. He reportedly joined up with the Walker Party when they established the first mining district in Central Arizona.

King Woolsey was one of the first to mine along Lynx Creek in the heart of Yavapai country. His ranch, which he homesteaded on the Agua Fria River, provided refuge for many settlers during the Indian wars in Central Arizona.

Gov. P.K. Safford, third territorial governor, designated Woolsey, whom he considered "a prominent citizen of the territory, rancher and owner of several mines," as one others might look to in times of trouble. Woolsey organized citizen volunteers for repeated expeditions against the 'hostiles' and gained fame and popularity as a successful Indian fighter.

The press announced in 1860 that Woolsey led a party of 100 men to prospect for gold, silver and 'copper-colored wretches.' Without exception, these volunteers sought vengeance. The barbarism of one member of the group in particular, Sugarfoot Jack, was so horrifying it even shocked Woolsey.

On several occasions, Sugarfoot Jack tossed crying Indian babies into the flames of burning wickiups during raids, and on one occasion, bounced a screaming toddler on his knee until it stopped crying. When the baby finally smiled at him, he shot it in the face. Nevertheless, Woolsey's comment on the subject of Indians was, "I choose to fight the broad platform of extermination."

Another famous member of the Walker Party who joined in the effort to exterminate Indians in order to preserve his own mining interests was Jack Swilling. Swilling owned several rich mines in Yavapai country. As a member of the famous Walker Party, he too was among the first to discover gold in the Bradshaw Mountains.

A former Confederate officer, Union Scout and "all around hellion," Swilling organized the Swilling Irrigation Company in

1867. His company set to work cleaning out ancient Hohokam canals leading to the Salt River. As a result, farmers once again made the desert bloom with crops, and the city of Phoenix eventually was born.

Swilling bore wounds from his numerous shoot-outs with Indians. These caused him great pain and eventually he succumbed to morphine and whiskey in his later years. He died in Yuma Prison in 1878, accused of a crime he did not commit.

From September to December of 1863, three more mining districts were established in the heart of Yavapai country, and by 1867, over 8,000 mining claims had been recorded in this same district. Indian raids and depredations increased. In order to deal more effectively with their Indian problems, the citizens of Prescott joined in what later became known as the infamous "Pinole Massacre."

In early January of 1864, the Yavapai and Pinal Mountain Apaches were invited to a "peace feast" in which all the food for the Indians was poisoned. Thirty-six Indians died. This affair also has been referred to as the "Incident at Bloody Tanks." It is an event which has attracted considerable attention through the years. Those who participated, defended their actions for the rest of their lives. Charles Poston, a pioneer and Arizona Territory's first Superintendent of Indian Affairs, explained that King Woolsey (who was in charge of his volunteers during this escapade) saw at once that either the Americans or the Indians were to be slaughtered, so he said, "Boys, we have got to die or get out of this." According to Poston, who defended Woolsey's actions, "they proceeded to do the latter by poisoning the Indian's food."

A conflicting report states that the food was not poisoned, the Indians were simply shot outright during the 'peace negotiations.' Regardless of how they were actually killed, the Yavapai realized they had little choice but to join with the Apaches in their war against the whites.

By February 2, one month after the Pinole Massacre, Yavapai Chief Qua-shac-a-ma warned Indian Agent Bennett against any more white encroachment on Yavapai lands.

The Chief told Bennett that white people had come into his country and taken some of the best planting places and told his people not to plant there any more. These whites had also driven all the game out and now his people were starving. The Chief's warnings were ignored and by March 3, the Yavapai began attacking ranches and driving off stock in order to survive.

On April 11, King Woolsey, his volunteers along with soldiers from Ft. Whipple retaliated by attacking Yavapai rancheras. By now, Woolsey had launched his second major expedition of citizens, (mostly miners numbering 100 men, with the view of not only making war on the Indians, but also exploring potential mining sites.) That same month, N.H. Davis, Assistant Inspector General of the U.S. Army, informed General Carlton that Woolsey was a man well fitted to lead companies of miners against the "Apaches."

By June 1, King Woolsey lead yet another expedition against the Yavapai in chief "Big Rumps" Valley. Wah-poo-eta or "Big Rump" was a major war chief who was considered a Yavapai by some and a Tonto Apache by others. His nickname, Chil-chee (Red Ant) was pronounced Delchay by the whites. During his time, he became as notorious a renegade Indian outlaw as Geronimo.

In September of that same year, Captain John Moss succeeded in making a treaty with the Yavapai to keep trails and roads free from their hostile raids. The following month, a memorandum was sent to the U.S. Congress requesting $150,000 to place Arizona Indians on reservations.

"From 1864, the army began building camps and forts throughout Yavapai country. The army wanted the Yavapai to settle in reservations around these forts. They told the Yavapai they would give them food, cloths, horses, cattle wagons and houses. First the Yavapai believed them and went to Camp Date Creek and Fort McDowell. But when the people were there, they found they did not get what the white people promised them. There was very little and poor food. The soldiers abused their women, shot their men and gave them terrible diseases. Many of the Tolkopaya (McDowell people) died from small pox after they had been given infected clothes. So the Yavapai did not want to live on these reservations and left." (THE YAVAPAI OF FORT MCDOWELL).

On September 26, 1864, the First Territorial Legislature met in Prescott. King Woolsey, at 32 years of age, became the second youngest member of the legislative council. He was made chairman of Militia and Indian Affairs as well as being appointed to other committees on Finance, Agriculture and the Judiciary. He also successfully voted to make Henry W. Fleury, a self-proclaimed atheist, "chaplain" of the legislative body.

The most pressing concern before this first legislative session was the need for troops to make war against the "Apaches." Although there was a shortage of governmental funds, lawmakers appropriated $1487.00 to reimburse Woolsey and others for their expeditions against the Apaches. By now, both Yavapai and Apaches were considered one and the same.

On May 20, 1865, the Yavapai again made an effort to live in peace with the white population. Twenty-seven of them agreed to work on the Ft. Mohave Toll Road under the 'protection' of Superintendent of Indian Affairs, G.W. Leihy. All 27 Yavapai were attacked and shot down by soldiers from Ft. Whipple.

Four months later, the Yavapai joined forces with the Mohave and Yuma tribes (their linguistic cousins) in a war against Piutes and Chemehuevi Indians in retaliation for their serving as army scouts.

Peace talks were once again initiated on April 13, 1866 between the Yavapai and the military. This time, a Yavapai band under Chief

39

Echa-waw-cha-comma (Hitting the Enemy), met the soldiers near Grapevine Springs in Skull Valley for purpose of this treaty. Troops from Ft. Whipple ambushed them, killing 30 Yavapai and wounding 40, despite the fact that Echa-waw-cha-comma traveled to this meeting with a note from Superintendent of Indian Affairs, Leihy, granting his band immunity.

"East of Prescott is Skull Valley. It is called that way because people found many bones and skulls scattered throughout that place. These bones and skulls were from Yavapai. The soldiers called Yavapai from all over to this place. They told them they would give them wagons and horses and many other good things if they came to this place. When the Yavapai arrived, the soldiers started shooting them. Some of the Yavapai escaped and told others about it. But most of them got killed and were left lying there. Skull Valley is called after the skulls of the Yavapai." (from THE YAVAPAI OF FORT MCDOWELL).

Four months later, 100 Yavapai attacked the army at Grapevine Springs in Skull Valley, but were repelled after 45 minutes of fighting. Later that same month, the Yavapai took control of the country around Skull Valley. They ordered the whites out and charged a toll on livestock and goods going over the roads.

These toll roads had been established because the First Territorial Legislature knew they could not afford to build wagon roads. They authorized a half dozen toll roads which they hoped would span the territory. It was one of these vital toll roads that the Yavapai had seized. The following month, on November 10, Superintendent of Indian Affairs, G.W. Leihy and his clerk were killed by the Yavapai at Bell Canyon near Prescott.

Special Order #16 established a military camp and reservation along Date Creek on January 23, 1867, to be named Camp McPherson. The post was later re-named, Camp Date Creek.

"Maj. Gen. Henry W. "Old Brains" Halleck directed that a permanent military camp be founded on Date Creek and named for Gen. J.B. Mc Phearson, killed in the battle of Atlanta in 1864. Halleck picked this location because of its strategic location in the heart of Yavapai country, 60 miles from Prescott, and less than 30 miles from Wickenburg. Settlers lived along the banks of this creek, miners prowled the surrounding mountains, and to the north were the ranchers in Skull Valley. Also, the main stage and freight road from La Paz on the Colorado River to Prescott ran near, and crossed this creek." (Sidney Brickerhoff - THE SMOKE SIGNAL - Fall 1964)

Two months after the establishment of this reservation, the Yavapai attacked a wagon train eight miles west of Camp Date Creek, which prompted a military troop to pursue them and launch a surprise attack on them in Hell's Canyon. Several days later, this same troop under Capt. Williams and the 8th Cavalry attacked and destroyed 30 Apache lodges in the Black Hills. Williams and his troops engaged the Apaches in a running battle near the Verde

River, followed by two other battles in the Black Mountains. Throughout the summer and into the fall, raids and battles between citizens, the army and the enraged Indians continued at a relentless pace.

Before the year was over, Gen. Gregg and the Yavapai met to explore peace proposals once again. Due to poor interpreters, the peace efforts failed.

Gen. Gregg, a dashing senior cavalry officer and seasoned combat veteran of two wars, was overzealous and inexperienced when dealing with Indians. Inadvertently he created new problems and quickly became involved in controversy with the Bureau of Indian Affairs. Confusion over policy in Indian affairs negated most of his victories over the Apache and Yavapai. As a result, the citizenry continued to lose confidence in the military and more and more chose to take matters into their own hands.

Before the close of 1867, the population of Yavapai County totaled 2,337. The most prominent occupation of the majority of Yavapai County citizens was recorded as 'miners.' Considering that the entire population of Arizona Territory that year was 7,136, it seems significant that almost 1/3 of that population was concentrated in north central Arizona.

With the war between the Indians and whites accelerating, Gen. Gregg declared all Indians in Arizona 'hostile' and revoked all passes and permits. This only made matters worse. The raids, killing and hatred on both sides increased even more. When twelve Yavapai gathered for a peace conference at La Paz on September 24, 1867, they were gunned down and all were killed.

By the summer of 1868, troops in Northern Arizona recorded 46 expeditions against the Yavapai and Apaches during that fiscal year. Despite army reports that 114 Indians had been killed, 35 wounded and many rancheras burned, Indian attacks continued to increase, and the Indians seemed to be gaining the upper hand.

On May 6, 1869, one hundred Apaches attacked a military wagon train at the foot of Grief Hill within sight of Camp Verde. It was a massacre for which the Indians claimed victory. Two days later, the Yavapai burned down a ranch owned by Abraham McKee and a Mr. Harding in Mint Valley.

The months between 1869-70 finally reached the intolerable point for the white population of north central Arizona. The low morale of the regular troops, whose numbers were dwindling and whose supplies were grossly inadequate, allowed the Indian raids to continue unabated. There was also a high level of confusion regarding Indian policy. But by the close of 1870, the army sent an increased number of troops into the territory. Thereafter, desertions decreased and the troops, under new command from Gen. O.C Ord, became better trained and more disciplined. Ord also ended confusion regarding Indian policy. His orders: "I believe the hostile Indians of Arizona should be destroyed, and I encourage troops to capture and route out Indians by every means, and hunt them down as wild animals." This became the popular 'extermination' policy regarding the 'Indian problem.'

By July of 1870, the Yavapai requested peace treaty talks with the military at Camp Date Creek, and finally Chief O-hat-che-come-e and 225 of his people succeeded in following through with this treaty. It by no means ended the Indian battles... and before long, even this chief was back on the war path.

On September 9, 1871, the Yavapai and military fought in Chino Valley resulting in death of one citizen. Before this encounter, twenty-five men of the Third cavalry with Scout Dan O'leary and his Walapai tracker leading, had lost the trail of these hostiles near Chino Valley.

Two civilians volunteered to go in search of the Yavapai if they could borrow the Walapai tracker. Later, when these same two citizens returned, they threw down a scalp and said they had run into four Indians and killed one. Eventually they admitted this was a lie. The scalp actually was that of the Walapai tracker. "What the hell," they said, "he was only an Indian."

One month later, on November 5, a stagecoach was attacked. Known as the "Wickenberg Massacre" this stagecoach, traveling with eight people on board, was attacked and six persons were killed outright. Another died later of wounds. Among those killed were three members of the George M. Wheeler surveying party. One was Frederick W. Loring of Massachusetts, a young writer widely known in the East.

Initially there was some confusion over who perpetrated the attack. At first the Prescott papers reported it was the work of Mexican bandits from Sonora. Following his investigation, Col. N.A.M. Dudley wrote the U.S. Board of Indian Commissioners that he did not believe there was an Indian in sight of the murders because Indians would have taken the blankets and horses. What was taken was a valuable shipment of gold bullion.

The sole survivor of the massacre, Molly Sheppard "a notorious courtesan from Prescott," claimed it was the work of white men. Nevertheless, it became more expedient to blame the Date Creek Indians under Chief O-hat-che-come-e, who with his followers, had bolted the reservation months earlier because of a malaria epidemic.

By August of that year, five Indians a day were dying of malaria at the Camp Date Creek reservation. Because of this, many Indians fled. Indian scouts were dispatched to track them down and kill them.

Gen. George Crook, who was called to duty in Arizona in 1871, proclaimed in General Order #10 that all roving bands of Indians were to be on reservations by Feb. 15, 1872 or be treated as hostiles.

Crook was considered one of the most successful men in dealing with the Indians that the United States ever had in its service. His

Dr. Wm. Corbusier, 1870s. Renowned Post surgeon at Fort Verde. [FVSP]

Ruins of hospital at Fort McDowell, 1990. Yavapai claim it is haunted. (photo by Kate Ruland-Thorne)

Gen. George Crook on his favorite mule "Apache" and accompanied by Apache scouts, tours San Carlos in the 1880s. [FVSP]

policy was "first justice, then the sword." Before his death in 1890, Crook emphatically stated that "greed and avarice on the part of the whites - in other words, the almighty dollar - was at the bottom of nine-tenths of all our Indian troubles."

From the spring of 1872 through September, the raids and killings on both sides continued at an accelerated pace. On September 1, 1872 the Indian population at Camp Date Creek doubled as a result of Crook's relentless campaign to force them back on this reservation. By September 7, Crook called for a meeting at Camp Date Creek with Chief O-hat-che-comma-e, the Yavapai leader accused of the "Wickenberg Massacre."

O-hat-che-comma-e and fifty warriors arrived for this meeting armed and painted. One of the chief's oldest enemies, Mohave Chief Irataba, pointed him out as the one responsible for the Wickenberg Massacre. When a soldier moved forward to make the arrests, one of the Yavapai pulled a knife and stabbed him. Gun fire broke out between the Yavapai and soldiers. Gen. Crook was nearly killed in the turmoil. Soldiers finally seized O-hat-che-comma-e and took him to the guardhouse.

That night, the chief attempted to escape through the guardhouse roof, but not before being pierced with a bayonet. He killed the guards, but died later in the hills north of the post. The following day, the cavalry clashed with O-hot-che-comma-e's followers near Camp Date Creek. Most of the Indians were captured and jailed.

On December 28, 1872, the "Skeleton Cave Massacre" in which 100 Yavapai men, women and children were killed during a surprise attack, finally broke the spirit of all Yavapai resistance.

Although newspapers, and army reports, described this as one of the most "terrible battles in Apache history," and reported 75 'hostiles' killed, 25 captured, the Yavapai consider it the most horrible 'massacre' in their history.

"It was in that cave that so many of our people got killed," said John Williams, a Yavapai from Fort McDowell. *"There were no Apaches there, all Yavapai. My grandfather died there. They lived in that cave and had plenty to eat. The Kakakas (mountain spirits) warned the chief in that cave to get out, but the chief wouldn't listen. He sent a boy out to bring more of our people there to come and eat with them. The soldiers got that boy and made him show them where our cave was. The next day when the people were having breakfast, the soldiers came and shot them all. The soldiers shot into that cave. The bullets hit the wall and ricocheted. All the people in that cave, men, women, children, babies got killed. Only one escaped from that cave. A girl jumped down a cliff, but broke her hip. The soldiers thought she was dead, so they left her. Later she went to Saddle Mountain where the others were. It took her two weeks to get there. No one knows how she did it. The people prayed over her and they sang over her. Later she could walk again, but not straight. She was a cripple.*

"Many sensational stories have been written about Skeleton Cave, where a band of 'bloodthirsty Apache' had been killed. These

The Gaan perform the Crown Dance at Camp Verde, 1990. (photo by Kate Ruland-Thorne)

Members of the Fort McDowell Indian community make 1990 pilgrimage to site of the "Skeleton Cave Massacre." (Louis Hood - Ft. McDowell)

Grave at Ft. McDowell containing bones of 75 Yavapai women, men and children massacred by soldiers in 1873. (photo by Kate Ruland-Thorne)

people who got killed were no Apache. They were Yavapai who did not want to leave their homeland and were hiding from those who wanted to chase them out. Not one soldier was killed or hurt during this event. But white people call it a 'battle'." (Compiled from John Williams' interview with" James Cook of the Arizona Republic in 1970; and from THE YAVAPAI OF FORT MCDOWELL).

On April 6, 1873, Tonto Chief Cha-lipun surrendered with 2,300 men, women and children to Gen. Crook at Camp Verde.

Cha-lipun's Apache name meant "Gray Hat." He was the leader of a group who lived under the Mogollon Rim from South of Bill William's Mountain to the Young area. Also surrendering with him was Hosteen Nez, leader of a group living above the Mogollon Rim from Bill William's Mountain to the Haber area. Delshay also surrendered his group from the Tonto Basin.

"We give up," said Cha-lipun, "not because we love you (Crook), but because we are afraid of you, and because we have not only white soldiers to fight, but our own people, too." He was referring to the Indian Scout Service.

By August, Camp Date Creek was abandoned as a military post and all Indians were moved to the Rio Verde Reservation. One month later, Delshay and twelve followers fled due to another outbreak of malaria.

Delshay was a mighty outlaw warrior, although later disclaimed by both the Yavapai and Tonto Apaches. He thoroughly hated and distrusted the white man. Like Geronimo, every depredation which could in any way be linked to him, was. Delshay was a symbol of hostility and for awhile was one of the most wanted renegades in Northern Arizona. By September 13, over 100 Indians on the Rio Verde Reservation had died of malaria, according to army reports. Yavapai historians tell another story.

They say people did die, but not from malaria. The troops, they claim, fed adults poisoned meat, and small children and babies, brown sugar laced with strychnine "which ate away their lips and gums."

On February 27, 1875, The 1500 surviving Yavapai and Tonto Apaches were removed to the San Carlos Reservation on what the Indians refer to this day - as the infamous "Trail of Tears."

"In 1873, most of the Yavapai and Tonto Apaches had been gathered in the reservation near Camp Verde. A few managed to hide out in Red Rock country around Sedona. At the reservation they were told to make irrigation ditches and start farming. There were no white man's tools for the Indians to work with. They worked with their own tools (usually sticks) and did well. But living conditions at the reservation were bad. Too many people were crowded in a small place and there was not enough food. A disease, (malaria, the whites say) killed hundreds of Yavapai. There were so many dead that the living could not gather enough wood to burn them. Despite this, the first harvest of the Yavapai turned out well. When the white settlers around the reservation saw how well these people were doing despite all their hardships, they wanted the Indians

An elderly man carries his crippled wife in a burden basket through the 180 mile journey, uncomplaining. Illustration by David Sine.

removed all together from this area. They were afraid the government would establish water rights for the Indians and give them more land. The white settlers sent delegations to Washington and told the government that the Indians on the reservation near Camp Verde all were 'Apache' and therefore should be sent to an Apache Reservation." (THE YAVAPAI AT FORT" MCDOWELL)

A notorious group known as the Tucson Ring, who profited by selling inferior goods to Indian reservations, also had a hand in this removal. Only 1361 Indians would survive this "Death March" to San Carlos.

DEATH MARCH TO SAN CARLOS

"Our Indian policy, or rather the lack of a sane one, marked by broken treaties, dishonest, ignorant, and tactless handling of the entire subject and the infliction of untold misery on our Indian wards, has been such that an army man who has had to stand by with hands tied, can hardly keep within the bounds when writing or speaking about it." Brig. Gen. Wm. C. Brown. 1875.

"Somebody make bad medicine," murmured Pa-ka-ki-va, son-in-law of old war chief, Delshay. Dr. Corbusier, attending physician at the Rio Verde Indian Agency, agreed. The promises of seeds and farm equipment had been 'delayed' too many times. Corbusier also noted a strange disinterest on the part of agent Chapman toward the Indian's eagerness to plow, and enlarge the acreage that had produced such good crops the previous year. When Lt. Walter Schuyler (5th Cavalry, Company K), who was in charge of the Rio Verde reservation, received a letter from Gen. Crook, he too, became alarmed. Crook's letter had ominous overtones. It instructed Schuyler to call on Col. Brayton (Commander at Camp Verde 16 miles away) "in case of any trouble." There was no explanation as to what that" trouble might be. By now, Corbusier and Schuyler were convinced that someone indeed was 'making bad medicine'.

The chiefs of the 1,500 Tonto Apache and Yavapai people, who lived on the Rio Verde River reservation, were just as suspicious. They asked Lt. Schuyler and the doctor to find out why Indian agent Oliver Chapman was evasive when asked about the delay in the seeds and farm equipment. Why, they also asked, did issuing day come and go with only a portion of their rations being distributed? The excuse given by Chapman was "the supply train had broken down." Not a single chief believed him.

Then pandemonium erupted. Two Apache runners from the San Carlos Reservation (who had relatives at Rio Verde) sneaked into the reservation and warned the chiefs that the San Carlos Indian agent was preparing to receive more Indians. The Rio Verde Indians, who for nearly two years had been peaceful and productive, now exploded into hysteria.

Chanting and wailing filled the air. Dr. Corbusier and his wife, Fanny, were besieged with questions from the Indians who had come to rely upon and trust them. Torches flickered all night in the disturbed mountain camps. When a band of Tontos, dressed in war paint, loomed before agent Chapman's tent and made threatening gestures, the agent panicked. A courier was dispatched immediately to Camp Verde. After receiving it, Gen. Crook alerted all the troops at nearby posts to prepare for possible action.

Within days, special agent Edwin Dudley arrived with his assistants and informed Indian agent Chapman that General Grant wanted all the Indian families at the Rio Verde Reservation moved to San Carlos - IMMEDIATELY!. Like a blast from a Winchester rifle, word shot through the reservation nearly causing a riot.

Small groups banded together with the intention of killing Dudley. Once again, Dr. Corbusier and his wife managed to calm the Indians. But, when Dudley ordered the chiefs to meet with him the next day, each one flatly refused. Again, Dr. Corbusier was called in to assist, much to the chagrin of Dudley.

By now, Dudley had announced his intention to move the Indians across the mountains, instead of on the roads that traversed around them. He would take them on a route across old Indian trails from Camp Verde south to East Verde, then through the valley to Rye. From there to the confluence of the Salt River and Tonto Creek, to Globe and San Carlos. Foolishly he ignored the pleas that followed.

Both Corbusier and Schuyler begged Dudley not to inflict such hardships upon these people. "It is the dead of winter," they argued. "Please, use the wagon roads around the mountains instead. Then teams can be used to transport sufficient supplies, and some of the older people and children."

Dudley vigorously shook his head - no. "Going" over the mountains is the shortest route," he shot back. "I must get them there quickly."

"But, not even beef-on-the-hoof can tolerate such rugged country, especially at this time of year," pleaded Dr. Corbusier.

"It is your duty to protect these people," shouted Schuyler - "not order them on such a difficult march!"

"I come from the highest authority in the country," Dudley bellowed. "My word is the law. Besides. . .they're only Indians. Let the beggars walk!"

The madness of these shocking official orders sickened and disgusted both Corbusier and Schuyler, but they knew there was nothing they could do to stop it.

Despite the tense circumstances, Dr. Corbusier dutifully circulated among the chiefs and persuaded them to meet with Dudley the next morning. Young bucks, stripped down and ready for action, joined the chiefs as they gathered in front of Dudley's tent. Nearby, Schuyler, his troop and Indian scouts watched. . .and pretended to be unconcerned about 600 well-armed Indians. Dr. Corbusier later recalled that cold, snowy February morning in the book, VERDE TO SAN CARLOS.

"After the chiefs had assembled, and waited about a half-an-hour, Dudley came out of his tent. He leisurely threw a buffalo robe on the step, sat down on it lopped over - resting one elbow on the robe as he talked. I stood just back of the crowd in order to listen to what might be said by the onlookers. Dudley spoke in thickened English while the interpreter translated his remarks.

"I heard a buck say in a low tone, 'He is drunk,' and turning to me, he repeated the remark. I just pointed and told him to listen."

Through an interpreter, Dudley read his orders to remove the Indians. He emphasized that they would be going to a much better place, where they could be together with their friends. Then, for no apparent reason, Dudley abruptly stood up and walked back into his tent.

"He went to get another drink, one of the chiefs murmured. This suspicion spread throughout the assembly. When Dudley returned and flopped back down on the buffalo robe, the crowd was dead silent. Two rifles clicked. Dr. Corbusier leaned against the bucks who had cocked their rifles. They let their hammers down. Dudley resumed talking, his words incoherent, even to the doctor. When Dudley finished speaking, Captain Snooks, spokesman for the chiefs, stepped forward.

"We will not go where we will be outnumbered by our enemies," he said. "Our fathers and grandfathers were born here and died here. Our wives and children were born here. The father in Washington promised that the country along the river and 10 miles on each side would be ours forever. This is little enough land for people who are accustomed to roaming for many miles before the white man came and stole our land from us."

Dudley yawned and stared blankly at the Indians. Snooks speech had not made any impression. Snooks moved closer and continued to plead. His speech was a masterpiece of oratory. He asked Dudley not to drink any more whiskey, so that he might know what he was asking of them. Other chiefs stepped forward and joined in the plea. Dudley waved them away and returned to his tent. The meeting was over.

Six days after his arrival at Rio Verde, Dudley started 1500 Indians, all on foot, across 180 miles of rough trails, over high mountains, and through numerous streams that were likely at any hour to rise many feet and become impassable. Not a single conveyance was provided to carry their extra loads.

Non-Indians who accompanied the exodus consisted of Indian agent Chapman and two assistants; Commissioner Dudley and two assistants; Chief of Scouts, Al Sieber and a small contingent of his Indian scouts; Harry Hawes, chief packer and four muleskinners; and Lt. George Eaton commanding a troop of 15 cavalrymen. Although he was not ordered to do so, Dr. Corbusier agreed to accompany these people whom he had befriended,

Yavapai woman carrying water to her 'wikiup.' By the 1900s, canvas had replaced brush thatch. [SHM]

Yavapai women at San Carlos c. 1900. [SHM]

because a group of chiefs insisted that they needed him along. Dr. Corbusier's family watched the sad procession...a sight his wife would never forget:

"On February 27, 1875, the long, silent and sad procession slowly passed. They had to carry all their belongings on their backs and in their V-shaped baskets, old and young with heavy packs. One old man placed his aged and decrepit wife in one of these baskets, with her feet hanging out, and carried her on his back, the basket supported by a band over his head, almost all the way. He refused help, except at several stream crossings, where he was persuaded to allow a trooper to take her across on his horse. Over the roughest country, through thick brush and rocks - day after day, he struggled along with his precious burden - uncomplaining." (VERDE TO SAN CARLOS)

Mabel Dogka, whose parents were among the children forced into joining that cruel march, related her parent's version of the story. *"They told us this story over and over,"* said Mabel, *"so that we would never forget.*

"One day the soldiers came and told my people to move out. None of them understood English, so they don't know why they play this dirty trick on my people. The people had promised to farm if they could stay on their land. They had never been farmers before, but they were willing to do this.

"When they were moved, they had hardly any clothes and no roads to walk on. They wore moccasin shoes. Going through rocks, their shoes wear out. Some of them had to tear the blanket and wrap it around their feet. The river was really high. My people were afraid to cross it. But, the soldiers, they horse-whipped them and made them do it anyway. Since they had hardly any clothes on, they just bleed when they are whipped. Many of them died in that river. My mother (an Apache born at Indian Gardens) and father were very young at that time, but they went through it.

"My people had to carry their babies and all their belongings. Soon it was too much for them, so they had to hang their babies (who were in cradle boards) in cedar trees because they couldn't carry them any more. That's why they call it the March of Tears. My people cried all the way to San Carlos."

Dr. Corbusier reported that at least one baby was born each day on the march. "Whenever the mother felt the urge, she would go off into the bushes, unattended, and emerge later with a baby. There seldom was a blanket to wrap it in, so the babies made the trip naked, and many of them froze to death."

The medicine men, who saw evil omens at every turn, chanted and wailed, and daily reminded Dudley of the broken promises which had been made to their people. After only one week into the march, Dudley and his assistants already were sick of their jobs...in fact two of Dudley's assistants deserted, and were not seen nor heard from again.

Hunger and anger increased daily. Trying to drive cattle and footsore, frustrated people up steep, snow covered trails was becoming almost unbearable. When the group reached Strawberry Creek,

Lt. George O. Eaton, 5th Cavalry. [FVSP]

five miles south of the present day Childs, they found the usually quiet creek had become a raging torrent due to a huge storm the day before. Of the three crossings the Indians were forced to make, Strawberry Creek would become the most devastating. Al Sieber and Lt. Eaton urged Dudley to delay the crossing for a few days until the waters had subsided.

"You've impeded the progress of this journey long enough with your silly fears," screeched Dudley. Later, Dudley would write his official report about the crossing: "We fortunately found the 'stream' could be forded. . .sad duty to compel men, women and children, to 'wade' through cold water. . .even though they were 'Indians.' The water was about waist deep to a tall man, and the crossing was a pitiful sight."

One can only be amazed, given his attitude toward Indians, that Dudley expressed any sympathy at all in his report. But such as it was, 'pitiful' hardly seems the appropriate word. . .unconscionable would have been more fitting.

Strawberry Creek was a raging river, much higher than any 'tall man's waist,' according to Dr. Corbusier's report. Debris and rock had piled up forming dams that would suddenly break loose, furiously crashing into its human victims. Some sympathetic soldiers passed ropes to those who were less able to withstand the force of the rushing water. Others offered to carry babies, small children and the old across on their horses. Then there were those who followed Dudley's commands, and used their bull whips. For days after the crossing, Dr. Corbusier was kept busy applying splints to broken bones, and administering to the injured, sick and dying. Two more dangerous river crossings were forced upon the people. But these crossings were only a prelude to more unconscionable suffering which soon would follow.

By the second week, the beef and flour gave out, compelling the starving people to eat Canadian thistle (a poisonous plant) and the stalks of agave. There was plenty of game, according to Dr. Corbusier, but the Indians were not 'allowed' to hunt. One night when a confused deer wandered in above their camp, Al Sieber shot it. Then the Yavapais from above the camp and the Tontos camped below, descended on the carcass. There was a frenzied melee which ended in the Tontos emerging with the prize, driving all others away.

**Author's Note: *One wonders how a troop of 15 cavalrymen and a handful of scouts managed to keep 1500 starving Indians from hunting? Could it be that all weaponry was removed from the possession of the Indians prior to the march? Perhaps that might explain why unarmed Indians tolerated 'orders not to hunt' even though they were starving . . .they had no choice. It also might explain why these tormented people continued to remain on such a hideous march while under the guard of such a small contingent of well-armed soldiers and scouts. Members of the Yavapai tribe at Ft. McDowell informed this writer in July 1990, that*

"Broken Arrow" - *a classic movie filmed in Sedona in the 1950s starred Jeff Chandler (standing back) as Cochise and Debra Pagent (end left) as Apache love interest for James Stewart. Mabel Dogka (middle foreground) was one of the 'extras' in the movie. (courtesy of Mabel Dogka)*

Mabel Dogka - Oldest living member of the Yavapai-Apache people of Camp Verde and Clarkdale, 1990. (photo by Kate Ruland-Thorne)

not only were all rifles removed from the Indians before the march, but all knives and anything else that might be considered a weapon. This information will not be found in any official army reports. ***

Old feuds between the Yavapai and Tonto Apaches were soon rekindled, and spasmodic war dances began. (Their feuding originally began when the Yavapai joined the ranks as Scouts during their Date Creek Reservation years, and helped track the Tontos, whom they blamed for all their troubles.)

For the first time, Dudley realized he had reason to fear for his life. On March 8, twelve days into the march, all hell broke loose. Dr. Corbusier recorded the events as he remembered them: *"Just after we made camp on the East branch of the Verde River (near Bloody Basin), the Western and Eastern Yavapais came in fighting-hungry and in an ugly frame of mind. Their women began to shout, "Kill the Tontos." Shortly, fifty naked warriors charged passed us. Dudley, Agent Chapman and their men tried to drive them back by waving their arms and shouting, but to no avail. The Yavapais ran up a 20 foot bank of a mesa on which the Tontos were camped - dropped to their knees and began shooting. Dudley called Lt. Eaton, who with his men stood waiting authority to interfere. As the troops ran passed Dudley, Chapman and their assistants, the soldiers noticed them on their knees, under a tree - praying. The troopers then drove the Indians down the hill."* (VERDE TO SAN CARLOS)"

Author Dan L. Thrapp, in his book AL SIEBER - CHIEF OF SCOUTS, (University of Oklahoma Press), researched Lt. Eaton's account of this event, a manuscript written 50 years after his involvement, and found many discrepancies in his report. According to Eaton's report, *'a fight broke out between two Indian camps. He (Eaton) and his troops stood their ground between the warring factions - he with his hands upraised - and through an interpreter, called the three leading chiefs together and 'bawled them out.' After some difficulty,"* he said, *"he was able to call the fight off."*

Author Thrapp claims it was Al Seiber who actually stood amidst a "hail of bullets and cowed them (the Indians) into ceasing fire without he himself firing a shot."

Commissioner Dudley's report of the incident supports Thrapp's claim: *"A difficulty occurred,"* wrote Dudley, *"which resulted in a general fight between the two tribes. . .The escort under direction of Mr. Al Sieber, Chief of General Crook's scouts, at once took a position between two contending parties and made every effort to send them to their respective camps, and success attended their efforts. When the loss came to be counted, we knew of five dead, the Indians said seven, and ten wounded. Not a great loss when so much lead was expended."*

Dr. Corbusier stated that after the 'fight', he climbed to the top of the mesa and found 25 Indians sprawled out in various positions (he doesn't say whether they were wounded - or dead) and treated the 10 worst wounded. "Estimates of the dead varied up to 30," he wrote, "but I found four." (VERDE TO SAN CARLOS). Both sides do agree that none of the whites were shot.

Mabel Dogka claims there never was a 'fight' - only a massacre:

"When you drive to Phoenix, you see a sign that says 'Bloody Basin.'
That's my people's blood. That was when they said, no, we won't go any
further, so the soldiers opened fire on them and their blood just flowed
like a river. The same way with Skull Valley, it was full of Indian heads.
White man say that is where Indians kill white people. That makes me
mad. I want to stand up and shout, you're wrong. It was a place where
white people killed many of my people. They say it the other way because
they want their side to look good. Same way with making my people cross
the rivers. They don't tell how the soldiers whipped them with bull whips
to make them cross those rivers. There was not a wagon any where on
that trip to help carry my people, who were too old, or young, or sick
to walk."

David Sine, Yavapai-Apache, said that if a fight did erupt, there
were certainly no guns, so it was probably a free-for-all. Also,
he states, there was no division between the tribes at this time.
The Tonto and Yavapai were all one. It is likely, he contends, that
the soldiers simply took the 'troublemakers' to the top of the hill
and shot them, along with anyone who was too sick or weak to
continue the journey.

Dr. Corbusier reported that the ten wounded Indians were either
slung over the shoulders of some younger Indians, or carried in
a crude litter attended by the medicine men, whose piercing chants
echoed for days throughout the Mazatzal Wilderness.

The third cruel river crossing lay ahead (the Salt River) before
they faced the grueling climb up the steep Apache Trail near the
present Roosevelt Dam. The old and the crippled finally sat down
on the trail, unable to move another step. Soon, they were whipped
to their feet. The trail was so narrow that horses had to be led.
A few of the troopers carried screaming, terrified children, who
clung to them desperately. Suddenly a mule lost its footing and
plunged into the river far below, carrying with it what was left of
the much needed supplies.

By the next day, the Yavapai men had painted their faces for war.
Beneath the paint were penetrating looks of hatred. Dudley lost
no time in leaving his charges on the pretense of going ahead to
San Carlos to bring back food and fresh supplies.

Although Dr. Corbusier claims Dudley did meet them at their
next camp with these supplies, there is no official report of his
doing so. What is recorded, is that the San Carlos Indian agent
Clum, accompanied by Dudley - and very likely a contingent of
troops - met them at their next camp, and "escorted" the Indians
the rest of the way to San Carlos.

The Yavapai claim that "food was brought to the camp. The people were so hungry, they cooked and ate it right away. The food
was poisoned and many died. The ones who only held it in their
hands and refused to eat it (remembering past experiences), just
got sick."

Of the 1500 Indians who left the Rio Verde Reservation six weeks before, various estimates indicate that approximately 375 either escaped, or did not survive the journey. These estimates do not include the numerous babies who were born, and died along the way.

The March of Tears was the last act in Dudley's government career. He stated in his final report that the move was a difficult one, but successfully made. When he turned in his expense account, he found himself gypped out of all money. In his protest to Commissioner Edward Smith he wrote: *"Myself, the Indians, the employees who were with me, the military escort, the pack train - all took their lives in their hands and knew that at any time they might be in danger of losing their lives. And you sit in a nicely carpeted office and forget more in one day about this miserable place than those of us who came over it ever knew. I am aggrieved that you should fail to give me the small amount of money that was necessary."*

On his way back to San Carlos, Dr. Corbusier disinterred several heads of Indians killed at Bloody Basin and sent them to a medical museum. The skulls showed the so-called explosive action passing through the skull, (gatling guns?) which broke it into many pieces. (De Coursey 1951: Letter). This seemed a curious thing for the doctor to have done.

Following the March of Tears, and the closing of the Rio Verde Agency, Corbusier continued to serve as Post Surgeon for the army at 15 other Indian agencies throughout the country.

During the expedition to the Philippines in 1898, he organized the Red Cross Society and initiated the first "dog tags" issued to soldiers. He also organized and trained the first female nurses to serve in the United States Army. He retired from active service with the rank of Lt. Col. in 1908 at the age of 64, only to be recalled again at the outbreak of World War I to serve in Court-Martial duty. Dr. William Henry Corbusier was finally relieved from active duty in 1919, following a distinguished and humanitarian career.

Agent John Philip Clum who took charge of the Indians at San Carlos was only 23 years old at the time. Although a "greenhorn" when it came handling Indians, he nevertheless was one of the few Indian agents who tried to be honest.

Nominated by the Dutch Reform Church to the federal government post at San Carlos, he promptly made himself "boss" of the Apaches and severed all relations with the Interior Department. Against army regulations, Clum organized the first Apache police force and Apache Court. When Geronimo bolted the reservation in 1877, Clum and 40 members of his force, walked all the way to Santa Fe and arrested 17 renegades, including Geronimo.

By 1877, however, Clum left the service in a huff, frustrated by the constant obstacles put in his path. He would go on to found Tombstone's famous EPITAPH newspaper, as well as become the town's mayor and postmaster. Unfortunately for the Indian people at San Carlos, one of the most corrupt Indian Agents ever to hold that position, would take his place - J.C. Tiffany.

SAN CARLOS TO THE PRESENT

The various bands of Apache and Yavapai people who were finally gathered together at San Carlos in 1875, did not constitute a united people. Separated by the Gila River, the Yavapai lived south in an area called the Mineral Strip, and the Tontos were located to the north. But separation did not prevent the suspicion and hostility which raged between them. The only thing anyone agreed upon was their hereditary hatred for the white man, and their unified dislike for the hot, unhealthful San Carlos Reservation. Every Indian there longed to return to his ancestral land.

By 1882, the Indians at San Carlos had been treated so outrageously by Agent J.C. Tiffany that many were once again on the war path. One major outbreak resulted in the Battle of Big Dry Wash in the Verde Valley following "The Cibicue Massacre." On September 4, 1882, General George Crook was recalled to command the Department of Arizona.

When Crook arrived at San Carlos, he found out just how badly things had gone during his absence. Crook protested vehemently against the government policy of forcing these people together initially. No one had listened. Now he saw first hand the consequences of this policy, and the monumental task that lay before him.

On his mule, Apache, Crook rode throughout the reservation and listened to each grievance. Immediately he expelled from the reservation all squatters, miners and friends of the Indian agent who had been plundering the Indians and the government for years.

The second month after Crook's arrival, a Federal Grand Jury concluded that, *"for several years, the people of the Territory have been gradually arriving at the conclusion that the management of the Indian reservations in Arizona has been a fraud upon the government; that the constantly reoccurring outbreaks of the Indians and their consequent devastations were due to criminal neglect or apathy of the Indian agent at San Carlos; but never until the present investigations of the Grand Jury have laid bare the infamy of Agent Tiffany could a proper idea be formed of the fraud and villainy which were constantly practiced in open violation of the law... and in defiance of public justice...and is a disgrace to the civilization of the age and a foul blot upon the national escutcheon..."* Washington relieved Tiffany of his office, but the damage had already been done.

Geronimo and Nachez and 120 men, women and children soon bolted the reservation again and dealt death and destruction everywhere they went. The Yavapai and Tonto Apaches, both men and women, volunteered as Scouts after Crook promised that all Indians who helped catch Geronimo, could go back to their homeland. Three years after the campaign began, Geronimo, Nachez and their band were rounded up on September 8, 1886 and put on a train for Florida. A Camp Verde Scout by the name of

Captain Smiley was instrumental in Geronimo's final capture.

By the following year, the settlers in the Verde Valley were alarmed to learn that the Yavapai and Apache had been given permission to return to their homeland because of their outstanding service for the government. Immediately political pressure was applied to stop their return. A letter writing campaign was initiated by the Valley's prominent citizens to the 7th Territorial Governor, C.M. Zulick:

> *Sir:*
>
> *The undersigned citizens of the Verde Valley and vicinity wish to enter a protest against the settlement of Indians upon the Camp Verde Military reservation.*
>
> *The actual settlers here who have acquired title to the government land feel that it would be an act of injustice to destroy the prospect of making future homes here by having a band of uncivilized Indians moving in our midst.*
>
> *That whereas now peace and order are the rule, with the addition of Indians, all sense of security would be gone.*
>
> *The Indians themselves would destroy confidence in the community, and added to them would be the camp followers who are less desirable than the Indians.*
>
> *Homes are being built up here and improvements made with the expectation that we were forever free from Indian intrusion. With their coming, all progress and social prospects cease.*
>
> *The fact that there are 300 families settled along the narrow valley, all prosperous, who shudder for what the future might bring if they are driven out by having a band of lawless Indians forced upon them as neighbors.*
>
> *We hope that you will represent our case to the authorities in Washington and show our many good reasons for objecting to their transfer to this valley.*
>
> > *Respectfully,*
> > *W.G. Wingfield,*
> > *J.B. Ricketts,*
> > *and J.G. Crum - farmers.*

The Yavapai and Apaches were not allowed to return, but in 1900, they simply walked away from San Carlos - wisely not bothering to ask permission. When the Wipukapayas and Dil'zeae arrived in their beloved valley, they discovered the best land had been taken over by white settlers. Mabel Dogka picks up the story:

"My people left San Carlos...even the mineral strip that was given to them and the cattle. They don't want any of it. They just walked away and came back to the Verde Valley where they had lived and roamed for all time. When they came back, they found there is a mine going on (Jerome), and they know why they were sent away in the first place. My mother and father came back with their people." Mabel's father, who had been a member of Agent Clum's celebrated Apache Police (called "Catch Thems") later took the surname of Kitchiyan, which means Catch Them.

"My mother would go to white houses and make a gesture of

Each year, Yavapai and Apache people gather at Camp Verde on February 24 to commemorate those who suffered and died on the terrible "Death March to San Carlos" in 1875. (photo by Kate Ruland-Thorne)

"WE ARE YAVAPAI" - Today, the People of the Sun are trying to re-establish their identity, which they feel was taken from them along with their lands when early white settlers and miners mistook them for Apaches in the 1860s.

Modern day 'social dance' at Camp Verde, 1990. (photo by Kate Ruland-Thorne

Miss Yavapai-Apache, 1990, Lisa Jackson, talented young Yavapai woman, and honor student at N.A.U.

washing clothes, to let them know she wanted to earn money washing their clothes. My father chopped wood for the white people. We lived in a teepee house (wickiup). Some of my people squatted on company land which belonged to the United Verde. The company let them do this if they worked in the mine.

"My family lived close to where the smelter was to be built (Clarkdale). When they were ready to build the smelter, we were told to move. There was a white man who had an orchard near there. He told us not to move, but we were afraid that if we didn't move, they would send us back to San Carlos.

"There were three or four families who had to move. The white man's name was Walter Jordan. He was a nice man and good to the Indians. Jordan let the Indians gather apples. The Indians put the apples into barrels and let them ferment. They added malt and mixed it with sugar. Pretty soon, the Indians would be hollering and screaming all over the place. Jordan let them do that.

"Jordan was the one who Christianized the Indians. They don't know what a church was then. He (Jordan) was a real Christian. He gave my people vegetables, watermelons and things and paid them to pick for him.

"It makes me sad that my people have let their traditions go." (The Apaches on the other hand have retained their traditions.) "It is not good for their future. There are benefits through the tribe now, for students who graduate from high school. Everyone who does, can get a $5,000 scholarship to college. This is good."

Today, remnants of the once proud and prosperous People of the Sun and Dil'zeae move into the 21st Century with determination, purpose and the hope for long-range financial independence. The Tolkepaya, or Western Yavapai, whose boundaries once extended from the Bradshaw Mountains to Yuma are now known as the "Yavapai-Prescott Tribe, and have 115 registered Yavapai on their reservation." In 1935, 75 acres of land was transferred to them from the old Fort Whipple Military Reserve. This created the only reserve just for Yavapai Indians.

In establishing the reservation, the government also issued two cows to each family as a potential source of income. Over the years, the increasing size of this herd led to the government's decision to add 1,320 acres, also on the military reserve, to the Yavapai-Prescott Reservation.

With the establishment of the reservation, Sam Jimulla (Gee-mu-la) was appointed Chief of the Prescott Yavapais by the Commissioner of Indian Affairs, and simultaneously elected as Chief by his own people. He was succeeded by his wife, Viola following his death in 1940. A devout Christian, Viola organized the first Indian Presbyterian Mission and was known for her talent as a basket weaver. At the time of her appointment, she was the only woman Chief among American Indians. After her death in 1966 at the age of 88, Viola was inducted into the Arizona Women's Hall of Fame.

In the 55 years since they became an official reservation, the

Violet Jimulla - First woman "chief" in America and leader of the Yavapai-Prescott tribe. [SHM]

Women of the Yavapai-Prescott tribe revive their ancient art of basket-weaving. 1940s. [SHM]

Tolkepaya, or Prescott Yavapaies have set aside portions of their small reservation for The Sun Dog Industrial Park on Highway 89, one of their first ventures, and the Sheraton Resort and Conference Center which opened in 1988 through the efforts of developer Bill Grace. The tribe is now working with Grace to develop a 30-acre shopping center fronting Highway 69 to be anchored by Wall Mart. In addition, the tribe's bingo and Smoke Shops were relocated on Hwy. 69 near the Sheraton Resort and planned shopping center. Presently the tribe is working with the city of Prescott to provide educational resources for their youth, and are striving to revive and preserve the rich heritage of their culture.

The Kwevikopaya, or Southeastern Yavapai who lived in the Mazatzal-Four Peak and Superstition Mountain region were granted a 24,689 acre reservation in 1903 at the old Fort McDowell Military Reserve. This is the largest of the Yavapai and Apache's three reservations in terms of acreage and it is certainly the most valuable.

Located at the confluence of the Salt and Verde Rivers, the Fort McDowell "Mohave-Apache" reservation is situated in the heart of two of Arizona's most expensive developments - Scottsdale and Fountain Hills. Since 1910, members of this tribe have had an ongoing, non-stop battle to retain this valuable piece of real estate, and their invaluable water rights to the Verde River.

The 1910 Kent Decree stipulated that the Fort McDowell residents should be moved to the Salt River Pima Reservation, where their water rights would have been reduced considerably. For over 25 years, the tribe continually blocked these relocation efforts. Dr. Carlos Montezuma, a Yavapai captured as a boy by the Pimas, sold into white society and educated as one of the first American Indian medical doctors, was instrumental in blocking the relocation efforts and saving the reservation for his people. In 1923, Montezuma, who became one of the most famous Indians in the United States from 1890 until his death, chose to die among his people in a wikiup on the Verde River at Fort McDowell in 1923. It was Montezuma who initiated the drive to give Native Americans the right to vote, and one year after his death, in 1924, this long over due privilege was finally granted.

Presently the Fort McDowell tribe (whose enrollment is 688 Yavapai and Apache), is fighting government attempts to build the Orm Dam, a component of the Central Arizona Project, which would cover most of the reservation at Fort McDowell with water. Such a dam would provide water considered 'essential' for the swimming pools and golf courses of their wealthy nearby neighbors. The "Indian Wars" are not over yet. They just take place in courtrooms now, instead of mountains, and water has replaced gold as the source of contention.

The Wipukapaya, people of the red rocks, and the Dil'zeae whose land once ranged from Bill Williams Mountain to Granite Peak

"Wassaja" with Carlos Gentile. Gentile bought Wassaja for $30. This five year old Yavapai child, who was captured in a Pima raid in 1872, was renamed Carlos Montezuma, educated in the east and became one of the first American Indian medical doctors. After a visit to his people at Fort McDowell in the 1900's, he helped save them from being relocated to the Pima's Salt River Reservation. He also was instrumental in getting American Indians the right to vote in 1924 and was one of the most famous Native Americans in the country from 1900 until his death in 1923. Arizona State University - Heyden Collection.

Grave of Carlos Montezuma at Fort McDowell. When Dr. Montezuma realized he was dying of tuberculosis, he returned to his people at Fort McDowell, shed all white trappings and stayed in a wikiup near the Verde River where he later died. Members of his family insisted on taking care of him despite his warnings against it, and all died of tuberculosis as well. (photo by Kate Ruland-Thorne)

65

near Prescott, (the Dil'zeae roamed from Bill Williams Mountain to Show Low and Young and throughout the Tonto Basin) returned to the Camp Verde area in 1898 with nothing but hope that land would still be available. What they found was only a future of hard labor and sacrifice. Things have never been easy for them, even to this day. "Our neighboring communities still do not understand why we are here," said David Sine, a respected member of this tribe. "They only see us a people who stand in the way of their progress."

Today, the 1,092 Yavapai-Apache at Camp Verde hold 653 acres of land which includes a 150 acre farming cooperative in Middle Verde on land sold to them by the Wingfield family. North of the town of Camp Verde near where old Fort Verde is located, the tribe has built the Yavapai-Apache Visitor's Center and Cliff Castle Lodge in order to serve the thousands of annual tourists who visit their 'place of the origin,' Montezuma Well, as well as Montezuma Castle and the Tuzigoot ruins. Their land holdings were recently increased by 54.4 acres when the Phelps-Dodge Corporation granted land to its Indian employees at their copper mine outside of Clarkdale in 1969.

All three groups are striving for self-determination and self-government, education for their children, and an ability to stand proudly alongside all of their American neighbors.

In the 1960's, the Tonto and Yavapai tribes united to make claims against the U.S. Government for the lands taken from them in the 1860s. A court settlement awarded them fifty cents per acre for the 10 million acres that had once been their home.

It does seem ironic, however, that each of these small Yavapai and/or Apache reservations now provide a refuge for them on or near the very forts which were historically established to exterminate them as a people.

◆

Looking to the future, which is in the hands of the young.
(photo by Kate Ruland-Thorne)

BIOGRAPHY

Kate Ruland-Thorne was born in Colorado where she began her writing career in 1976. She specialized in human interest, art, personal profiles and historical subjects, several hundred of which were published in regional magazines and newspapers including the DENVER POST. Her first book, LION OF REDSTONE (Johnson Publishing, Boulder) is an acclaimed history of one of Colorado's infamous coal barons. After moving to Sedona, Arizona in 1984, she served as editor for the SEDONA MAGAZINE AND VISITORS' GUIDE, and was the first woman editor of the Sedona RED ROCK NEWS. She also is a regular contributor to SOUTHWEST ART MAGAZINE among others. In 1987, she formed THORNE ENTERPRISES with her husband Keith and son Reed Thorne. This is the company's third publication.

ACKNOWLEDGEMENTS

My very deepest gratitude goes to David Sine, Mabel Dogka, "The Elders of the Tribe" and Vincent Randall of the Yavapai-Apache Tribe of Camp Verde and Clarkdale who spent hours going over my chapter and making changes and suggestions, and to Nancy Quaid, historian for the Yavapai-Prescott Tribe, also to Louis Hood of the Fort McDowell Indian Reservation, all of whom provided encouragement and information that was invaluable.

Chapter Three
WHITE EYES, LONG KNIVES
AND RENEGADE INDIANS

General Crook, Indian Scouts
and The Pony Soldiers of the Verde Valley
By Dr. V. Keith Thorne

*he labors, endurance and combats of the western regular created the framework of law and order that made settlement and social development possible. As members of the Regular Army, these men formed an important segment of our usually slighted national military continuum, upon and around which our massive armies have been created in times of crises."*

Don Rickey, Jr.

Forty Miles A Day On Beans and Hay

What was it like to live in the Verde Valley following the ending of the Civil War in 1865? This beautiful area stretching from red rock country (Sedona) to the lower valley where cottonwood trees line the banks of the Rio Verde, was a pioneer's dream. But, until 1882, it was too dangerous a place to settle down.

The early settlers' efforts to grow crops, raise cattle, build homes and establish a community, brought on inevitable attacks by Indians. The Verde Valley was the stronghold of the Yavapai and Tonto Apaches, who fiercely fought against this white invasion, and the intrusion on their way of life.

Because of this conflict, Company K, 1st Cavalry, consisting of one lieutenant and eighteen "pony" soldiers (the nickname for the cavalry), were sent from Fort Whipple in Prescott to the Verde Valley upon "urgent report."

Indians referred to settlers and miners as "white eyes," and troopers were called "long knives" because of the sabers they carried in the early part of the Indian Wars.

Company K established a tent camp, known as "The Camp on the Clear Fork of the Rio Verde." It was located near a small Verde Valley settlement and by the end of 1865, was officially named Fort Lincoln.

Within a few months after their arrival, this small detachment of troopers became engaged in its first battle with the Tonto Apaches. Five of the 'hostiles' were killed. Throughout the rest of that year, the Yavapai and Tonto Apaches continued constant raids on the ranchers and settlers, often escaping with large amounts of livestock and cleverly avoiding direct contact with the soldiers at Fort Lincoln.

Recognizing the need for more help, Company E, Fourth Infantry, marched from Fort Whipple to Fort Lincoln the following year. This time a Captain, two lieutenants and 129 soldiers arrived, and soon were engaged in another confrontation with the Tonto Apaches. The 47 soldiers engaged in this conflict suffered no casualties, but did manage to kill 17 Apaches and took a large number of them prisoner.

By 1871, due to the unsanitary conditions and rampant malaria at Fort Lincoln, the tent camp was moved one mile south to its present location on higher ground, and construction of a more permanent fort began. Officers quarters, stables, barracks and a hospital were built and an area cleared for a parade ground. Eight years later, this new site was designated Fort Verde, replacing the name "Fort Lincoln." Despite this more fortified establishment, hostile raids continued and the threat of death hung over settlers, troopers and Indians alike.

In the summer of 1871, some 56 Tonto Apaches were killed by Fort Verde soldiers. The soldiers once again escaped causalities.

When not engaged in combat, the life of the frontier soldier was best described as a boring, lonely life filled with constant danger from his hostile environment. Not only did he face threats from marauding Indians - his living conditions were unbearable. Stifling desert heat, disease, blowing dust, snakes, scorpions, poor rations and clothing, bad equipment, poor quarters in isolated camps and forts in waterless, desolate regions were his daily companions.

The possibility of being wounded and taken alive, then slowly tortured by being placed on an ant hill, or perhaps roasted alive instead, head down over a campfire. A horrible mutilation usually followed. And all for the great sum of thirteen dollars a month.

Modern movies and writing portray the frontier regular as a dashing, romantic figure - or brand him as a squaw or baby killer, who degraded and oppressed the 'Noble red man' by intruding into his land. In truth, the trooper of the Regular Army was a professional made up of recent Irish, German, English and Slavic immigrants. There were many Civil War veterans who enlisted after 1865.

Most were illiterate, neither able to read nor write, and took to the army in order to survive. As individuals, they were psychologically and physically isolated from their fellow Americans, (as were the Viet Nam veterans of modern times.) It remains a national disgrace that more recognition hasn't been given to these men who sacrificed not only their lives, but their dignity as individuals. They fought under untold hardships in a guerrilla warfare for which they were not trained. In some cases, they fought

an enemy who had been supplied with superior weaponry by the U.S. Government.

During the Civil War, many of these men were indeed heroes, but little concern was given them when they fought the Indian Wars. They were heroes, of course, to the settlers in the Western plains and Southwest desert. Without their protection, settlers, miners, and railroad workers making their way west would have suffered even more, had not the cavalry played a major part in their survival.

The daily routine of garrison duty was often dull and boring. A trooper, or soldier with any experience or skill as a carpenter, barber, tailor, or cobbler was usually given this duty. The men got their hair cut once a month by the company barber and were required to shave twice a week. The barber did this on his own time and was paid fifty cents per man each month. However, this did not excuse him from his regular duties as a guard or for cleaning details.

Men detailed as cooks and bakers, which provided necessary troop services, received neither pay or special rank. Men often served as blacksmiths, wagoners and farriers (responsible for shoeing all horses in a company which totaled at least 65 horses. Farriers also helped keep wagons in good order).

Thirty-five cents a day was paid to the post school teacher who had a background of some education, such as writing, reading and arithmetic. He taught those enlisted men, and officer's children who desired further education.

Being a 'Striker' was usually considered the most desirable duty. In contrast to barracks duty, the Striker was freed from routine duties, because he was associated with his officer's family. He thereby received special privileges and much better food. He waited on the officer and his family's every need, usually enjoying extra pay from the officer he served.

Most troopers resented, and somewhat scorned the officer's Striker, much as children would a teacher's pet. As a result, these servants were derisively known as "dog-rubbers."

But given the monotonous routine and the soldier's daily menu, one can hardly blame an enlisted man for offering his services as a Striker. For one thing, he ate better food.

Sgt. Pearly S. Eaton, who was stationed at Camp Verde, described in his diary the typical menu that was the daily fare of the soldier:

"For breakfast we had dry sliced bread (no butter) and coffee (no milk); For dinner, sliced beef, dry bread and coffee; for supper, coffee straight - just dry bread and coffee . . . the food was very poor."

Army rations did not include milk, butter, or eggs. Soldiers often used company funds to purchase these items. Commissary supplied rations did not include fresh vegetables - the enlisted men had to obtain these for themselves from whatever available source they could find.

Soldiers at Fort Verde at camp during a "long" scout." 1870s. [FVSP]

A typical young Fort Verde soldier in winter dress - 1870s. (Fort Verde State Park [FVSP]

FORTS WITHOUT WALLS Fort Whipple was typical of forts established in Arizona and the Southwest during the Indian wars from 1860s - 80s. Apaches and other 'hostile' tribes rarely if ever attacked entire forts, preferring instead to employ guerrilla tactics (fighting in small groups acting independently). It was common, however, for them to initiate early morning raids on livestock at these forts. (Sharlot Hall Museum [SHM])

Troops sought assignment to extra duty for reasons other than pay, for they could be excused from some guard duty and drills. For twenty-five cents a day, hospital duty entitled a trooper extra pay and he was excused from other routine chores.

As in most armies, the non-commissioned officers, First Sergeants, were the key personnel in the smooth operation and maintenance of the required daily routine and discipline. They acted as executive officers to their commanding officers of the troop to which they were assigned.

During drills on the parade ground, the entire procedure was under the close control and observation of the 1st Sergeant, with seldom an officer present. The officer rarely was in close association with members of his troop, and was usually somewhat aloof.

Practically all the forts in Arizona and New Mexico were abandoned during the Civil War. It is reported, that following the outbreak of the Civil War when these frontier soldiers were removed from Arizona Territory, less than 200 civilians stayed behind . . . the rest fled to safer country. Although most of the people in the East looked upon the Indians as noble red men, settlers in the plains and desert considered them "Red Devils", and feared for their lives. They knew there would be an increase in massacres once the soldiers left...and there was.

The Indians interpreted this exodus of soldiers as a sign that they had run them out with their harassing and villainous attacks. None were more surprised than these same Indians when the soldiers returned four years later.

Cochise and Magnus Colorado, with enthusiastic cooperation of other Apache leaders, laid waste to all the Southwest. All the mines were closed, even those at Tubac, and one after another of the cities were abandoned. Only Tucson survived this devastating upheaval that made a smoking, smoldering, wasteland out of Arizona and New Mexico, while Plains Indians further north took advantage of the Civil War to devastate large areas in the Northwest.

White-eyes, as the Indians called the settlers and miners of Arizona and the Verde Valley were, according to the Indians, formidable foes. These foes were different from their Mexican prey, in that they were never without their deadly rifles and were extremely accurate with their guns. They were very difficult to kill, and even while dying, thought of only one thing - to take with them as many of their enemies as they could into the shadows of death.

In 1871, General George Crook was put in command of the Department of Arizona by order of the Secretary of War. With Fort Verde as one of his bases, Crook launched a campaign against the Yavapai and Apaches, and did not let up until his mission was accomplished. Because of the unique tactics he employed, it took him less than two years to bring an end to the Indian Wars which had been raging in the Southwest for over 300 years.

GENERAL GEORGE CROOK (1829 - 1890)

General George Crook was known to the Indians as Nan-Tan-Lupan (Chief Grey Wolf). His attitude toward the Indians was different from that of his predecessors. He had a better understanding of the Indian's problems, and more compassion toward their plight, even though many of the present-day Apaches and Yavapai may not agree with that assumption. As to General Crook's appearance, a description by Captain John Bourke, who served under him, details it best:

"His personal appearance was impressive, but without the slightest suggestion of the pompous and overdressed military man; he was as plain as an old stick, and looked more like an honest country squire than the commander of a war-like expedition. He had blue-grey eyes, quick and penetrating in his glance, a finely chiseled Roman nose, a firm and yet kindly mouth, a well-arched head, a good brow and a general expression of indomitable resolution, honest purpose, sagacity, and good intentions. He had an aversion to wearing a uniform, and to the glitter and filigree of the military profession. He was essentially a man of action, and spoke but little, and to the point, but was fond of listening to conversations of others. He was at all times accessible to the humblest soldier or the poorest "prospector," without ever losing a certain dignity which repelled familiarity, but had no semblance of haughtiness. He never used profanity and indulged in no equivocal language."

His chosen mode of transportation was his favorite mule, Apache. Capt. Bourke also noted: "Crook's council of war differed from those of any general he had known. He never asked anyone for an opinion, and never gave one of his own."

General Crook graduated from West Point in 1852, and in 1862, was wounded during the Civil War. He retained the rank of Major General before the conflict between the states ended.

Following the Civil War, Crook continued his army career, this time as an Indian fighter. Although Crook has gone down in history as one of this country's greatest Indian fighters, there are some historians who believe General Crook was too timid, slow, cautious, and at times failed to press attacks even when he had superior forces.

One interesting example was the criticism he received for his action (or non-action) when in command of a large force driving up from Fort Fetterman to protect the southern flank during the June, 1876 drive to the Little Big Horn.

General Terry and General Gibbons coming down from the north and from the east with their contingents of infantry and cavalry, were to meet with Lt. Col. George Armstrong Custer and his 7th Cavalry at Little Big Horn on June 26, 1876. Their purpose was to surround and drive renegade Indians back to the Rosebud Reservation.

Coming up from the south, Gen. Crook encountered a large band of these Indians, painted for war at the Rosebud, and a battle ensued. Although greatly outnumbering the hostiles, Crook failed to press his advantage and instead proceeded an orderly retreat. He reasoned that his line of communication might become over extended. He also believed he had suppressed an Indian attack, a victory of its own. The Indians, on the other hand, saw this as their victory. They believed they had turned away a large army contingent and went wild with excitement. If General Crook had pressed forward and taken the field, demoralizing this marauding group of hostiles, Custer's defeat at Little Big Horn several days later, might not have taken place.

As it was, the Indians returned to their encampment filled with 'war power' which incited the 4,000 other renegade warriors to stay their ground. Custer never knew his southern flank no longer existed, and his fate was sealed. Discovered by the Indians on June 25, a day before his reinforcements were to arrive, Custer was forced into an unexpected battle with the Indians, who outnumbered him tremendously, and the rest is history.

Prior to this infamous event, Crook had already made a name for himself in the Southwest, where his final victory over Geronimo was the climax of his military life. Crook was known for his skill as a leader against tribes, and was respected by the Indians for his honesty in dealing with them. All in all these factors helped shorten the Apache Wars and in some people's opinion, benefited both whites and Indians in the long run.

Gen. Crook had his base of command at Fort Whipple, Prescott, where he laid down his policy toward the Indians in his General Order:

"The Commanding General, after making a thorough and exhaustive examination among the Indians . . . regrets to say that he finds among them a general feeling of distrust and want of confidence in the whites, especially the soldiers; and also that much dissatisfaction, dangerous to the peace of the country, exists among them. Officers and soldiers . . . are reminded that one of the fundamental principles of the military character is justice to all - Indians as well as white man - and that a disregard of this principal is likely to bring about hostilities, and cause the deaths of the very people they are sent here to protect. In all their dealings with the Indians, officers must be careful not only to observe the strictest fidelity, but to make no promise, not in their power to carry out; all grieving arising in their jurisdiction should be redressed, so then an accumulation of them may not cause an outbreak."

Gen. Crook next ordered all squatters and unauthorized miners to remove themselves from the Camp Date Creek and Camp Verde Reservations. He even started an investigation which resulted in the reorganization of the Indian Department, and the discharge of some agents and higher-up officials in the same department.

Next, he established a military trail, which today is known as General Crook's Trail. This trail began at Fort Whipple in Prescott, and ended at Fort Apache. Both of these forts, and the Crook

YAVAPAI SCOUTS - 1870s. Chief of Scouts Al Sieber preferred the Tonto Apache scouts over Yavapai because the Yavapai insisted on four days of a purification ceremony following each scouting expedition, particularly if any killing was involved. Tontos did not adhere to such requirements, and therefore did not slow expeditions down. [SHM]

Capt. J.C. Burke, Capt. McGonigle and General George Crook. 1880s. [SHM]

.rail, are still in existence. The 175 mile-long trail traverses the Verde Valley, cuts through the pine wilderness of the higher terrain of the Mogollon Rim, and ends at Fort Apache in the White Mountains.

In her delightful book, VANISHING ARIZONA, Martha Summmerhayes recalled her own excursion along the Crook Trail in the 1870s. She relates her experience as a young Army wife, accompanying her Lieutenant husband to Fort Apache. She was the first woman to travel by wagon along Crook's Trail.

Camping along the trail at night, Martha could not free herself from anxiety of an Apache attack. Everywhere she looked, she imagined a fierce Apache behind a dark tree trunk. Seeking assurance one night from her husband, he patted her lovingly and told her she could feel safe about going to sleep. "The Apaches never attack at night," he said. Several minutes later, Martha whispered..."When do they attack?"..."Just before dawn," he yawned.

Unbeknownst to Martha Summerhayes, she had as much reason to fear the Yavapai warriors as she did the Apache. By the 1870s, both of these distinctly different tribes had joined forces to fight for their sacred lands in the Verde Valley. Yavapais are not Apaches, but even Crook did not bother to make this tribal distinction. This error on his part, and that of other white Americans, caused untold hardship and suffering for this Yuman-speaking tribe, who initially tried in vain to avoid war with the U.S. Army.

The major reason for Crook's eventual success in the "Apache Wars" was his establishment of the Indian Scout Service. Crook used one Indian band against another, relying on the traditional enmities that often existed between them. In his war against the Tonto Apaches and Yavapais for instance, Crook employed Scouts from the White Mountain band, whose historic association with their northern brethren rarely had been friendly. The man Crook chose most often to lead these Scouts was Chief of Scouts, Al Sieber.

INDIAN SCOUTS VERSUS INDIAN OUTLAWS

General George Crook proved that Indian Scouts were necessary in the successful elimination of Indian hostiles in Northern Arizona. The main figures in that triumph were the civilian and army leaders who controlled, managed, led and inspired those Indian Scouts. They were known as Chief of Scouts. Normally they were not the officers in command, but as head of all Scouts, they were actually in command in the truest sense of the word. Commanding officers learned quickly while in the field to base their decisions upon whatever their Chief of Scouts advised. Such were the likes of Al Sieber, Tom Horn, Dan O'Leary and Mickey Free, and others, all well-known Chief of Scouts in the Verde Valley.

Mickey Free had been captured by the Apaches when he was a boy, and had not been treated well by them. As a Scout, he

Mickey Free, one of the least trusted and least liked scouts among the Indians he led. [FVSP]

Al Sieber, Chief of Scouts, 1870s. [FVSP]

Tonto Apache scouts at Fort Verde, 1870-80s. [FVSP]

Al Sieber (middle) with Tonto scouts, 1870s. [FVSP]

delighted in their suffering, and took great satisfaction in helping to exterminate them whenever possible. Of all the Scouts, he was the least liked and respected by Indian people. Al Sieber, who worked with Mickey Free, once described him as "half" Mexican, half Irish and whole son-of-a-bitch."

Cochise, the famous leader of the Chiruachua Apaches, was wrongly accused of Free's childhood kidnaping in 1860. It was because of this, and the unbelievable bungling by a greenhorn lieutenant, that one of the most vicious Apache uprisings in the Southwest erupted.

In 1861, Cochise was accused of stealing Mickey Free from a ranch near Fort Buchanan. Like most Apaches, Cochise had a bitter hatred and distrust for all white men, which stemmed from an incident in which his wife and children were slaughtered.

But Cochise had been at peace for awhile when the 7th Cavalry camped near his stronghold on Apache Pass. One Lieut. George Bascom was sent to retrieve the child, Mickey Free, from Cochise' encampment. Cochise, along with some warriors, came to Bascom's tent to talk to him. As soon as Cochise arrived, the soldiers tried to take him into custody. Cochise drew a knife and slashed his way out of the tent, leaving his fellow warriors to be seized as hostages. Cochise immediately captured several white men to assure an exchange of prisoners. Due to Bascom's bungling, the exchange never took place. Furious, Cochise saw to it that the white men were tortured and put to death. The soldiers retaliated by hanging the Indians, and a vicious war began again.

During this war of hatred, it is a known historical fact that Cochise tortured at least 16 prisoners by dragging them behind horses with a rope until they died. He was known to have burned 18 men alive at the stake, and tortured many others by cutting flesh slowly from their bodies until they died in agonizing, screaming pain. With this kind of statistic, one can only believe Cochise was a murderous, sadistic outlaw, and truly an uncivilized savage by white man's standards. Despite Hollywood movies to the contrary, he was never of the same mold as Chief Joseph of the Nez Pearce or Crazy Horse and other respected warriors.

But, there were those who viewed him differently. One doctor, A.N. Ellis, observed Cochise during a peace conference with Gen. Granger in 1871.

"While he was talking, we had a fine opportunity to study this most remarkable man. Evidently he was about 58 years old, 5'8" tall, in person lithe and wiry, every muscle being well-rounded and firm. A silver thread was now and then visible in his otherwise black hair which he wore cut straight around his head, about level with his chin. His countenance displayed great force.

"General Granger expressed the White Father's" desire for peace. He reiterated that the land, mountains and valleys he was now in, would be part of his reservation. Cochise, expressing his doubt,

gave his speech - a sad speech, relating the unsolvable problems revolving around the white man's intrusion of his sacred homeland. Cochise stated . . ."when I was young, I walked all over the country, east and west, and saw no other people than the Apaches. After many summers, I walked again and found another race of people who had come to take it. How is it? Why is it that the Apaches want to die - that they carry their lives on their fingernails? They roam over the hills and plains, and want the heavens to fall on them. The Apaches were once a great nation; they are now but a few...many have been killed in battle...tell me, if the Virgin Mary has walked throughout all the land, why has she never entered the land of the Apache?"

Cochise ended this oratory stating he would never consent to life on the Tularosa Reservation in New Mexico. "That is a long way off," he stated. "The flies in those mountains eat out the eyes of the horses. The bad spirits live there. I have drunk of these waters...I do not want to leave here."

In spite of General Granger's promise that he would not be sent to the Tularosa Reservation, within months, that is exactly where Cochise and his people were ordered to go. Cochise kept his promise. He fled into his beloved mountains. Once again, the Apaches were on the warpath. Some 56 raids were made in the year that followed. Over 45 white people lost their lives as a result, and the numbers of wounded and amount of livestock stolen, soared.

The white man's inability to follow through on his promises, always reaped death and destruction. For the Tonto and Yavapai people of Central Arizona, however, such men as Crook and Al Sieber went out of their way to be honest and straight forward in their dealings with the Indians. After Crook took control in Central and Northern Arizona in 1871, the Indian Wars came to a speedy conclusion, simply because men like Crook and Al Sieber kept their word.

Al Sieber was not only honest in his dealings with the Indians, he was considered a gentleman among his own people. Tom Horn, another respected Chief of Scouts, and Al Sieber were great friends and shared many adventures together. Like Sieber, Horn was known as an excellent Chief of Scouts. Unfortunately, Horn was hanged in Montana many years after the Indian Wars, for a crime he did not commit.

In the final containment of the Southwest, the value of Crook's Indian Scouts proved a case in point. During the period between 1872-74, fewer than 20 hostile Indians were killed or captured by the regular army without using Scouts. Whereas the army units who took advantage of the Indian Scout system, killed 275 hostiles and captured more than 330 during that same period. Needless to say, the value of the Scouts during the Indian Wars of Arizona Territory, was invaluable.

The way that General Crook persuaded Indians to become Scouts against their own people was by telling them: "I expect good men to help me to run down bad ones. This is the way white people do it; if there are bad men in neighborhoods, all law-abiding citizens turn out to assist the officers of the law in arresting and punishing those who will not behave themselves. I hope that you will see it's your duty to do the same."

Being fed and clothed and put on the payroll of the U.S. Army, helped persuade many to join up. Scouting was an easy thing to do, particularly when tracking old tribal rivals. They had been doing this for centuries.

Crook used as an example to them, that the white man had outlaws too. Men like Frank and Jesse James, the Dalton Gang and Cole Younger were bad men who needed to be hunted down, just as Indian outlaws like Geronimo, Cochise and Delshay.

Not all Indian Scouts were Apaches in Arizona. To fill out the ranks, General Crook enlisted Yavapais, Walapais, Pimas and Piutes, among others. Both Crook and Sieber preferred the Tonto Apaches overall, and considered them the best Scouts. Yavapais were excellent Scouts also, but they required a four day purification ceremony following an engagement in which there was killing, and this simply slowed things down too much.

Men like Al Sieber were put in control of one Company of Indian Scouts, usually consisting of 26 Indians, who were attached to a column of cavalry. Sieber became one of Gen. Crook's most renowned Chief of Scouts.

Al Sieber was born in Rhineland, Germany in 1844. His widowed mother brought her family to America when Al was still a boy.

As an adult, Sieber stood six feet in height, and was a man of strength, and powerfully built. He had penetrating blue eyes, and wore his blond hair short. He always sported a mustache, which was common during this period.

An excellent shot, Sieber never hesitated to take aim and kill when the need arose. He maintained a loyalty among his Scouts both through fear and honest dealings. He said, "I do not deceive them, but always tell them the truth. When I say I'm going to kill them, I do it, and when I tell them I'm their friend, they know it." There was rarely a deserter among Sieber's Company of Indian Scouts.

Sieber arrived in Central Arizona during the height of the gold rush in the late 1860s. This was also the time of the Yavapai and Apache Wars in that area.

Violence raged on both sides as Arizona soil became drenched with the blood of men, women and children, both red and white. To pluck a gold nugget out of the soil, one had better be prepared to fight for it. Of course the "ignorant" Indians never understood why they had to give up their hunting grounds and way of life to satisfy the white man's lust for gold.

When Sieber arrived in Prescott in 1867, it was an established gold camp with a population of around 500. He arrived after mustering out of the Civil War, working his way westward doing odd jobs. Just 25 years of age, and without funds, he signed on to ride guard for Teamster Dan Hazzard. It was a dangerous job to bring freight into Prescott through hostile territory. From behind any bush or rock, there was a constant threat of being attacked by either marauding Indians, Mexican bandits, or plain-old outlaws. Soon Sieber made friends with such Indian fighters as Dan O'Leary, John Townsend and Ed Peck. Dan O'Leary, possibly the most famous Indian fighter up until 1868, had guided a survey party for General William Jackson Palmer when he was looking for a railroad route through Northern Arizona in 1867. O'Leary and Ed Peck were always in the news during the decade of the 60s, because of their continued success in fighting Indians.

Eventually Sieber became foreman of a large ranch near Prescott. Here he was called upon to fight Indians on a regular basis. With the help of Dan O'Leary, he became most proficient in learning the rudiments of scouting. Sieber developed the keen ability to hear, see and smell, and accumulate and evaluate evidence. Upon this basis, he could make fast decisions about what was happening, what might happen and why it was happening at all. From his friend O'Leary, Sieber learned and learned well.

When Gen. Crook arrived in Arizona with orders to crush Yavapai and Apache resistance, Al Sieber was one of the first Crook sought to train and oversee his companies of Indian Scouts. Crook immediately admired Sieber's worth, and could see that he was a knowledgeable Scout.

General Crook needed men like Sieber, whose skills he described as extraordinary. Crook placed equal value on his other Scout leaders like Dan O'Leary, Archie McIntosh and Tom Horn.

Crook's plan to subdue the hostiles entailed placing small commands into the field to saturate the territory and either fight or keep Indians so stirred up that they would choose to surrender rather than starve or be routed out and slaughtered. Winter snows aided in this operation.

Crook's ruthless plans involved destroying the Indian's food supply and not only subjecting them to starvation, but also to freezing. In the later part of the Indian Wars, this became the general procedure of the army who used the winter months as their ally to hunt down, capture or kill Indians during their most vulnerable time.

Throughout the winter, soldiers and Scouts attacked, burned and destroyed encampments, wiped out food supplies and killed off the Indians' half-starved pony herds. After the Superstition Mountains were cleared of hostiles, the war moved east and west of the Verde River. By the first week of April 1873, bands of Indians began to surrender, most of them at Fort Verde. They complained that "every rock had turned into a soldier and that soldiers sprang from the ground."

The only one who did not surrender at first was the murderous renegade Delshay, also known as "Big Rump" and the "Red Ant." This Northern Tonto was the scourge of the Verde Valley, and every bit as elusive and treacherous as Geronimo. Just like Geronimo and Billy the Kid, Delshay was feared by his own people. In spite of the surrendering of these hostiles, this was not the end of the Indian troubles in Northern Arizona. Nevertheless, most of the white Scouts were discharged at the end of April, 1873. Archibald McIntosh and Al Sieber were not among those discharged, but were retained to mop up the remaining renegades. Sieber was assigned to Fort Verde. From 1873 to 1879. He was the only regular guide and Chief of Scouts at Fort Verde during that time, and was continually in the field. Because the Indians at the Rio Verde Reservation, 16 miles from Fort Verde, were of mixed tribes, old feuds erupted regularly among these 2,000 people. It was common for many of them to bolt the reservation and have to be brought back. Sieber was convinced that regardless of the trouble at the Rio Verde Reservation, it was usually the old renegade Delshay who was at the bottom of it.

Delshay was as mean-tempered and sadistic as Geronimo. He was a powerful man, incapable of compassion, who cleverly was able to avoid capture. General Crook finally put a price on his head - literally. Payment would be received if Delshay's head was brought to him. Delshay's distinguishing feature was an earring which he wore in his right ear.

Three Tonto Scouts were sent out for the proposed capture or decapitation. Returning from their escapade, they claimed they killed Delshay at Turret Mountain on the 29th of July. They brought in a scalp with part of the notorious earringed ear as proof. Crook paid them for the scalp. On at least two different other occasions, Delshay's head was presented again to Crook, earring and all. Crook paid off all three parties. It wasn't until the final surrender of the Verde Valley Indians at Camp Verde on April 27, 1873, that Crook came face to face with Delshay, head in tact, when Delshay surrendered.

Six months previously, Delshay had 125 followers. Now only 20 existed. Delshay complained, "there was a time when we could escape the white-eyes, but now the very rocks have become soft. We could not put our feet anywhere. We could not sleep, for if a coyote or fox barks, or stone moves, we are up - the soldiers have come."

Delshay was finally killed by his own people on July 7, 1874. They were tired of being punished for his murderous behavior. His death was a real relief to Sieber. It finally gave him some spare time, to poke around for the yellow metal.

It is likely Sieber's Indian friends showed him the ancient mines near Fort Verde on what later became known as Jerome's Cleopatra Hill. Unfortunately for Sieber, he never filed an official claim on the hill that later became the "Billion Dollar Copper Camp of Jerome." But in those days, copper had no particular value, the famous hill's gold and silver was buried too deep for him to know about, and the turquoise nuggets lying around were prized only to the Indians.

In 1875, Sieber was ordered to accompany 1,500 Indians from the Rio Verde Reservation on their infamous forced "March of Tears" to the San Carlos Reservation. After the Apaches and Yavapais were settled on this reservation, they entered into a new relationship with the white man. For many of them, their roaming days were over, and they wanted to live in peace. They were encouraged to forget their old ways and start raising corn instead of scalps.

After arriving at San Carlos, Sieber was assigned to be in charge of the first Apache police force, established by Indian Agent, John Clum. When Geronimo first bolted San Carlos in 1877, Sieber, Clum and 40 Apache policemen captured him and brought him back. When Geronimo escaped again in 1882, Sieber was once more put on his trail. This time, Geronimo's escape was precipitated by the Cibicue Mutiny of 1881. This was one of the only times when Indian Scouts mutinied against the U.S. Army.

CIBICUE MUTINY - AUGUST 30, 1881

In the majority of cases, a crooked Indian Agent could foment such trouble as to provoke an uprising on an Indian reservation. Such was the case of Indian Agent J.C. Tiffany at Fort Apache, who cheated in the issuing of rations, stole cattle meant for the Indians, and held back stores of supplies, selling them to unscrupulous others and pocketing the money.

The Office of Indian Affairs in Washington finally relieved him of his position, but it was too late. The harm had already been done.

A year before, a Piute medicine man named Wavoka had a vision in the Northern Plains of Nevada (Pyramid Lake) and the Ghost Dance was introduced. Shortly afterwards, the Indians at San Carlos adopted it.

Nockay-del-klinne, a White Mountain Apache, came forth with his own version of this new religion. His doctrine promised the resurrection of all ancestral Indians, dead warriors and relatives, and the restoration of land stolen from Indian people. Nockay-del-klinne envisioned the death and removal of all white men from their sacred homeland by the time the corn grew tall.

Ten years earlier, Nockay-del-klinne had been sent on a peace mission to Washington, and conferred with President Grant. Although only in his twenties, this young Apache was a man of some influence and considered a man of peace. Upon his return, he enlisted as an Apache scout, and was one of the first such scouts used by General Crook to track down hostile Indians.

In 1881, just before being relieved of his Indian agency control

- the corrupt Agent Tiffany informed Col. Eugene A. Carr, commander of troops at Fort Apache, that Nockay-del-klinne was to be arrested, or better yet be killed if he showed any signs of resistance. This Ghost Dance had to be stopped.

Col. Carr left Fort Apache with 23 White Mountain Indian Scouts, ten civilians, and three troops comprised of 121 troopers. Their destination was Cibicue Creek where they were to arrest and bring back to Fort Apache this young prophet of the new religion. This religion was particularly alarming because, for the first time, traditionally hostile bands of Indians were dancing the Ghost Dance - together. The overriding fear among the soldiers was that this dance would incite another major uprising.

There are two versions of what happened next - The soldiers' version and the Indians' version. According to army reports, Nockay-del-klinne agreed to come peacefully after considerable arguing and pleading on the part of the soldiers. The Indian version states that a Captain Hentig forced his way into Nockay-del-klinne's wikiup and dragged the young medicine man out by his hair, enraging the assembled Indians. Nockay-del-klinne was then put under guard in a tent.

The troopers and their entourage then made camp around or near the Indian encampment. Sergeant Dead-Shot, a White Mountain Apache Scout, asked permission of his officer to move his Scouts closer to the Indian campsite, because of supposed ant hills in their designated area. Suddenly, after they had moved closer to the Indian camp, Sgt. Dead Shot let out a war-whoop. He and his fellow scouts started firing into the soldier's camp, much to the surprise and horror of the soldiers. Capt. Hentig, the one accused by the Indians of humiliating their medicine man, was the first to be shot - in the back - as were five other troopers. The guards near the horses and grazing mules were killed instantly, and the herd driven off by the Indians.

When the firing started, the Sergeant guarding Nokay-del-klinne did as he had been ordered by Gen. Carr. He promptly shot the medicine man in the head. Nokay-del-klinne did not die immediately, and tried to crawl from the tent. This time, the troop bugler, seeing him trying to escape, shot him again in the head. This shot was fatal. Other witnesses say that a seargant grabbed an ax and decapitated Nokay-del-klinne. The fighting continued until night fall, after which the troopers buried their dead, eight in number. The bodies of 18 Indians including Nokay-del-klinne, his wife and six of the betraying White Mountain Apache Scouts, were left lying on the ground.

The Cibicue Mutiny provoked a whole new uprising. Raids continued against settlers and soldiers alike. Eventually, arrests were made of some of the White Mountain Apache Scouts who were involved in the Cibicue Mutiny.

In March of 1882, three White Mountain Apache Scouts: Sgt.

Geronimo, 1870s. [FVSP]

Dead-Shot, Skippy, and Dandy Jim, were found guilty of treason. They were publicly hanged at Fort Grant. Out of grief, Sgt. Dead-Shot's wife, it is reported, hanged herself from a tree at San Carlos that same day. As far as the military command was concerned, Carr had not used good judgment in engaging White Mountain Scouts to help him arrest a White Mountain medicine man.

Just before they were hanged, the doomed Scouts placed a curse on the attending priest and commanding officer. Both died of natural causes a short time later.

THE DEMISE OF GERONIMO

Because of the Cibicue Mutiny and the subsequent uprising, General Crook was called back to Arizona. He left San Bernardino with a company of 30 civilian volunteers, around 200 Apache and Yavapai Scouts, serving under Lieut. Gatewood, and Chief of Scouts, Al Sieber. Crook had successfully negotiated with the governors of Sonora and Chihuahua, Mexico, to have permission to cross over one another's border without consequences when in hot pursuit of hostiles. This, he believed, would ensure the capture of these renegades, who up to this time, roamed freely back and forth from one nation to another to their sanctuary in Mexico's Sierra Madre Mountains.

This new arrangement did indeed bring about the surrender of the most hostile Apache outlaws: Chato, Nana, Loco and the most infamous of all - Geronimo.

But once again, a familiar scenario developed - the first night after Geronimo and the others had been returned to the San Carlos Reservation, Geronimo got drunk, and away he went. Nana, Chato and their followers left with him. As a result, Crook came under severe criticism from General Sheridan in Washington. Crook tendered his resignation. It was accepted.

General Nelson Miles was assigned to replace him. Upon taking command, and not having the faith that Crook had regarding Indian Scouts, Miles dismissed most of them and replaced them with 5,000 white troopers.

Now we have an assembly of 5,000 troops, being called upon to destroy Geronimo and his enormous force of 38 renegades. Without using the Indian Scout Service, it took Miles 15 months to accomplish this feat.

One of his first efforts was to set up 30 heliograph stations to flash Morse messages from mountain top to mountain top. This network of stations was set up from Fort Verde to Fort Huachuca. Over 800 messages were sent during one period of four months. When Geronimo saw these mirror flashes, he thought they were magic and avoided the mountains all together.

Shockingly, another of General Miles' first orders was to exile all Mimbres and Chiricahua Apaches, including faithful Scouts from those bands, to a Florida prison. Among them was Geronimo's

Capt. Adane Chaffee [FVSP]

Out in the field, this was the method used to carry wounded back to camp. [FVSP]

own family.

Although General Miles took full credit for the final capture of Geronimo, in actuality it was Lieut. Gatewood and a company of reinstated Tonto Scouts from the Verde Valley led by two Tonto Apaches, Captain Smiley and Ed Joe. It is to them that the credit should have been given for finally locating Geronimo again in the Sierra Madres Mountains. Gatewood, with the help of two Chiricahua interpreters, convinced Geronimo to give himself up. As their reward, Miles shipped all these Scouts and interpreters off to a Florida prison along with Geronimo and his followers.

For the record, Geronimo was perhaps one of the most captured renegades in Arizona history. Among those who laid claim to his capture on various occasions were General Crook, John Clum, Lieut. Emmett Crawford, Lieut. Gatewood, and of course General Nelson Miles. History has never credited the real heroes in Geronimo's repeated captures - The Indian Scout Service of Arizona.

After serving two years at the Florida prison, Geronimo lived the remainder of his life in Fort Sill, Oklahoma. He often collected money by posing for photographs, autographing picture post cards of himself, and carving bows and arrows for children. He was quoted as saying, "I am no longer an Indian - I am a white man." He bragged that it took 5,000 soldiers 15 months to finally capture him and his 38 followers.

Geronimo died of pneumonia following a drunken stupor, after falling out of a wagon in a shallow pool of water, face down in the mud.

BATTLE OF BIG DRY WASH

The Battle of Big Dry Wash, took place almost a year after the Cibicue Mutiny, and was a direct result of it. Some of the White Mountain Scouts involved in that mutiny, joined a small contingent of Apaches led by a renegade named Nan-tio-tish. Their bloody escapade would come to a violent end in a remote canyon in the Verde Valley.

When the army command returned to Fort Apache two days after the famous mutiny, they found that word had spread about the death of the beloved medicine man, Nokay-del-klinne. Enraged Indians went on the war path again. Renegades by the hundreds fled the reservation and began a relentless series of raids against civilians and soldiers alike. Almost immediately, 11 troopers and seven civilians, mostly farmers and ranchers, were massacred within weeks of the incident.

For five years, the Verde Valley had enjoyed relative peace. Because Fort Verde was inactive, it was ordered to be abandoned in December of 1880. Most of the troopers were sent north to fight the Plains Indians. The Army officially closed Fort Verde in July 1881.

Fort Verde Today - Looking across the parade grounds toward the Commanding Officer's house (right) and the home of the Post Physician. photo by Alan Caillou.

Officers and their wives on a post porch at Fort Verde, 1880s. [SHM]

The more than 200 people who had settled in the Verde Valley, hated to see the troopers go, and even protested the decision. Three months after its abandonment, the events at Cibicue and San Carlos, caused the Fort to be re-garrisoned on October 26, 1881.

By July 6, 1882, a band of 54 Cibicue White Mountain Apaches, led by Nan-tio-tish and some renegades, including Indian Scout deserters involved in the Cibicue Mutiny, went on the war path. These hostiles raided the San Carlos Agency, killed the Indian police Chief and seven other Indian policemen, then stole supplies, horses, guns, ammunition and headed north.

Brevet Major General Orlando B. Wilcox - commander of the Department of Arizona ordered the activation of twelve troops of cavalry, and two companies of Indian Scouts. The following troops were immediately called to duty:

WHIPPLE BARRACKS: Capt. Russell, 3rd. Cav., commanding, left Whipple Barracks with 3rd Squadron consisting of his own Troop "K" and "H," 3rd Cavalry, Lt. G. F. Chase, commanding plus - troops "H" 6th Cav., Lt. H. P. Kingsbury, commanding.

FORT THOMAS: Capt. Drew, 3rd. Cav. Troops "A" and "C" and "G." This column did not arrive in time to participate in the Battle of Big Dry Wash due to trouble with their pack train.

FORT MCDOWELL: Capt. A.R. Chaffee, 6th Cav., Troop "I" was in route from Whipple Barracks to his home station at Fort McDowell, when he was advised by messenger from Whipple to proceed immediately to Tonto Basin, Rye Creek area to contact and intercept Nan-tio-tish.

FORT APACHE: Maj. A.W. Evans, 3rd. Cav., left Fort Apache with Troops "E," Lts. Hardy and Johnson, 3rd. Cav. commanding with Company "I," Lt. Converse, 3rd. Cav. commanding. Troops "E," with Capt. Kramer and Lt. Cruse, 6th Cav. "K" Capt. Abbott and Lt. Hodgson, 6th Cav. Also Lt. Dodd, Scout Keogh, four Scouts, Co. "B" accompanied the above named companies.

The hero, one of many, was Capt. Chaffee, 6th. Cav. Troop "I." He sent a messenger to Fort McDowell for Chief Scout Al Sieber and Lt. Morgan's Scouts, Co. "E" to meet him at Rye Creek. They thus crossed Nan-tio-tish's trail on the Mogollon Rim. This was on the 16th of July that Maj. Evans came upon the trail of Chaffee, who was now only a half day's march away.

Evans sent a patrol forward to bring Chaffee into conference. Chaffee related that the hostiles were only a half-day's march ahead of him, and they had discovered the white horses ridden by his troopers.

Maj. Evans instructed Chaffee at daylight to pursue the enemy and that he would follow with his four troops in support. Evans advised him that Lt. Converse's white horse troop would be placed in front of his column to possibly mislead the Indians into thinking that only Chaffee's single troop was chasing them. Nan-tio-tish took the bait. He never realized he was being pursued by all these different columns. He thought his only threat was the forty white horse contingent that he planned to ambush - this was his fatal mistake. He delayed leaving his camp at "General Springs" until he could see the pursuing column of white horses advancing in the canyon below the Mogollon Rim.

When Chaffee reached General Spring Camp, he left a note for Maj. Evans to send Lt. Converse's troopers to reinforce him as soon as possible. About eight miles north of General Springs, where Nan-tio-tish planned his ambush, the trail descends 800 feet into the almost vertical canyon of Big Dry Wash. The Indians barricaded themselves behind rocks in order to guard the trail up from the wash. At this point, the canyon is a little over 700 yards in width. This planned ambush was discovered by Apache Scouts, and they warned Chaffee in time to avoid a disaster.

This engagement was to be fought on the high mesa of the Mogollon Ridge, set in an area with no shrubbery or underbrush, but thick with large pine trees. The crossing point in this canyon was held by the hostiles, and their fire covered every foot of trail coming up or going down.

Chaffee dismounted his troops on the south rim of the canyon. At this very moment, Lt. Converse, with his all white horse troops, dismounted and began firing across the canyon. Nan-tio-tish, thinking this group numbering 40 was all that he faced, was surprised to learn that the troops numbered more tan 80 with still more to came.

A few hours later, around 3 p.m., Maj. Evans arrived with four more troops, without the knowledge of the Indians. Chaffee reported to his senior officer and was amazed when Maj. Evans told him to continue his plan of attack, as he relinquished his higher rank in favor of "you found them - it's your battle - proceed as you planned." Maj. Evans dismounted his troops some three hundred yards from the canyon rim, unseen by the hostiles.

Chaffee immediately ordered Lts. Cruse and Kramer, Troop "E," plus his own Troop "I" with Lt. West commanding, to proceed in an easterly direction. He ordered Al Sieber's Indian Scouts to go east about a mile and flank the enemy to the right. Lt. Converse kept up a steady fire across the canyon. Indian Scouts under Lt. Morgan, 3rd Cav. plus Lts. Hardy and Johnson of the 3rd. Cav., Capt. Abbott and Lt. Hobson, Troop "K", 6th Cav. were sent westerly to cross the canyon and then were instructed to head east to outflank hostiles from the left, thereby preventing their escape. A small number of men were left to guard horses and protect the pack train in case the Indians filtered through the defenses. The troops commanded by Lt. Converse held the point, in case the hostiles tried to slip past the chasm.

During this engagement, a ricochetting bullet struck a lava rock sending a sliver into Converse's eye, wounding him and putting him out of action. He later retired from the army as a Colonel, wearing a black patch over his left eye from that day of battle.

Lt. Cruse and Al Sieber and their scouts were on the north rim of the Dry Creek Wash, scouting the east flank when they discovered the Indians' pony herd. At this same time, Lt. Abbott on the west flank opened fire. Confusion reigned as Indians didn't know which way to turn. They just wanted to get away, so they rushed for their ponies. The ambush had worked in favor of the soldiers. It was a trap that led to the Indians' death.

One of the mule packers with Al Sieber's Scouts reported, "right in the middle of the fight, one of the Scouts saw two of his brothers and his father with the hostiles. He threw down his gun and ran toward his kin. Al Sieber called out for him to stop, but he did not comply, so Sieber raised his rifle, fired, and shot his own Scout in the back of the head."

Against Al Sieber's advise, the young Lt. Cruse, with his seasoned Scouts, charged the Indian camp. A young Scotsman, Joseph McLernon, standing to the left rear of the lieutenant, was killed by a bullet meant for Cruse. Lt. Cruse fired and killed the hostile. Cruse was awarded the Medal of Honor for his charge upon the hostile camp. Two other officers, Lts. Morgon and West, also received this medal, as did 1st. Sgt. Taylor.

Thus ended a day of slaughter. A raging storm swept out of the west to put a stop to the carnage. Tom Horn, Indian Scout, called it the heaviest rain storm and hail he had ever seen. According to Lt. West, it was so miserable and paralyzing that "Maj. Chaffee got so cold and wet he had to stop swearing."

Under the cover of darkness and the storm, the hostiles who were wounded and were able to escape did so, making their way across the reservation line some 20 miles away. Troopers who came from Camp Verde via Crook's Trail, arrived at daylight the following day, "much out of temper," because they missed the fight.

The following day - details were sent out looking for bodies and hunting the wounded. They counted 22 dead hostiles with seven wounded. It was presumed that many others lay dead, their bodies concealed in cracks and crevices of the rocky formations. It was learned that many Indians died later from wounds received in the battle.

Lt. Hodgson, head of a patrol that occupied an area where the hostiles had been, heard groans during the night. The next morning while investigating, the troopers were suddenly fired upon. Gun smoke arose from behind a large boulder, betraying the direction of the shots. The soldiers took cover and opened fire. The troopers continued firing for a few minutes, but getting no response, charged and discovered a young Indian woman, about 18 years old, lying prone on the ground. She shielded her six month-old baby while drawing her knife. She attacked the soldiers who finally overpowered her and took her gun and knife. Three bullets was all that was left, the empty cartridges scattered beside her.

The young woman's leg had been shattered by a bullet. A makeshift stretcher was made and she was transferred for two hours on a tedious decent down the canyon wall to the soldiers' camp. She must have suffered terribly, but never a groan was heard, nor did she cry out when an Army doctor later amputated her leg without anesthesia.

The Battle of Big Dry Wash was the final major battle between Apaches and Troops in Arizona. Nan-tio-tish was killed and the question arises, what would Cochise, Geronimo, Victorio have done under the same circumstances that faced this renegade warrior?

Of the soldiers who participated in this final battle, two officers, and seven enlisted men were killed or wounded. Co. "E" of the 6th Cav. took the heaviest causality toll.

A SOLDIER'S STORY

Cpl. Cyrus Milner, Co. A, 5th U.S. Cavalry, Camp Verde, A.T. 1873

During his enlistment, Cyrus Milner wrote letters to his cousin, Amelia Milner. The following is a letter written by Cyrus Milner, the spelling, punctuation and grammar are the soldier's. The letter was contributed by Catherine B. Bowen to the Fort Verde State Park:

"Dear cousin;

As I have been on a scout for the last thirty (30) days you will have to excuse my not writeing (sic) sooner. We have been on the war path since the first of oct (sic) and have only captured on (sic) Indian and he was a very little fellow (sic) I guess about four years old.

"He is in the possession of Let. (sic) Woodson our present company commander. Other companies of my regiment have had better success. 3 of them G.H. and L. (sic) surrounded a rancheria last week and killed fifty-six and captured twenty-five squaws and papooses K. co. (sic) killed eight.

"The fifth cavalry (sic) has the name of having killed more Indians since they have been in the Territory then any other regiment that was ever in it (sic) But I must tell you how I spent Christmus (sic) and New Year (sic)

"Christmus eve (sic) we made a night march and it rained and snowed by turns all night the next morning we were sent out on foot to scout a creek about six miles off (sic) Walked thirty miles without any thing (sic) to eat and when we come back to camp found that they had moved camp four miles further (the Leut. & part of the company had been left in camp) so that it made 34 miles on a amty (sic) stomach and very little water (sic) we growled a little but after we Had (sic) something to eat the most of us could be heard humming a song as thought (sic) we had never been hungry in our lives or tierd (sic) either

"Newyears (sic) day I receaved (sic) permission from Lieut Woodson to go hunting So away I went with only one man with me We had only walked about five miles from camp when I discovered a large amount

of indian (sic) signs some of them made the same day so went back and reported to the Leut (sic) and he sent out ten men and me to guide them to the place (sic) I found the trail and followed it about two miles when we ran head first into a indian rancheree (sic) of about six huts the indians (sic) had just left about five or ten minutes before we arrived their fires were still burning and the huts had deer meat in them some of the men eat (sic) it but as I perfer my own cooking to that of an indian (sic) I did not indulge.

> *From your cousin*
> *Corporal Cyrus Milner*
> *CO E U.S. Cav*

Write soon

O I had almost forgotten to tell you that I have been promoted I was made Corporal the first day of december (sic) in 72 and as I am the first on the list of corporals and their (sic) is one of our sargents (sic) transfered to the General service I expect to be made sergent (sic) in a few days I was glad that was made for some of my relations had a fashion (sic) of saying that I would be good for any thing and I can show them that Im (sic) at least a good Soldier I am one of the best shots in the company and the men would rather go with me into danger than with an officer
But I must bid you good by (sic) and may God bless and preserve you"

Catherine Bowen best describes Cyrus Milner as a man of slight build, five feet five inches tall with light complexion, light hair and blue eyes. Until he enlisted in the U.S. Cav. on October 26, 1868 at Carlisle Barracks, PA., he lived at Port Deposit, Cecil County Maryland, where he was a farmer. It is interesting that Cyrus would choose military service since he was born of Quaker stock.

Cyrus stated in one of his letters that he loved to read, and that was his undoing on one occasion. His enlistments were relatively uneventful except for GENERAL COURT MARTIAL proceedings against him. The Board sat on November 16, 1869 at Fort Russell, Wyoming Territory. The charge was read, "Neglect of duty, to the prejudice of good order and military discipline."

One of the two prisoners who Cyrus was guarding escaped while Milner "was reading a book." He was found guilty and sentenced to five months of hard labor and forfeiture of $10 of his pay per month for the same period.

When Co. A. 5th Cav. arrived at Camp Verde on May 5, 1872, Cyrus B. Milner was with the unit. He described his duty there in letters written to his cousin, Amelia Milner, who later taught at the Carlisle Indian School, Pennsylvania.

In April 1869, Milner was assigned to Co. A. 5th Cav. under command of Lieut. Gordon. He served in that unit, except for a period between enlistments, until he was killed by Indians in 1876. Milner's enlistment time expired on October 26, 1873. He was discharged at Camp Verde on that date. Nothing is known of him from that time until he re-enlisted at the base on Jan. 1, 1875. He was then sent to Dakota Territory under the command of Gen.

Crook. He was on a side scout away from the main body of Gen. Crook's command, and was separated from his fellow troopers for a period of approximately 10 minutes. When they found him, he was dead, scalped, stripped and horribly mutilated. His clothes were never found, and he was buried on the spot where he was killed. At the time of his death, Cyrus Milner owed the U.S. $2.28 for tobacco, and $33.09 was due him for "clothing not drawn in kind." Final statement concerning this soldier was signed by Capt. C. P. Rogers, commanding, Co. A 5th Cav.

In a letter written to his cousin while stationed at Camp Verde in 1872, young Milner wrote saying he hoped he never had to kill an Indian - it's ironic that he met his death by those he confessed he didn't want to kill.

It was men like Cyrus Milner who made up the frontier army. Their dedication and loyalty to their comrades-in-arms, and faithful service to their country, made them unsung heroes. Lest we never forget, many gave their lives to their country for just $13 a month.

BIOGRAPHY

Dr. V. Keith Thorne, a native of southern California, has been a history and cavalry buff for over forty years. After retiring to Sedona in 1980, Thorne took up painting and sculpture, with his subject matter focusing on Gen. George Custer, the Indian wars and later, British Military history. He has written a number of articles on these subjects as well. Together with his wife Kate and son, Reed, Dr.Thorne established Thorne Enterprises, a company which has published Experience Sedona recreational map and Experience Sedona Legends and Legacies. The Jerome and Verde Valley Legends and Legacies is the third in their popular series.

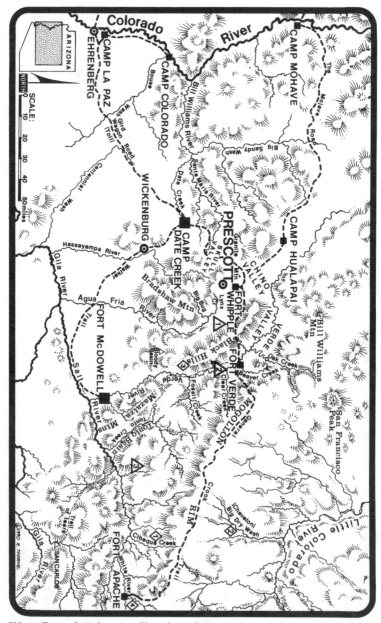

West Central Arizona - Showing places and names from this book.

⊙ Major Settlements   ■ Military Posts
△ Cattle Ranching: 1) King Woolsey, 2) William Wingfield, 3) Pleasant Valley.
◇ Indian/Military Skirmishs: 1) Cibeque, 2) Battle of Big Dry Wash,
3) Turret Peak, 4) Fort Apache

Chapter Four
ROUND-UPS, HOOTCH AND GOL-DERN CATTLE
The Ranchers Of The Verde Valley
By Linda Hiett Lawrence and Zeke Taylor

he Spanish explorer Antonio de Espejo rode the first horse into the Verde Valley in May of 1583. His very brief records don't impart much information about what they saw or thought of the area, but our imaginations can paint a picture of those first "vaqueros" (cowboys) as they rode their ponies down through the Mingus Mountain passes and stared at the changing clouds and the verdant rolling hills before them. The early ranches in Arizona were the legacies of these first Spanish explorers and later Mexican settlers.

These tenacious first ranchers established the beginnings of culture and civilization in the valley. In fact, they left their own brand on this beautiful valley. . . its name. The word "verde," as in Verde Valley, means green in Spanish.

The Anglo settlers who came to Arizona complemented the Hispanic culture and joined in the development of the ranching industry. James Parrish and John M. Swetnam were among the very first to taste the agrarian benefits of this lush valley. However, the outbreak of the Civil War in 1861 brought the infant ranching industry to its knees. As federal troops were needed in the war zones, the expansion of new forts in the West was curtailed and ranchers were left without even the promise of future protection from the marauding Apaches who preyed on Anglos, Mexicans, Yavapais and Hopis alike. Many felt that the risks simply weren't worth staying on. The prospect of wives and children abandoned as waiting victims, and hard-earned land improvements left to ruin, was enough to daunt any rancher, Anglo or Mexican.

When the Civil War ended in 1864, the Territory of Arizona was created under military rule, forts were established, and people slowly started to move back just in time for a boom in the eastern cattle markets. As the great Texas cattle drives were headed toward Kansas from established ranches there, an expanse of open range land in the Verde Valley and on Mingus Mountain was again tempting to settlers. In 1875 a cattle drive brought herds from Texas to this valley.

However, a bad drought in the '80s killed off most of the range grasses and was followed by a series of floods which washed away much of the topsoil and created a classic erosion scene. The result was serious harm to both the soil and the ranching endeavors. The ranchers in the valley never did make the big money associated with the large ranches in California and Texas, but they maintained orchards and field crops to supplement their beef sales. In fact, it is impossible now to separate the ranching and farming; their interdependence has merged them into one business and way of life.

The Hon. W.S. Head came to the Verde Valley from New York as the post trader at Camp Verde. Known for his sharp mind, he established a ranch and a store and was elected to the state legislature in 1877. During this service at the state capital, which was then in Prescott, he was dubbed "Boss" Head as a compliment to his ability to get bills passed that he thought were in the best interest of the Arizona Territory.

George W. Hance came to the area in 1862 from Tennessee with a group of people, many of whom were killed by Indians during the first year they were here. As a rancher and legal scholar, he served for 45 years as Justice of the Peace. He married Partheny Rutledge who had come across the plains to Arizona with her family from Alabama. Living on a ranch 10 miles from the nearest neighbor, she was known for her generosity and hospitality to cowboys and travelers. Dedicated to the youngsters of this community, Hance worked to found and develop schools in the area. His descendants are still active in Yavapai County; one of them carries on his legal heritage through the practice of law.

Another of the first of the big ranches was established in 1879 by William Wingfield, originally from Virginia. Shifting his focus back and forth between Arizona and California, he finally settled in Camp Verde. Married to Margrette Ann Pleasents, the first of their children was born in Arkansas. They bought the old Casner place and built the first privately-owned irrigation ditch, now known as the Upper Verde Ditch. The original stone house used by the Wingfield family is gone. However, the family had purchased the old Sutler's Store in Camp Verde from Boss Head, built on a cement addition and operated a general store. It eventually became known as Wingfield Store and was operated in Camp Verde for almost 100 years. A restaurant now occupies the building. The family developed the ranch on which the Montezuma Well is located, the Beaver Creek Ranch, and a ranch on Clear Creek.

Wales Arnold came from Massachusetts with the military, returned several times and finally took up ranching. Jennie Wells came around Cape Horn to San Francisco to the Agua Fria Valley. She married Wales Arnold in 1869 and ran the Sutler's store at its original location at Fort Lincoln. They eventually established the Flower Pot Ranch on the back of Squaw Peak. They later resettled

UPPER VERDE RANCH - 1887 *The Nichol's Ranch located 19 miles from Fort Verde epitomized the isolation and loneliness of the Verde Valley Ranchers. Courtesy of Fort Verde State Park (FVSP).*

Ranching family of the Verde Valley, 1887. Most of those who settled in the valley were poor people who came West in the hopes of providing their children with a better life. (Library of Congress)

nearer Camp Verde on what was later to become the Fain Ranch.

The Willard family came to the Verde Valley over a period of time during the 1870s and '80s. The first to arrive were four brothers who drove their herd of cattle from their Nevada ranch. Various branches of the family ranched and farmed in and around what is now Cottonwood, and participated in the original formation of the Cottonwood Ditch, so vital to the infant farming and ranching industry in that part of the valley. In fact, one of the Willard families recalled camping under a large cottonwood tree after which the town was named. The area was located where the Old Town portion of Cottonwood is now situated, but the huge cottonwood tree is no longer there.

On May 4, 1877, John and Jane Newman left Oregon with their eight children and headed for the Verde Valley. They established a ranch 10 miles west of the little settlement. However, John Newman became ill and died in November, 1878, leaving his wife and children in a new land with no resources except themselves.

They all worked hard and overcame many hardships. Many of the children, grandchildren, nieces and nephews are still in the Verde Valley. Zeke Taylor keeps their story alive by sharing it with local schoolchildren. And he tells them about his teacher, Ruth Jordan, who has lived in Sedona since the early days. Jordan Road in Sedona is a reminder of her family's early contributions to that area.

Ranching in the Verde Valley is young, younger than ranching in other parts of the state or the country. As a result there are still people living in the valley whose parents or grandparents were among the original settlers. This provides a rich and accurate account of how ranching was done and who did it. For example, buried in the old settlers' cemetery outside Camp Verde is Benjamin Franklin Taylor, one of the original ranchers. His son, Carl Godard, still lives in Camp Verde, and his grandson, Don Godard, lives in Cottonwood. Don Godard has continued his family's history of community service through his work on the school board in Cottonwood and is a driving force in the Verde Historical Society.

It is important to realize that ranching is a very individualistic business. And it's more of a way of life and a culture than it is a business. Most ranches in the United States have always been small. The huge ranching empires we read about or see on film are the exceptions. Ranches, both in the past and now, have seldom involved more that fifty or a hundred head of cattle. Most cattlemen have worked at another job or for other cattlemen in order to support their ranches and their way of life. In fact, there are several old sayings and jokes about the fact that a wife with a good job is the most necessary ingredient to a successful ranch.

Another point to keep in mind is that asking a man how many cattle he had was just as rude as asking him how much money

The Sutler's Store, Camp Verde - 1871   *Post trader, William "Boss" Head operated the store in 1874, replacing Wales Arnold. The store provided military personnel and civilians with both necessities and luxuries, and for several years was the only store in the Verde Valley. It also served as the 'nerve center' for the entire community. During the Indian wars, citizens grouped themselves together for protection and traveled to the store on Sundays.*

In addition to his other duties, "Boss" Head acted as a banker and postmaster. A room in the back provided three tables for card games and was used by the officers of the post.

In 1893, "Boss" Head sold the store to Clinton Wingfield and Mack Rodgers. Six years later, both were murdered in the store, reportedly by Black Jack Ketchum. The store, which is still in use today, was operated by a member of the Wingfield family until 1971. (FVSP)

The original sign for the Sutler's Store can now be seen at Lawson's Trading Post, located in the historic building. Photo by Alan Caillou.

Original home of "Boss" Head, Camp Verde 1990. Photo by Kate Ruland-Thorne.

he had in the bank. His cattle represented his entire worth. That's true today, too, but most city people don't realize their lack of etiquette when they ask that question.

This recent history also adds another dimension to the stories from the past. We find Model T's and buggies being used at the same time; windmills and electric pumps operate on the same ranch. The work of the cowboys was done the same way as 50 years earlier in other states, and Saturday night entertainment might include the silent movies. Pulled up in front of a summer dance might be a few horses belonging to some of the cowboys, a wagon driven by a ranch family and a new-fangled Ford motor car driven by a merchant from town. Ranching was and still is an occupation which truly bridges a simpler way of life to the modern machine age.

Even today such anachronisms exist. A visitor may see branding irons on the porch and horses in the corral ready for tomorrow's work, while a computer is used in the kitchen for keeping records of cattle or sales and doing taxes. The importance of the weather is still reflected in the discussions among the cowboys, but they're apt to be watching the latest cattle market prices from Wall Street on the television, too.

The open range ended with the building of fences to accommodate "civilization." And the building of fences on the open range in the 1930s signaled the end of some of the traditions that had developed among the cowboys and ranching families in the valley. Some feel that the end of the open range allowed environmentally destructive practices such as over-grazing to begin. They feel that cattle that were left to roam free naturally migrated to where the grasses were plentiful and did not remain to over-graze in one area.

One of the best examples of the cooperation among the ranchers and cowboys was the Association. The very last Association roundup occurred in 1930 when the fences were built.

THE LAST ASSOCIATION ROUNDUP

The Association wagon was loaded heavy with provisions. Pulled by four good mules, it lumbered along carefully chosen, but very rough, terrain. Charlie Mulligan was driving the wagon. He had a ranch at the foot of Round Mountain, but this year he was doing the cooking and sharing in the roundup work for some wages.

This wagon was a big one, not much different than the ones we used to see in movies, but not nearly so fancy or new. It had a lid that let down in the back and served as a work area, but all the actual cooking was done over an open fire. Loaded on the back of the wagon was a chuck box filled with necessary items such as spices, utensils, tin plates and matches. The whole front end of the chuck wagon was bursting with huge sacks of beans, flour and sugar, cans of shortening, coffee, milk, vegetables, syrup, lots of dried and fresh fruit, and salt pork for flavoring the beans. In addition to all these food items, all the tools necessary for

*C.W. Norwood's
Blacksmith Shop,
Camp Verde 1895.
(FVSP)*

George Hance (FVSP)

*Wales and "Aunty"
Arnold - 1879. One of
the first settlers in the
Verde Valley, Wales
Arnold operated the
Sutlers store and served
as an Army Scout for
many years. (FVSP)*

doctoring men, horses and cattle were packed in with branding irons, horseshoeing equipment, horse hobbles, and anything else anyone thought might be needed.

There was a second wagon following the chuck wagon which carried the bedrolls. The cowboy who drove this wagon had hitched his horse to the wagon, drove it behind the chuck wagon to the next campsite, collected enough wood for a pretty big fire, built the fire, and generally helped Charlie get things ready.

"The Association" had been organized by the ranchers in the Verde Valley to help them doctor, brand, and generally "work" their cattle. The range where everybody's cattle roamed and grazed was over 1,000 square miles. There were no fences, so the different ranchers' cattle were running together. The Association ranchers worked together to help each other find and care for their cattle on the vast range.

The wagon "Boss" had been elected by the ranchers and there were definite rules about behavior during the annual trek:

1. You washed your hands before eating or handling food.

2. Rest rooms were at least two or three hundred feet from camp. Most of the time, you rode horseback out to find a suitable place.

3. No vulgar talk or improper behavior in camp.

4. No standing around the cook's fire. You stood around the "B.S. fire," out away from the cook's fire where dust couldn't be kicked up around the food being cooked.

5. There was a "chap rule." If you failed to obey any of the rules, you were spread-eagled over a bedroll and your butt was whipped with a pair of leather chaps. I never saw the "chap rule" used. Everyone always obeyed the rules.

6. You kept a horse saddled, ready for use, 24 hours a day.

7. Each cowboy had to have at least ten horses in his "mount."

8. You never swung your rope out wide around the horse herd; you pitched it out to catch your horse.

Charlie planned huge meals three times a day. The cowboys worked hard and really chowed down every meal. They stood around the B.S. fire and shot the breeze while Charlie got the last things ready. They waited for him to bang on a Dutch oven with a gaunch hook, making such a loud noise that you couldn't miss it. He'd yell, too.

The cowboys filled their plates with meat and beans or "Son-of-a-Bitch" stew (this was called Forest Ranger Stew if ladies were around), and biscuits baked over the fire. After eating, they took their dishes to the big dishpan so the cook could wash them all. (Another RULE.)

Each day another part of the range land was covered, rounding up all the cattle. Clear Creek, Wickiup Gnat, Cedar Flat, Soda

Judge John Goodwin, 1886. "Uncle Johnny" was the Justice of the Peace in the little settlement along the upper Verde River. (FVSP)

The Casner Family, 1912 all dressed up and going to the county fair. (FVSP)

Camp Verde School (year unknown). Children of early pioneers, many of whose names are still found on area streets and landmarks. The teacher, Frank Holder stands with his 41 students, many of them with the last names of Wingfield, Van Deren, Price, Gillett, Guthrey, Hance, Turner, Stephens and Wright, among others. (FVSP)

Springs, Walder Creek and Wet Beaver Creek areas were all covered. Oak Creek, House Mountain, and Rattlesnake Canyon were worked and the last year, the Apache Maid Ranch marked the end of the work in the valley. The gnats, the heat, and the thirst made the work almost unbearable. Cowboys sometimes carried smoldering cow chips on a stick to help keep the gnats away.

Then the really hard work began. The spring branding on the mountain required riding some pretty rough country. Five-mile Pass, Tin Roof, New Tank, Horse Knoll, and Home Tank were the local names of some of the areas on Mingus Mountain that had to be covered. After the whole valley and the mountain had been covered, it was over until the fall roundup. Then the whole process was repeated.

The way the Association organized the job was just a larger example of how it has always been done, except that before the Association, a cowboy or two worked it alone or a few families worked together in a smaller "association."

It is estimated that there were probably about 2,350 calves, 2,350 mother cows, 650 dry cows (with no nursing calves), 2,300 yearlings and heifers left from the previous year, and about 200 bulls by 1930. That total of 7,850 head would have the entire Verde Valley, including Mingus Mountain and clear up to Stoneman Lake, to graze on. The cattle tended to naturally move over the land so that none of it became over-grazed. It was only with government interference and regulation that over-grazing became a problem rather than a rarity.

FAMILIES AND THEIR BRANDS

Ranchers branded their cattle to identify ownership on the open range. The brands were sometimes unique and there was an art to reading them. All brands must be registered with the state government and there is still a state brand inspector in most states to ensure an orderly record of the ownership of livestock.

A brand is read from top to bottom and from left to right. (If you play Arizona Trivia, that's an answer you'll want to remember.) Early ranchers and those who were just setting up their outfits used a "running iron" for making their brands. A long iron rod was heated at the end in the flames of an open campfire and then the brand was drawn on the hide of the steer. Brands are more commonly and properly made with a branding iron. The shape of the brand is forged out of metal and welded to the end of an iron rod. This "iron" is heated the same way as the running iron and the brand is then "pressed" into the hide of the steer. The following are some of the early families in the Verde Valley and their brands:

WINGFIELD
The Wingfield brand has been in use since the early days. They had several brands.

BEN TAYLOR
B-A-T

ZEKE TAYLOR
T-BAR-S

ALBERT FAIN (A Fain now serves on the board of Marcus J. Lawrence Hospital in Cottonwood. The Fain place was bought by the Grosetta family who still ranches it today.)
X-TRIANGLE

JOSIE FAIN (Ab's wife)
BROKEN-BOX

RALSTON (owners of the Apache Maid Ranch)
T-BAR-S

IRVIN WALKER
M-DIAMOND

GILES GOSWICK
TRIANGLE-J-E-A-6

"DADDY PA" CLAYTON
LINK-DART

GEORGE HANCE
BROKEN-H

WALES ARNOLD
FLOWERPOT

DAVE STRAHAN
CIRCLE-S

JIM WILLARD
J-W

CHARLIE MULLIGAN
H-BAR-S

 CHARLIE HOLLINGSHEAD
A-BAR-Z

 DAN MARR
T-BAR

Some of the old brands are still being used, but some of them have been bought up or have just disappeared. For example, some were bought by a group who formed the Vee-Bar-Vee outfit. It was eventually sold to Marcus J. Lawrence and Bruce Brockett. The Marcus J. Lawrence Hospital in Cottonwood serves the entire Verde Valley, which includes Sedona, and is one of the best small hospitals in the country. It was named after this same Lawrence by his mother, who endowed the hospital in his memory. Zeke Taylor's brand was sold to Larry Mellon, a relative of Andrew H. Mellon, a United States Treasurer.

The following poem was written by one of the Valley's natives and portrays the feelings and the details as one of the early cowboys felt and saw them:

ROUNDUP OF 1896
by M.O. Dumas
The old boys of 1896
Have ridden their last Round Up
Out in the sticks
They rode over the hill
One at a time.
Though through the dim mist
They left a plain sign,
They rode on and on,
And never looked back.
But we can easily follow
For they left a plain track.

Now there's old Lute, Haydee and Joe,
Who rode with those pokes
Of a long time ago.
That same trail
We shall sometime follow
Up that same hill
And down yon hollow.
Boys, keep the camp-fire burning
To light up the way,
For we shall surely join you
And join you to stay.
When we register
For that last call,
It will be on that grand Round Up
Later in the Fall.

(From Those Early Days - printed
by The Verde Independent, copyright 1968, The Sedona Westerners)

COWBOYS AND HOOTCH

Another interesting thing about being such a young area is the mixture of eras that has resulted. We usually don't think of prohibition and cowboys together, but here in Arizona they mixed. In the early '30s, a man had the largest still ever found in Upper Fossil Canyon. It had 3 huge copper vats about 4 feet in diameter and 6 feet deep. The ground around the still was white like it had snowed when it was found. But it wasn't snow; it was sugar! The owner and operator was a well-known rancher from the northern part of the state. He was sent to Alcatraz, but 2 weeks after he was released he had an even bigger still going. He only ran it for 6 weeks. That was all the time he needed to make enough money to pay everything off and set himself up again. He didn't sell to locals, but packed it on a burro to the rail line to be sold in the midwest.

The local cowboys bought their moonshine from two locals who had a small still. They would stop at the moonshine cabin on their way to a dance and buy a little courage for meeting the girls. The whiskey was kept in a large keg and bottles were re-used as containers. They weren't very careful, and the floor was covered with whiskey and the smell was pretty strong.

THE SMELTER AND THE RANCHERS

As the smelter became more and more active, the effects of the poisonous fumes and smoke spewing into the air began to be seen, and not just in the air. The wild grasses depended on for grazing, and the crops grown for human and cattle consumption began to die or be stunted by the refuse in the air. Engineers were sent to study the problem, but nothing was done. Finally the Verde Valley

Farmers' and Stockmen's Protective Association was formed to deal with the problem. This effort by the farmers and ranchers was the first formal attempt at curbing the pollution caused by the smelter.

The smelter and those it controlled and influenced maintained that the smelter fumes had no effect on the ranches, but their view was certainly not shared by the ranchers, who claimed that the sulphur smoke from the smelters in Clemenceau and Clarkdale had destroyed range grasses in the valley and that the effects of the sulphur would eventually destroy the valley and put the ranchers out of business. (By the way, Georges Clemenceau was a friend of the Douglas family and visited the area. You will see his name on several buildings, such as the Clemenceau School at the corner of Willard and Mingus in Cottonwood. The Verde Historical Society and Museum and the school district offices now occupy the restored building.)

The ranchers and farmers individually instituted lawsuits against the smelter company for damages. Each year the company would settle out of court by paying a lesser amount to each claimant. After several years of this, the company began buying up tracts of land and trading ranchers a new ranch for their old one. The new ranch would be out of the path of the pollutants. As a result, each year the number of lawsuits decreased until finally every rancher had been bought out. Only one rancher never sold and continued to sue the smelter every year.

WATER, WATER, WATER

The single most important resource of the Verde Valley is water. The source of that precious commodity is the Verde River and the smaller tributaries which flow into it. For both domestic and agricultural purposes, the use of water and disputes over it have been of concern for over a hundred years.

There are several ditches which are fed from wells near the river where the water table is shallow. A formal organization of water share ownership determines who gets how much water and when. There have been more than a few disputes over alleged misuse of water shares but, in general, there is a spirit of cooperation because of the ranchers' mutual dependency on the "ditch."

On the range land shared by the ranchers, there are man-made watering holes for the cattle. The cattle are driven from one area to another according to the availability of water and to prevent over-grazing of the land. The United States Government has strictly enforced regulations concerning the protection of the grazing lands. This protects not only the land, but other forms of life as well.

THE ENVIRONMENT AND RANCHING

It is due to the efforts of ranchers that many of the pristine areas in the Verde Valley have been preserved. Areas which have been under the control of the government have sometimes been sold to developers or homebuilders. Some of the riparian areas located on private ranches which have been retained in the hands of the original or subsequent ranching families have been protected. This is not to say that the original ranchers were unusually environmentally conscious. The actions of some resulted in damage to rivers and the land. On the other hand, the actions of the federal and state governments also resulted in like damage. It must be remembered that much of the wrong that was done by ranchers and government alike was done out of ignorance, not intent. Most ranchers and other land users are the most vocal opponents of uncontrolled and unsupervised growth or development. It is in the best interest of ranchers that the land and the waterways be protected.

FEEDING THEMSELVES, THE COUNTRY AND THE WORLD

The ranchers of the Verde Valley have continued the tradition of ranchers throughout the United States, Australia, Asia and South America. The romance, the adventure, the hardship and the economic perils of ranching are all a part of the rich tapestry of service to our country and to the world. The fearless and hardworking ranchers of the nineteenth century in the Verde Valley established the values and economy of this beautiful area. They forged the link to the rest of the ranching industry in the country who fed the soldiers during the Spanish American war, the First World War, the Second World War, and the several perils of the country since.

The early cowboys and ranchers in the Verde Valley were the fathers, sons and cousins of pioneers. Some of them came to escape debts, relatives, criminal records, or just to search for adventure. But most came in search of opportunity, free land, and a chance to prosper even if they weren't rich or educated. They had been warned about all the hardships, especially for women and children, but they were willing to take those risks on the chance that they or their children would succeed.

In imagining those "good old days," we must picture how it must have been to be a woman having babies and pulling weeds, nursing hurt and ailing cowboys and animals, worrying that sick children and husbands would die due to lack of medicine and doctors. It was a hard life, a good life, a productive life. Without their sacrifices, we would not enjoy the standard of living that allows us to visit or live in this beautiful Verde Valley.

Mysterious Sarcophagus, 1898
found hidden in a mesquite grove near the rubble
of an old home on a remote valley ranch.
Apparently the husband of this young wife did not
have the heart to bury her in the ground.
Photos by Kate Ruland-Thorne.

Infant mortality on the frontier
was high.
Photo by Kate Ruland-Thorne.

Women died young on the frontier,
often in childbirth.

Clear Creek Cemetary lies in the shadow of Squaw Peak Mountain and is the final resting place for many Verde Valley pioneers. Photo by Kate Ruland-Thorne.

Cattle Ranch on the Verde River - 1990. Photo by Kate Ruland-Thorne.

BIOGRAPHY

Dr. Linda Hiett Lawrence is the granddaughter of Arizona pioneers. Her grandparents came to the Salt River Valley in the Glendale and Mesa areas in a covered wagon, establishing ranches and farms around the valley. Her education includes a B.A. from the University of Arizona, and a Masters and Doctorate from Arizona State University. A teacher and principal for 25 years in the Phoenix area, she is now Superintendent of Schools in the Cottonwood-Oak Creek School District which includes Sedona, Cornville and Cottonwood. Dr. Lawrence' family has been involved in ranching near Camp Verde for over thirty years. In addition to education-related writing, she teaches at Northern Arizona University and actively participates in the operation of the family ranch.

BIOGRAPHY

Ezekiel B. (Zeke) Taylor was born in Phoenix, Arizona, in 1913, and was brought by his pioneer parents to the Verde Valley six months later. Zeke is the nephew of John D. Newman who came to the valley in 1877, from Tennessee, with his wife Jane. Zeke was a thirteen year old cowboy on the 1926 Association roundup and shared his own and his family's history through the writing of *Reflections of the Past As It Rolled Along* in 1987. The book was written particularly for his grandson, Daniel Taylor, but has become a favorite of the entire valley. He shares his knowledge and history with schools in the area and is a leading force in the Verde Historical Society.

Early prospectors in Jerome. (KTVK-TV Collection)

Chapter Five
HIZZONER, BAKING POWDER BILL
AND RAWHIDE JIMMY
Jerome's Mining History to the Great Depression
By Jeanette Rodda

early two hundred years before American colonists declared their independence from England, Europeans rode into Central Arizona's lush Verde Valley in search of silver and gold. These imperious Spanish conquistadores, dispatched from Mexico City, commanded trains of common soldiers, native guides and bearers, priests, and assorted camp followers, penetrating north as far as modern Kansas. The conquistadore, Antonio de Espejo, first European to explore the Verde Valley, found native Yavapai Indians engaged in exploiting the region's mineral wealth in 1583. Yavapai men, women, and children, wearing crosses tied in their hair, led Espejo along a steep mountain trail high above the valley floor to a mineralized outcrop of rock. Here he observed native miners working above ground and in tunnels, chiseling off richly-colored blue and green pigments with stone tools; dyes from the pigments decorated bodies, clothing, blankets, and utensils. Over four-hundred years later, the outcrop marked the site of the richest individually-owned copper mine in the world.

Espejo later toured underground salt mines on the valley floor, from which the Yavapais extracted this valuable mineral for local use and trade. Early twentieth-century miners working these mines sometimes discovered grizzly reminders of their ancient counterparts: skeletons preserved in salt; the fossilized bones of a human hand and forearm at a depth of seventy feet; and a skull split in two by a stone hammer.

The Spaniards left the valley to the Yavapai and did not return. Abundant water, arable soil, and potential native converts and workers did not interest them with no gold or silver in the bargain. Espejo sought neither prime settlement land nor copper. He complained in his journal of the high copper content of the outcrop, how it obscured and locked in meager streaks of silver and gold. Only modern smelting methods would release the wealth of precious metals embedded in the rich copper ore: eighteen and a half million ounces of silver and over half a million ounces of gold by 1922.

The Yavapai saw no more whites in their valley until the early nineteenth century when white trappers, including Kit Carson and the tragic-comic James Ohio Pattie, cleared the Verde River of beaver. Like the conquistadores, these colorful and destructive individuals moved on quickly. The close of the Civil War brought a third wave of whites. Mainly Anglo-American farmers and ranchers, they pushed into the valley from the Territorial capital at Prescott, eager to graze their stock on the tall, dense grasses of the Verde and to plant crops on the fertile river terraces. Understandably, the Yavapai vigorously resented this rude intrusion on their ancestral lands and launched raids and other forms of guerrilla warfare against the settlers.

Only after the U.S. military crushed native resistance did these first settlers dare venture into the surrounding mountains on prospecting trips. In June 1876, Morris Ruffner and his wife, Sarah, valley ranchers of modest means, filed claims on and around the outcrop noted by Espejo, dubbing one the "Eureka" and one the "Wade Hampton", after a hero of the Civil War. A few other ranchers filed claims as well. Ruffner insisted to his neighbors that someday his mine would be worth millions. With the nearest railhead in Abilene, Kansas, Ruffner's friends met his declarations with skepticism; they knew profits depended on cheap rail transportation from the mine site. Ruffner managed to convince brothers George and Angus McKinnon, Prescott shopkeepers, to take two-thirds interest in the claims in exchange for a grubstake. The partners, with pick, shovel, and the most primitive of hoisting equipment, dug a forty-five foot shaft and drove a tunnel.

In 1882 Ruffner and the McKinnon brothers sold their mine. Profitable underground mining requires extensive capitalization in addition to modern transportation. The partners brought up copper ore assaying high in gold and silver values but hauling this ore to the surface proved the least of their problems; the small grubstake provided by the McKinnons covered neither crippling freight charges to a railhead by ox team nor smelting costs at distant plants. Besides, the McKinnons did not share Ruffner's blind faith in the mine. They worried that the ore would pinch out, a reasonable assumption, considering that the majority of mining claims barely kept their owners in beans and bacon. A typical prospector vainly shoveled and sweated his way through the day and at night attended to aching muscles, severe blisters, and perhaps a smashed finger or toe. Only in his dreams did he strike the motherlode. Holding majority interest, the McKinnons placed the claims on the market.

Among mining experts sent to investigate the property was Dr. James Douglas, co-inventor of the Hunt and Douglas process for refining low-grade copper and later, president of the Phelps Dodge Corporation of New York. Dr. Douglas travelled from the East to Arizona Territory in 1880 to solicit copper for custom smelting

United Verde miners at old Jerome yard prepare to go underground in the 'cages' (1913). Courtesy Jerome Historical Society.

United Verde tractor shovel underground (1920s). Courtesy of Jerome Historical Society.

at his small plant in Pennsylvania. Two Philadelphia capitalists, anxious to invest in Western mines, hired him to make a side trip to Ruffner's mine. Douglas recognized the ore's potential but advised his clients to reject the property because of transportation difficulties. One Philadelphian, Charles Lennig, disregarded Douglas' recommendation and purchased the Eureka claim.

By 1882, capitalists, both Eastern and Western, controlled the claims. Arizona Territorial governor, Frederick A. Tritle, appointed in 1882, engaged his own at-large expert in the mining field, one Frederick Thomas of California. Thomas had wide experience on the Comstock in Nevada. He met with Angus McKinnon in Prescott and the two rode over the mountains to the little shaft near the blue-green outcrop; after he examined the work in progress, Thomas urged Governor Tritle to take an option. Tritle, always a little short of cash, roped his friend, William Murray, into the deal; Murray, in Prescott for his health, had wealthy connections in the East. Tritle, Murray, and Thomas took a $500 option on the Wade Hampton claim, agreeing to pay Ruffner and the McKinnons $45,000 on expiration. To avoid future apex litigation over the property, the new owners bonded several more claims in the immediate vicinity of the Wade Hampton. Ruffner headed south, richer by $15,000, invested in a Gila River irrigation project, and lost the entire amount. He died in Phoenix in 1884, impoverished and disillusioned.

Tritle hit on the idea of drawing Eastern capital into the new partnership when he realized that in his enthusiasm to acquire the mine, he did not allow sufficient money to pay off Ruffner and the McKinnons. At his suggestion, partners Murray and Thomas sped back East in late 1882 to drum up some quick cash. In New York, Murray solicited funds from his uncle, Eugene Jerome, a banker and financier. Jerome conceded to his nephew the thrill of gambling at cards and at the horse track but held that the thought of risking money on a hole in the ground left him cold. Murray's petition, however, caught the fancy of Jerome's wife, a rich woman in her own right. She drew her sister into the scheme and the two raised $200,000 in development money, transferring it to the delighted Murray. With his wife's money irretrievably invested, Eugene Jerome, an able manager, took an active interest in the remote Arizona mine. Thomas later designated the infant camp sprouting up adjacent to the mine "Jerome", in honor of the family name. Neither Jerome nor his wife ever visited their namesake. Their nephew, Frederick Murray, did not care much for the rough little camp either; he doubled as both company agent and postmaster in Jerome, but being a Yale man, he preferred the bright lights and more civilized attractions of Prescott.

Additional investors included James A MacDonald, president of the Queen's Insurance Company of New York and Charles Lennig of Philadelphia, holder of the Eureka claim. On February 23, 1883,

Work crew at surface of the United Verde mine, Jerome, turn-of-the-century. (KTVK-TV Collection)

William Andrews Clark, owner of the United Verde Mine. (KTVK-TV Collection)

the new owners incorporated the United Verde Copper Company (UVCC) under New York laws with MacDonald as president, Lennig as vice president, and Jerome as secretary-treasurer. The Arizona partners, being only minor investors, were given charge of the more strenuous on-site development work.

By this time the Atlantic and Pacific Railway (later the Santa Fe) had reached Ash Fork, Arizona Territory, and the new mine owners built a sixty mile wagon road from the mine to the railhead. The company freighted in two small smelting furnaces by bull team over this rough road. Frederick Thomas made a fine show of superintending the UVCC, considering the primitive conditions he encountered. Surface ores ran high in gold and silver values -- so high that for a time, precious metals paid operating costs. Copper, for which a major market was just developing, amazed the mine managers with its purity and sold for fourteen cents per pound. Thomas reported an initial profit of $80,000, with which the company paid all debts and issued the first dividends.

In December 1884 company executives shut the mine down in response to plummeting copper prices and depletion of gold and silver in the rich surface ores. High freight charges and an inability (or reluctance) to invest heavily once again spelled disaster for hopeful investors. Governor Tritle, whose faith in the property matched that of its original locator, Morris Ruffner, leased the mine in the summer of 1887, but a dearth of capital vanquished him permanently. The UVCC unceremoniously cancelled his lease within two months. When mining experts pronounced the remaining ores to be "spotty" or irregular in quality, executives decided to sell.

Once again, the United Verde mine went on the market. Dr. James Douglas, who had investigated the property in 1880 and now worked for the Phelps Dodge Corporation as a mining expert, urged his employers to take an option. Now a front-leader in Southwestern copper mines, Phelps Dodge began negotiating, at which the UVCC promptly raised the asking price. Phelps Dodge just as promptly bowed out, leaving the field open to a most extraordinary man.

William Andrews Clark, copper king, industrial giant, Montana senator, and philanthropist, first noted UVCC ores in 1884 when he represented Montana Territory as commissioner to the New Orleans Exposition. As one of America's foremost mining men, well-versed in all technical and practical aspects of the craft, Clark recognized the Arizona ore samples as superb. At this time, Clark's Butte (Montana Territory) mines poured gratifying profits into the vaults of W.A. Clark and Brother, his privately-owned Butte bank and he toyed with the idea of expanding his empire. Clark kept his eye on the United Verde mine.

A few years later the Port Orford Copper Company of Verde Point, New Jersey, failed, becoming hugely indebted to Clark in the process. Poring over the company's books, Clark noticed that United Verde copper bullion, which the firm processed, assayed

United Verde smelting works, Clarkdale, circa 1918. (KTVK-TV Collection)

United Verde smelting works, Jerome, circa 1903. (KTVK-TV Collection)

high in gold and silver content. This strengthened his interest. When Clark learned the mine was for sale, he summoned Joseph Giroux, superintendent of one of his Butte mines, and the two travelled to Jerome to look over the United Verde.

A small, wiry man with meticulously barbered whiskers and disorderly dark red hair, Clark paid painstaking attention to his elegantly subdued wardrobe. Yet never did he allow vanity to interfere with sound business principles. Thus, on his arrival in Jerome, Clark and Giroux both donned hardrock miners' overalls, boots, and hats and spent the major part of three weeks underground, carefully taking ore samples at twelve-inch intervals throughout the workings. Previous experts sampled carelessly at five-foot intervals and missed rich veins. Clark, a trained metallurgist, personally assayed the samples, confirming his earlier opinion that the United Verde contained bonanza ore. He took a $30,000 three-year option on the property at once.

Unlike most business tycoons of his time, Clark avoided mergers and partnerships, preferring, when necessary, to take on tractable family members as associates. His huge fortune, among the very largest in America, allowed him this luxury. True to form, Clark moved to gain personal control of the United Verde mine. Under the conditions of the option, Clark agreed to take one-half the mine's profits and turn the remainder over to company shareholders.

Clark's first ninety day run of ore yielded a $180,000 profit. His portion went toward the purchase of 160,000 shares of UVCC stock at one dollar per share and made him the company's largest stockholder. As profits soared under Clark's management, he continued buying shares until he controlled some ninety-five per-cent of UVCC stock. Only UVCC President James MacDonald refused to sell out, remaining the sole outside stockholder; his foresight made him a fortune.

From the beginning, Clark stoutly declined to disclose particulars of the mine's finances and underground development to the press or to government officials. It is difficult, then, to determine the exact purchase price of the mine; most historians estimate $200,000 to $300,000. The mine eventually netted him at least $50 million in profits. Clark turned down offers of as much as $90 million for the property from the world's great mining companies. To all offers he said simply, "The United Verde mine is not for sale at any price."

Clark considered the United Verde mine to be the jewel of his empire, a financial kingdom that included prosperous mines in nearly every Western state, Mexican rubber and coffee plantations, sugar factories in Southern California, and America's largest bronze factory in New York state. He built the San Pedro, Salt Lake, and Los Angeles Railroad early in the twentieth century, founding Las Vegas, Nevada, in the process. Grateful citizens named Clark County, Nevada, in his honor. Americans marveled as Clark spent

Swimming Pool, Jerome, built by the United Verde Copper Company. (KTVK-TV Collection)

Clubhouse, Peck's Lake golf course, built by the United Verde Copper Company. (KTVK-TV Collection)

extravagantly from a seemingly bottomless purse. He built fabulous houses in Butte, New York, and Santa Barbara, and travelled incessantly to Europe, collecting masterpieces of art for his renowned collection, now housed in the Corcoran Museum in Washington, D.C. His New York mansion, a prime example of the ostentatious tastes of the very rich of the period, contained four private galleries where Clark spent many hours contemplating his treasures. Indeed, as his holdings multiplied, Clark admitted that he could not list every one from memory.

People admired Clark as a self-made man. Born on a farm in Pennsylvania, Clark relocated with his family to Iowa to settle on more fertile land. Here he attended school and farmed with his father and brothers. He worked his way through Iowa Wesleyan University and accepted a teaching job in Missouri. In 1862 he followed a gold rush to Colorado and here obtained employment as a miner, learning the business from the ground up, so to speak. Clark's involvement in the Civil War is a mystery; he fought briefly with the Confederate Army in Missouri and may have been wounded. He followed another gold rush to Bannack (Montana Territory) in 1863 and filed a claim at nearby Horse Prairie. In his first season on the placers, he washed out $3,000 in gold, having entered Bannack with five dollars in Colorado gold dust in his poke.

Unlike most young men in frontier camps, Clark refrained from spending his money on women, whiskey, and gambling over the cold winter, though he appreciated all three. Instead, in the late autumn of 1863, he rode south to Salt Lake City where he invested in dozens of eggs, an item his fellow miners craved. He freighted the eggs back to Bannack through a severe blizzard and eager miners snatched them up at three dollars per dozen. Ambition and initiative characterized Clark's career from this time; he had an exceptional knack for merchandising, banking, and generally being in the right place at the right time. His early merchandising efforts earned him the nickname "Baking Powder" Bill, a sobriquet he soon outgrew. Instrumental in the development of Butte, one of the world's great mining centers, Clark made his home and fortune there and always claimed Montana as his state of residence.

Throughout a stellar and honorable business career, Clark practiced a typical but shrewd philanthropy. He believed a "free" ride eventually crippled able-bodied adults but held that working men and women deserved comfortable housing, pleasant and wholesome leisure activities, fair wages, and safe working conditions. From the Paul Clark Home for Orphans and the Columbia Gardens (a deluxe resort for the workingman) in Butte to the model town of Clarkdale in Arizona; from the Mary Andrews Clark Home for Working Women in Los Angeles to the Katherine Stauffer Clark Kindergarten in New York, Clark used the finest building materials and the most modern equipment. He incorporated his philanthropic principles into solid brick and tranquil green retreats.

The ingenious and sometimes unscrupulous role William Andrews Clark played in Montana's War of the Copper Kings eclipsed an otherwise honorable career. In this fierce struggle for control of Montana's mineral resources, Clark played the lone wolf against corporate giants like the Amalgamated Copper Company, a piratical brainchild of Standard Oil executives. Clark took up the weapons of his enemies: money, a controlled press, and carefully orchestrated lawsuits. With these and his huge popularity in Montana, he stormed his way into the U.S. Senate against all odds and held the corporate octopus at bay in Butte for years.

In Butte, Clark's enemies pointed to his benevolence and projects to better his employees' lives and working conditions as inducements to garner votes in his bids for the Senate. Personal political considerations did not motivate Clark in Jerome, though he occasionally involved himself in Arizona politics for business reasons. His career in the Jerome district provides a far more accurate measure of the man than his actions in Montana.

Clark's development of the United Verde mine demonstrates his acute business sense. When he acquired control, Jerome clung to the mountain near the mine, a sorry jumble of rickety cabins, canvas tents, and a store or two; in ten years the United Verde was Arizona's top copper producer. The original smelting works consisted of Tritle's two water jacket furnaces and little more, while most of the mine's underground workings had barely penetrated the surface ore. Clark judged it a promising property but he could not be certain he had a bonanza on his hands. Previous UVCC capitalists wavered when it came to heavy investing in the property, especially in the area of modern transportation, the mine's biggest problem. Clark, on the other hand, staked much of his burgeoning fortune on the chance that he owned a big producer.

Six years of intense development work followed; money poured into the mine and copper flowed out. Clark's most ambitious project was the construction of a twenty-seven mile-long narrow-gauge railway, the United Verde and Pacific, completed in 1895, which zig-zagged its way from the mine over the mountains to connect with the new Santa Fe line at Jerome Junction, between Ash Fork and Phoenix. By this time, hardrock miners had drilled and blasted their way underground to a depth of five hundred feet. Veteran miners daily exposed an orebody that waxed in size and richness until it appeared to have no limit. Assay and progress reports elated Clark, as well they might, for deep under the booming camp of five hundred rested the largest deposit of high-grade pyritic copper ever discovered in the United States and one of the most extensive in the world.

As news of Clark's discovery circulated, miners, prospectors, and those who pocketed their earnings converged on the camp. A cosmopolitan population, typical of boom towns, thronged Jerome's boardwalks and rutted streets. From boarding houses and saloons jammed with miners there issued the clamor of a dozen languages. Excitement reigned in old Jerome but, as in most camps, beauty and gracious living sat below the salt. Prospect holes scarred the mountains and urban planning was unknown. To remove unwanted sulphur from the ore before transfer to Clark's new smelter, heaps of roasting ore smouldered at the mouth of every tunnel. The sulphur-laden smoke, a common sight in camps at the time, stung the eyes, caused paroxysms of coughing, and killed every trace of vegetation in town. Mules hauled the ore to the smelter, located for topographical reasons directly atop the underground workings. At the smelter, modern in every respect, workers produced a constant stream of gleaming copper bullion and a smaller amount of gold and silver. Mining experts and the few visitors allowed in the smelter remarked on the top-of-the-line machinery and equipment Clark installed, and the rigid safety measures he required his men to follow on pain of dismissal.

Before the turn of the century, Clark was shipping sixty-million pounds per year of copper bullion from Jerome and his personal profits from the property exceeded ten million dollars. United Verde profits plus millions more generated by his far-flung interests made Clark one of America's richest men; some "experts" in the field of estimating other peoples' fortunes declared that Clark's hidden wealth, in the form of buried ores in his many mines, made him far richer than John D. Rockefeller, then deemed America's wealthiest citizen.

Barring a few brief shutdowns, the UVCC operated steadily over the years. Clark conferred routine management of the company on his sons, Charles and William, Jr. Both executed their duties admirably but always looked to their father for guidance. Until his death in 1925, Clark made all major decisions. In 1912, the senior Clark announced a grandiose project, the biggest he ever undertook. An underground fire in the main orebody, ignited by the friction of a cave-in in 1894, put the smelter and surface works in danger of collapse. Slowly-burning timbers under the smelter caused the ground to give and workmen continually shored up loose foundations. Clark spent heavily to extinguish the fire but to no avail. Perhaps the man could not move the mountain but he could move the smelter.

In 1910 Clark bought a number of ranches in the Verde Valley below Jerome, along with water rights. Here he would build not only a new reduction works, but a model town to attract and hold stable family men who would become loyal and steady employees. He set the best mining engineers and architects to work and by the summer of 1913, construction crews filled the once peaceful valley, stirring up great clouds of dust and cursing their mules.

Railroad men laid out tracks for three lines: the Verde Valley Railway, a thirty-eight mile broad-gauge running from the townsite

James Douglas, Jr., owner of the Little Daisy Mine. (KTVK-TV Collection)

to Drake on the Santa Fe line; the Verde Tunnel and Smelter Railway (VT&S), an eleven- mile road between the mine and townsite which transported ore and passengers; and the electric Hopewell Tunnel Railway which hauled ore through the 7200-foot long Hopewell Tunnel at the 1000-foot level of the mine to connect with the VT&S line. Clark's new brick plant near the townsite turned out thousands of bricks each day to be used for the smelter buildings and town. He required all construction, including the business district to conform to unusually high standards.

Clark's Upper Verde Public Utilities Company (UVPU), an umbrella organization which provided water, light, and power for Jerome, administered and owned Clarkdale. From garbage crew to police department, Clark and his managers controlled the town through the UVPU. An enlightened concern for employee welfare helped to offset this circumscribing paternalism.

Brick houses (patio-style in the Hispanic section) boasted maple floors, screened sleeping porches, indoor plumbing, electricity, and free water each summer for lawns and gardens. Employees were offered modern electric ranges at cost; Clarkdale had more of these per capita than any town in America. Broad streets surrounded a spacious central plaza, planted in grass, trees, and shrubs; Clark ordered that no "Keep Off the Grass" signs be posted. After hours, employees and their families might stroll to the clubhouse and check out a library book, go for a swim, play a game of tennis, attend a hotly-contested baseball game with Jerome or play a round of golf; the UVCC donated first-class accommodations for all these activities. A mining town with no saloon is unthinkable; Clark allowed three to operate but forbade a red-light district.

Clark's will stipulated a $100,000 endowment for the construction of a new clubhouse. This superb example of Spanish-style architecture, embellished with copper, housed a bowling alley, billiard room, auditorium, lounges and cardrooms for men and women, soda fountain, and library -- most facilities were free of charge for employees and families. Clark's heirs spared no effort to equip the clubhouse with the finest furnishings. Clark spent at least six million dollars over the years on Clarkdale.

As company officials fired up the new smelter in May, 1915, and Clarkdale assumed the air of a model town, a new Jerome mine owner dazzled the mining world. James Stuart Douglas came to Jerome in 1912 to look over the Little Daisy mine, owned by the United Verde Extension Company (UVX). Many called him "Rawhide," not for any trait of character but for a rawhide device he concocted in Mexico to save wear on mining machinery. "Rawhide" suited him though; Douglas was a block of a man, with a disarming smile that tempered somewhat rugged features. His mercurial temperament intimidated some, yet many remarked on his generosity and sense of fair play. His father, Dr. James Douglas, famous in mining circles, presided over the Phelps Dodge

*Vertical stope drilling under-
ground - United Verde (1925).
Jerome Historical Society.*

*Leyner on a tripod - United
Verde branch of Phelps
Dodge Mining Co. (1941).
Courtesy of Jerome
Historical Society.*

Corporation for many years and devoted his later years to good works. Dr. Douglas had inspected the United Verde mine for investors twice -- once in 1881 for the Philadelphia investors and again in 1888 for Phelps Dodge. He showed less enthusiasm for the Jerome district than for the copper districts to the south.

If Dr. Douglas made no great splash in Jerome, his son certainly did. "Rawhide" James Douglas, born in Quebec in 1868, like Clark, embodied that unrestrained boldness, focused ambition, and strong independence that characterized so many prosperous nineteenth-century businessmen. In the West, these qualities almost always guaranteed success (or a jail term). Young Douglas did not gravitate at once to mining; it had ruined his grandfather financially and frustrated his father for years. Instead, Douglas, an asthmatic, chose at age seventeen to homestead, alone, on Manitoba's Red River. He farmed, but not well, and supplemented his income freighting supplies for the Canadian National Railway, then under construction.

Five years later, in 1890, Douglas moved on to Arizona Territory where he raised strawberries in Cochise County, location of Phelps Dodge's most productive copper mines. Farming defeated him a second time and forced Douglas, a proud young man, to make use of his father's influence to gain employment. The Phelps Dodge Corporation took him on as an assayer in Bisbee and a year later sent him to Prescott in the same capacity at the company's Big Bug, Senator, and Commercial mines. Company officials quickly recognized young Douglas' managerial talents and promoted him to superintendent of the Prescott properties where he remained until 1900. During this time, he became familiar with the Jerome district.

From 1900-1913 Douglas supervised Phelps Dodge's Picacho and Canannea mines in Sonora, Mexico, where he increased production by cutting expenses and modernizing mining methods. Occasionally he ran afoul of the local populace in his efforts to economize and once had to flee the country for three days when his miners walked off the job and threatened to ride him out of town on a burro. Blame for the strike cannot be placed entirely on Douglas; all of Mexico seethed with revolution at the time. Douglas' thrifty ways ended his association with Phelps Dodge when he made unwelcome attempts to cut expenses at company headquarters in New York. When executives took offense at what they perceived as a young upstart's impertinence, he resigned.

When Douglas came to Jerome in 1912, he had found his niche in mining, banking, and promotion. He still worked for Phelps Dodge and divided his time between Mexico and the American border town of Douglas which he founded and named for his father. He grew wealthy in real estate speculation and established the banks of Bisbee and Douglas. Like Clark, Douglas diversified, having many interests outside mining.

In Jerome, Douglas examined the Little Daisy mine, property

of the UVX Company. J.J. Fisher, a surveyor, located the Little Daisy claim in 1899 in the maze of claims in and about Jerome; prospectors overlooked this tiny fraction of ground in the rush to lay claim to the mountain in the wake of Clark's great success. Fisher convinced L.E. Whichner, a Boston capitalist who owned claims in Jerome, to back the sinking of a shaft. Whichner halted the flow of capital in 1901 because of poor ore showings. In 1902, though, Whichner regained his enthusiasm and acquired four claims adjoining the Little Daisy. Whichner, Fisher, and a few others merged interests, organizing the United Verde Extension Company the same year. With depth the quality of ore improved. Whichner, in need of more capital, joined forces with Douglas in 1912.

The Little Daisy came to Douglas' notice through Major A. J. Pickerell, a UVX stockholder with great faith in the mine and a friend of Douglas. In 1911 the Major urged Douglas to evaluate the Little Daisy, hoping he would kick in some working capital. Douglas liked what he saw and tried to interest Phelps Dodge in a partnership option. For a second time, the company turned down a stake in Jerome, ostensibly over a problem with title to the mine but more probably because Phelps Dodge feared apex litigation with Clark, a veteran of many apex suits in Butte. Pickerell tried a new tack; he urged Douglas to undertake the option himself. Douglas hired the famous mining geologist, Ira Joralemon, to make a final report before leaping in. Joralemon told Douglas the odds were good on a money-making prospect. Douglas leapt.

At this point in his career, Douglas had made the acquaintance of a number of wealthy capitalists and expert mining men. He did not have the resources to tackle the Little Daisy venture alone so appealed to these men. George E. Tener of Pittsburgh, a director of Jerome's Calumet and Arizona Company, agreed at once to invest. Tener and Douglas took an option on shares then fired off letters to prospective investors.

Among those who bought in were Chester Congdon and James Hoatson, associates of Tener; Henry Hoveland of Live Oaks (Arizona) Development; Arthur James of Phelps Dodge; and John D. Ryan, president of Amalgamated Copper Company of Butte. Whichner, the previous owner, sat on the board of directors. The inclusion of Ryan among the UVX stockholders jolted Clark, who possessed no greater enemy than Amalgamated, which after years of struggle, forced a sell-out of his Butte copper properties in 1910.

Clark naturally took an interest in UVX progress. He noted the thousands of dollars that went into development and the thousands more that company president, Douglas, requested from share-holders. For two years, a small force of hardrock men probed Little Daisy ground and Douglas assured the people of Jerome that a great copper deposit would be found. The first big ore strike came in December, 1914, when Little Daisy miners cut into an immense vein of 45 per-cent copper ore. It is easy to imagine

Clark, in the privacy of his New York offices, grimly bemoaning the discovery of bonanza ore right under his nose; especially so, because originally the Little Daisy and the United Verde ore bodies were one. An ancient geological accident separated a sizeable chunk from the main body.

Clark's own discovery of ore attracted many lesser companies to the mountains around Jerome, all intent on striking it rich. These organizations invested heavily in their claims from 1915 on, but not one approached the wealth of the United Verde. By the time of Douglas' discovery, geologists proved that only one deposit of high-grade copper existed in the district. Millions of years before, a fault cut through the top of this pipe-shaped structure, slicing off the top, which then slid off and buried itself somewhere in the vicinity. Mining men knew of the fault and the possibility of more bonanza ore; Douglas took a calculated risk that he owned the missing section and won.

Dividend payments from Jerome's two great mines tell the story; the Little Daisy yielded $52 million in dividends, split by a number of shareholders, before final shutdown in 1937; the United Verde paid several million before 1900, at least $60 million between 1900-1927, and millions more to Clark's heirs. A further indication of wealth buried beneath the surface of the United Verde is that Phelps Dodge paid over $10 million to the heirs for the property in the midst of the Great Depression, and realized a further profit of some $40 million before final shutdown in 1953.

Clark and Douglas never became implacable rivals. Though embroiled in litigation between 1916-1922 over which company owned title to disputed mining stocks, both men put aside their differences in 1917 to form a mine owners protective association with a view to putting down labor unrest, a rarity in the district. Profit always took precedence for both men. Political differences never developed; as Democrats and mine owners, both had a vested interest in pro-company legislation and cooperated to that end. Clark's sons followed the lead of their father and lived peacefully with Douglas.

The Jerome district boomed through World War I. Clark, now in his seventies, made annual inspection trips to Jerome and Clarkdale but spent most of his time in New York. Douglas began building a fine mansion in Jerome near the Little Daisy and when the Great War broke out, volunteered his services. The Red Cross accepted his offer and gave him charge of all the organization's warehouses in France. He became a lover of all things French during his stay, another trait he shared with Clark.

After the war, Douglas built his own smelter and support city, naming it after his new friend, Premier Georges Clemenceau of France. The Premier made Douglas a Chevalier of the Legion of Honor in 1927 for his Red Cross work. Douglas did not establish Clemenceau on nearly so grand a scale as Clarkdale, but he built it with genuine concern for the well-being of his employees. Unlike Clark, Douglas had balky stockholders to contend with when making improvements or attending to employee welfare. Douglas built the handsome and spacious Little Daisy Hotel near the mine to house his men, and a modern company hospital to care for their medical needs.

Clark and Douglas both shut down their mines in 1921 in response to a nation-wide post-war slump. As America recovered, so did Jerome; through the remainder of the twenties, the district's smokestacks emitted choking white smoke day and night, skips roared up and down mine shafts, mine sirens shrieked, long trains of ore cars clacked along to smelter, and the streets of Jerome, Clarkdale, and Clemenceau swarmed with three shifts of miners and smeltermen. Only Clark's death in 1925, of pneumonia, at age eighty-seven, caused activity at the UVCC to cease; all operations stopped for a day in his memory. His sons effected a smooth transition and the good times continued until the Great Depression.

The UVCC shut down in the early years of the Depression, partly in response to low copper prices but also because both Clark's sons and his grandson, Tertius, heir apparent to the Clark empire, died. His daughters, Mary and Katherine, inherited, but sold out to Phelps Dodge in 1935. The Little Daisy played out in 1938, and James Douglas, in a fit of pique over Roosevelt's New Deal Program, renewed his Canadian citizenship, making his home in Montreal until his death in 1949 at eighty years of age. As long as he lived, Douglas returned regularly to Jerome to visit old haunts.

William Andrews Clark and James "Rawhide" Douglas are long dead, but visitors to Jerome see everywhere evidence of the King and the Crown Prince of Copper. Well worth a side trip, Clarkdale itself is a monument to Clark, a man who succeeded brilliantly in the material building of the West during a time when most Americans considered progress and growth to be nothing less than humanity's highest goal. Clark built many of Jerome's historic buildings; his influence permeates the town. Douglas stamped his image over a more limited area, perhaps, but his presence remains strong. His elegant mansion is now headquarters for the Jerome State Historic Park, a fine museum and park devoted to Jerome's mining history. Clemenceau is gone but the skeleton of the Little Daisy Hotel remains, as does the site of the fabulous Little Daisy Mine.

While Jerome stands, Clark and Douglas live, symbols of a past era, one in which anything was possible, when remarkable men wrested fame and fortune from the earth.

Chapter Six
THE OUTLAWS
The Verde Valley's "Friendless Men"
Who needs a friend if you have a gun...?

irst of all, what exactly is an outlaw? The word itself is self-explanatory - he (not she), is someone 'outside the law.' And how did this all come about? Modern thought seems to suggest that the difference between an outlaw and your ordinary day-to-day criminal is a matter of notoriety.

Not so; the difference is far more clearly delineated. In Europe's older culture, originating in Scandinavia of all places, the word was *utlagi,* and the judicial declaration 'outlawry' meant that the poor fellow who had evaded justice by deciding not to present himself in Court when charged as a common criminal, preferring simply to disappear off the face of society, was officially declared, in the legal Latin of the time, to be *Libera Lex,* or no longer enjoying the protection of the law. In English Saxon times (like it or not the basis of all modern American/English law), he was even known as *caput lupinum,* or 'wolf-head', because under that law, any Tom, Dick, or Harry, on meeting with one of these villains, was permitted to bash him over the head as one would a wolf, and drag him off to the Shire Riff (read 'County Head') for suitable punishment, which usually meant a friendly village gathering for the hanging...

We are thinking now of some eleven hundred years ago, and the outlaw had, in those wonderful, far-off days, other descriptive titles too; the Judiciary of the time called him *civiliter mortuus* which meant that he was not entitled to sue in any court of Law. But the common people, who spoke no Latin, called him simply *friendlessman* because he had forfeited his friends.

Understandably so; any of his friends suspected of helping him was subject to the same punishment as he himself received when, finally, he was caught and strung up for the pleasure of the populace. What a splendid idea.

And outlaws were always men, not women. There were many famous ladies who slipped beyond the law and were subject to the same discomforts as their male counterparts. But, correctly, they are not called "outlaws." They are called *"Waives."*

141

But who, in Arizona's lovely Verde Valley, ever heard of a *Waive?* Pearl Hart, who, with her friend Joe Boot, pulled off Arizona's last-ever stagecoach hold-up, in 1899, was known simply as an *outlaw,* just like her lover Joe, and to the devil with the niceties of language. There were not very many of these ladies; and when they finished up in Yuma's Territorial Prison - they were all known by the staff as a damn nuisance to everybody, and were therefore released under one pretext or another as soon as might be politically practical; pardons by the Governor of the moment were very popular.

But in the meantime, they shared their dismal cells and their tawdry meals with such celebrated criminals as the famous Elena Estrada, a lady convicted of killing her lover, one Refugio Bindiola, by gutting him with a sharp kitchen knife to the stomach. She was widely known also to have cut out his heart and thrown it into his face; but of this, the local press said little. Indeed, the Graham Sentinel reported, simply and with remarkable journalistic inexactitude: "There is no doubt at all that it was she who fired the fatal shot..."

(Senorita Estrada, incidentally, was sentenced to seven years for her butchery, and was pardoned by Governor Nickols after four.)

In the United States, outlawry never existed in civil cases, only in criminal law.

And finally - the term "outlaw" became legally obsolete in 1910. One wonders why...

So what was it that made the Verde valley so happy a home for so many of Arizona's infamous outlaws?

We must remember, first of all, the violent history of that vast and wonderful land that today we know as Arizona, more vast than wonderful, perhaps, to the first Europeans to come here, whose homeland, Spain, comprised a mere one hundred and ninety thousand square miles and who found themselves colonially confronted with more than twenty times that space, not even counting their even vaster conquests in South America.

Their Northern territories reached from Mexico north to way beyond San Francisco, and the more adventurous of them were even squabbling with Russia at the border of Alaska.

It meant that the individual Spaniard in the Americas was one in a million, and moreover - meeting hostility wherever he went. Whether that individual Spaniard was himself an "individualist" really doesn't matter very much; because in the course of time he must certainly have become one, learning very quickly that his well-being and his life very often depended on his skill with his weapons and the speed of his horse.

He was governed only by the laws of his distant homeland; here, the concept of Law existed in a vague sort of way, but whose laws were they? The assorted laws of the varying savages who occupied these huge, sparcely-occupied territories? They must have meant nothing to him as he drove North and East in the compulsive search for gold - or better still, for the legendary "Cities of Gold" of which he must surely have read so much in his rigid childhood, before soldiery replaced the very nationalistic studies of his earlier years. History records that here, in our territory, he rode unbelievable distances to find wealth, or to save his own skin. He fought, and he died; but the loneliness lived on...

South from "New Spain," reinforcements were arriving constantly, but to the North, the numbers were always pitifully small; even as late as the year 1777, the Spaniards' only miltary post in Arizona, at their tiny settlement of Tubac, some 50 miles south of today's Tucson, was manned by no more than fifty men, armed with muskets, swords, lances - and four practically useless cannon.

Almost alone, driven by greed, contemptuous of whatever local laws there might hav been, dependent only upon his and his steed's competence, and with no-one in the local society to help him when he found himself in need...Was the lonely Spaniard the first of the *friendlessmen* in the State we now call home?

Can he legitimately be called an "outlaw?" He qualifies, so perhaps he can.

Did he, so long ago, unconsciously set the standards for our Arizona?

Perhaps he did.

But then, a mere seventy-two years later, the picture in the American West had changed completely with a new brand of goldseekers - the "forty-niners" - and the loneliness was no more; between 1849 and 1851, more than sixty thousand ex-Europeans, now called Americans, headed West in a furious and frantic search for gold and other minerals.

"Furious" is the operative word here; the dream of untold wealth was all-consuming, burning up any old-fashioned ideas of morality or even of common decency. Claims were staked out, and woe to him who dared trespass upon them; guns were fired, and dead bodies were legion, not often counted...or even reported.

The common good meant nothing now; it was the individual who mattered, and that seed of individualism sown by the lonely Spaniard in a territory ripe to receive it, was sprouting again. And it was more deadly now, because whereas in the old days it had been sword or lance against arrow or club, each contestant eye to eye with his enemy - today, a coward with a Winchester could kill a brave man at more than five hundred paces.

And he did just that, very often.

The plenitude of the friendlessman was bursting at the seams; now, with those valuable claims staked out and the only law a roving, often solitary Sherriff with a six-shooter, it was every man for himself, and the devil take the hindmost.

It was the birth of the philosophy: "My gun is faster'n your'n..."

Contempt for the law was bound to follow, and it did.

And this was the rebirth of the concept of outlawry, a concept that was to become so common that it almost earned social acceptability.

Until, that is to say, it all got quite out of hand. And what was it, then, that made the Verde Valley home to so many of these friendless men?

We must think in terms of water. Of course, there's the great Colorado River and the Gila, but in between them, in that enormous expanse of arid, deathly desert, there's very little except the Verde River. And it was to the waters of the Verde Valley that the settlers came.

One must imagine, here, the long, dry treks where a single mouthful of water meant the difference between life and death, not only for the single traveller, but for his women and children too. It was not enough that he had to defend himself against a justifiably angry Apache population, skillfully after his scalp, - dry and swollen-lipped, he had to worry himself sick about where the next supply of water was coming from.

His scalp? Scalping, the knife-removal of the skin of the head together with its trophy-hair, was not an exclusively Indian custom; it had been introduced here by those friendless Spaniards, and even as late at the eighteen thirties, the Sonoran Government itself was in the scalp-bounty business. In 1839, one American bounty-hunter was reported to have earned himself and his gang an incredible hundred thousand dollars for the scalps he turned in; they were not always Indian, as was the intent - the Mexicans were far easier pray.

The crescendo of violence was quite frightening now, leading inexorably to the lonely white man's explosive dependence upon his arms and his personal bellicosity; and the normally admirable idea of individuality was fast becoming a very serious danger.

Even when that lonely traveller was lucky enough to be in a wagon-train of perhaps forty or fifty people. . . it was still a case of the very few against a too-often unseen horde of a competent enemy out there who were accustomed, as he was not, to the merciless, intolerant, and quite unforgiving desert; and there still wasn't very much of a legal system to come to his rescue if, and when, he needed it.

It was one man against the world, and this meant, inevitably, the growth of the spirit of independence for which, even today, the Westerner in general, and perhaps the Arizonan in particular, has become famous. The wide-open West, historically, never was a good breeding-ground for wimps.

And this spirit was also the built-in philosophy of the outlaw. It is surprising, only, that there weren't far more of them, though by around the mid 1870's, general lawlessness - abetted at least in part by the venality of so many of the lawmen themselves, Sheriffs and Judges alike - was so rife that vigilante committees were

ARIZONA
TERRITORIAL PRISON
THESE SOMBRE WALLS HELD IN
BYGONE DAYS SOME OF THE MOST
NOTORIOUS DESPERADOES OF OLD
SOUTHWEST · HERE TERRITORIAL
JUSTICE WAS SERVED BETWEEN
THE YEARS 1875 AND 1909 · WHEN
THE PRISON WAS MOVED TO FLOR-
ENCE · ABANDONED AND LONG-
FORGOTTEN · THIS GRIM RELIC
WAS RESTORED BY THE CITY OF
YUMA IN 1940 AS A HISTORICAL
MUSE

Yuma, Arizona, June 5, 1905.

Mr. _____

The Sheriff of Yuma County, Arizona, announces that
on Friday, June 16, 1905, at the hour of 11 o'clock a. m.,

Martin Ubillos

will be executed at the jail yard in this city, for the murder
of Simon Aldrete. You are respectfully invited to witness
the execution.

Gus Livingston
Sheriff.

Typical invitation to a hanging. (Yuma Territorial Prison Museum) springing up everywhere.

At this time, the brutal murder of a small-town storekeeper and his wife so infuriated the local residents that they formed a posse, tracked down the three murderers, put them on what was called by a jubilant Press "a public trial," and summarily executed them while the assembled - and very angry - crowd cheered. In another case, local residents broke into the town jail, carted off two confessed murderers, and strung them up; and hanging undesirables from trees or telegraph poles was a very popular undertaking.

It was that wonderful Arizonan individuality at work - "If they won't do it for me, why then, I'll jes' take care of it myself..."

And long may it survive; in matters of law and order, a certain toughness was often quite necessary.

But there was another reason, too, for the popularity of the Verde Valley as a hang-out for the friendless men who had decided not to face their accusers but to keep their own lives intact for as long as possible by their own efforts and their own wits; the now-famous Red Rocks and the immediately surrounding countryside of what was to become the City of Sedona were almost impossible of access, threaded through as the forbidding mountains were only with Indian trails. It was perfect country for a fugitive.

Indeed, tracking them down was an almost impossible task, demanding the services of dedicated and indefatigable lawmen and highly-skilled Indian trackers - men who could recognize particular footprints or hoof-marks days, weeks, or even months after they had first been committed to memory, following hopeful tracks over hard rocks and wet mud alike, through thick forest and heavy undergrowth with the dogged persistence which was also part of that Western spirit.

It was never possible to hold to a track in this kind of country for more than a little while, for more than a short distance, but these men were driven by an obsession to find those tell-tale marks again, somehow, somewhere; and very often, they did.

There was acute danger for them, too; they were not hunting animals which would, for the most part, try to save their skins by seeking out hidden lairs and merely escaping. The outlaw knew that his capture only too often meant the rope, and once the pattern of the hunt was set, once he knew that the avenging law had picked up his trail - then the perfect set-up for an ambush was ready to hand.

A cluster of boulders, a darkly dense thicket, the high branches of a tree, with a rifle at the ready, it was all that was required.

The pursuers might have spotted a footprint, the Indian trackers might have told them it was recent. But how recent? A day or so? An hour or two? Or maybe only minutes? Was that dark shadow ahead someone lying in wait for them? Sometimes, the only answer to that question would be a rifle-shot and one of their number lying dead or wounded there.

Outlaw Francisco Garcia, (right) who killed his cell-mate, Simon Ardrete, (left). (Yuma Territorial Prison Museum)

Francisco Garcia, neatly dressed for his hanging. (Yuma Territorial Prison Museum)

Patience now. No good rushing into trouble, the gunman, skilled as they were themselves, would have gone, his quick escape-route already picked out. Besides, there was a casualty to attend to, and tomorrow was another day. At least, they knew that they were getting close now. . .

"Take care of Chuck here. Make camp. Sun-up tomorrow, we move on. West, he'll be heading for the creek, hide them tracks."

And then, more gently: "You gonna make it, Chuck? You better. And don't you worry none, we'll get him."

So many good men lost their lives along today's tourist trails of beautiful Oak Creek Canyon.

Sometimes, the outlaw won out, sometimes he lost and was quickly strung up; and sometimes, just like today, he wiggled till the yes or no was decided for him.

Take the case of one Francisco Garcia, alias Martin Ubillos, laborer, Mexican native, and murderer turned outlaw. Twenty-five years old, uneducated, and with no known relatives, a young trouble-maker from the banks of the Verde River in Yavapai County, Arizona, chased, and caught, and thrown into the infamous territorial prison in Yuma; for life.

But prison, it appears, did not cure his bad temper. Five months later, for refusing to work, he was put in solitary confinement for three days - and solitary in Yuma was no fun at all - a tiny, bare stone cell with all light excluded from it. Four months later, he was sentenced to a nasty 54 days there for assaulting a guard.

And then, on August 16, 1903, he killed his cell-mate, one Simon Aldrete, was charged with his second murder, and spent an incredible eight months in the dark of the cell, awaiting his trial.

In the end, the Judgement, dated Wednesday, April 13th, A.D. 1904, was clear and to the point:

THE TERRITORY OF ARIZONA VS
Martin Ubillos, indicated as Francisco Garcia, defendant.

Judgement

The defendant, Martin Ubillos, indicted as Francisco Garcia, being present in open court in person and by his council, (sic.) Heny Wrifferman Esq., and Frank Baxter Esq., also W.F. Timmons Esq., the District Attorney. And this being the time heretofore fixed for announcing sentence and judgement in this case; the defendant, Martin Ubillos, indicted as Francisco Garcia, was duly informed by the court of the indication found against him, for the crime of murder of the first degree committed on or about the sixteenth day of August A.D. 1903; of his arraignment and plea of "not guilty" as charged in the indictment; of the trial, and verdict of the jury on the seventh day of April, A.D. 1904, finding the defendant guilty, as charged in the indictment, and fixing the penalty at death.

The defendant was asked if he had any legal cause to show why judgement should not be pronounced against him, and no sufficient cause being shown or appearing to the court, there upon the court tendered its judgement: That whereas you, Martin Ubillos, indicted as Francisco Garcia, for the said crime of murder, committed as aforesaid, be punished in the manner prescribed by law, to-wit by the hanging of you by the neck until you are dead; and that you Martin Ubillos, indicted as Francisco Garcia, be taken hence and safely kept until Friday, the third day of June, A.D. 1904, and on that day, between the hours of eight o'clock in the forenoon and one o'clock in the afternoon, you be hanged by the neck until you are dead, and may God have mercy on your soul. The defendant was then remanded to the custody of the sheriff of said Yuma County, for the execution of the sentence and judgement aforesaid. Whereupon the said defendant, through his council (sic) filed notice in writing of his appeal from said judgement to the Supreme Court of the Territory.

Geo. T. Davis
Judge

June the 3rd came and went without incident, and twelve days later, the Arizona Sentinel took up the story:

WILL PROBABLY NOT BE HUNG: the story was headed, and it went on:

A few people, perhaps, have been wondering why there was not a hanging function in the Yuma County jail yard on June 3rd. As a matter of fact, the absorbing question of government irrigation and how to head off and capture the elusive almighty dollar has held the boards so exclusively that most people have doubtless forgotten that such a legal tragedy was to be entered. It is safe to assume, however, that one Martin Ubillos, a life convict, did not fail to congratulate himself and with satisfaction note that Friday, June 3rd, slipped by, leaving his still doing time at the old stand and in full possession of all his faculties intact. About a year ago, Martin killed a fellow convict, one Simon Aldrete. He was convicted at the April term of court and sentenced to be hung June 3, 1904. His attorneys, Henry Wupperman (sic) and Frank Baxter, took an appeal, which acted as a stay of execution until passed upon by the Supreme Court, which grants an extended lease of life to Ubillos at least until next January. The attorneys have filed a brief in behalf of their client in which a considerable portion of the testimony of the lower court trial is submitted tending to establish the point that the killing of Aldrete was not premeditated, but resulted from a duel, Aldrete himself being the challenger. The men had a falling out and subsequently quarreled often. Aldrete repeatedly challenged Ubillos to fight. On the fatal morning he told Ubillos that one of them must die and invited him to come into his cell and they would fight it out. The challenge was accepted, and the convicts fought with knives to the death. Through the persistent efforts of his lawyers, Ubillos may yet secure a commutation of sentence, which could not be less than life imprisonment. He is a life-termer now, so that the only way to inflict another such sentence would be to have it extended to the life beyond, and commission His Majesty the Devil to execute it, provided it is within his jurisdiction.

The last two entries in his prison record close this unhappy tale:

Francisco Garcia the record states: *June 16, 1905; By virtue of an order of the Court delivered to Sherriff of Yuma County for execution.*

And then, at long last on the same day:

When and How Discharged: June 16, 1905, Executed by Hanging at

11 O'Clock by sentence of Court.

This was just one of the outlaws, far removed in character from the conventional outlaw so long depicted by the novelists and by Hollywood. He was really just an angry young punk at war with the world and with himself. Four years previously, in a drunken bar-room fight, he had stabbed two companions, wounding one of them and killing the other, then eluding the deputies who had been sent to arrest him for three hectic days before he was spotted in another bar, and hustled off to the jail where once again his violent temper took possession of him.

"I charge you," said the Judge to the jury, "that no act committed by a person in a state of voluntary intoxication is less criminal by reason of his having been in such condition. . .unless such intoxication has been so protracted as to produce a real disease of the mind distinct from the ordinary effect of alcohol. . ."

And the outcome for poor, angry Francisco, could not have been much different in the long run. Hanging could never have been much of a comfort to the victim; but in those not-too-distant days, there was not always the heavy knot under the ear that would quickly snap the vertebrae. *Hung by the neck,* said the judgement, *until you are dead,* and that's how it was; slow and struggling strangulation that sometimes lasted for a very long time.

More in the accepted mold was the notorious train-robber John Halford, who got together a small band of five cronies (among them, one William Stiren, of whom more later,) with the Atlantic and Pacific railroad in his felonious mind. (The A&P was the first of the Southwestern railroads to be built, chartered by Congress in July of 1866; it was never much of a success.)

Hollywood brain-washed, we can imagine the sweating horses spurred on alongside the screaming train, the outlaws swinging aboard, but not stunt men now, the real thing. . .Only on this occasion, Halford and his men were less energetic; they merely waited at the Canyon Diablo station, calmly boarded the train, and held up the man who had the money; or, as the indictment described him so very meticulously: *one E.G. Knickerbocker who was then and there an express messenger on said railroad train and in the said railroad car, and which said express messenger was then and there an express messenger of Wells Fargo and Company, a corporation duly created, organised, and existing under the laws of the territory of Colorado, and which said railroad car was then and there one of the railroad cars of said railroad train.* . .etcetera and etcertera ad infinitum.

He was a young man, John Halford, only twenty-four years old at the time. He was tall and skinny, a skeleton of a creature who both smoked and chewed tobacco, fair-skinned and grey-eyed, and was relatively well-educated.

This was almost certainly not his first train robbery - he was suspected of engineering at least three others; it was just the first time he had been caught, and a heavy sentence was inevitable; on July 22nd, 1889, he was handed down a stiff 25 years in Yuma Territorial Prison.

There, it seems that he was a model prisoner, employed as the prison baker and liked by all the staff for his genial and gentle character. Even so, there were occasions on which the guards found it necessary to put him in leg irons for a while to inhibit the escape they always thought that a man of his undoubted intelligence would be permanently planning.

But the leg irons never worked for John Halford; incredibly, he always found a way to open their locks, and the most exhaustive research by the prison officers never found out just how he did it. Characteristically, his intent here never seemed to be an ettempt at freedom, but merely to find a strange sort of delight in frustrating his many friends among the guards.

None the less, the very severe strains of life behind bars weighed heavily on him, to the extent that Prison Superintendent Dorrington began to fear that his favorite prisoner was slowly dying; and through his efforts and the efforts of the prison staff in general, John Halford, twenty-five year convict, was unconditionally pardoned by Governor McCord on November 1st, 1897, after serving a little more than eight years.

And history records no more of him.

This was, in fact, the pattern. The outlaws seldom made their own history: but even so, in this lovely, verdant Verde Valley, outlawry had become so rife that in May of 1882, then-President Chester A. Arthur threatened to end the problem once and for all, by the imposition of martial law, a threat that was never carried out.

And so, the outlaws lived on.

Train and Highway robbery were the two crimes with which the ordinary outlaw was most commonly associated, perhaps because the public mind was so often centered on a galloping posse hard on the heels of galloping robbers. The local sheriff or deputy would ride fast from the scene of the crime up to the nearest sizeable town, and call for help, just like something out of "High Noon," and gather together a dozen or so honest citizens, if he could find any. (If not, almost anyone would do.) And they, in turn, would ride furiously off with him, deputized under hasty oath and thereby "licensed to kill." (One notorious Sheriff, named Frank Watron, encouraged his men not to bother bringing the culprits in for trial, telling them it made much more sense just to shoot them on sight.)

And this was always a little excitement in the rather drab lives of the townsfolk.

It meant that in the harsh desert heat and formidable landscape of the territory, the friendless outlaw always needed a good horse himself. Often, his mount would succumb to the harsh exertion of the constant hard-driving; and often, he would find himself sorely in need of something just a little better. . .

It meant that horse-stealing was high on the list of the outlaw's preferred activities. On his visits to the towns that, incognito, he wandered through for his supplies, he always kept a keen eye open for a really good horse that he figured was faster or had more staying power than the one he was currently riding.

One such outlaw was named Zack Booth, one of a large family of Booth sons who all lived on the wrong side of the law, and who claimed some sort of vague blood-relationship with President Lincoln's assassin, though no-one really believed them.

But this claimed relationship has an interest all its own: John Wilkes Booth was a murderer who had been shot to death for his crime, and had achieved lasting fame or notoriety. Many of the outlaws were hanged for their crimes, and this made them all, so to speak, brothers in arms, even though their reasons for their lawlessness were so different from his. It can easily be understood that these petty criminals might seek some sort of stature by aligning themselves, however nebulously, with such a famous name that was, after all, the same as their own.

Be that as it pathetically may, Zack Booth was a suspect in half-a-dozen horse thefts, and the Sheriffs had been after him for more than three years before, at last, they caught up with him.

His brother John was already in the penitentiary and serving a four-year sentence for burglary; brother Nick was in for three years on a charge of forgery; but Zack outclassed them both by getting himself twelve years. And he, it seems, was the only one of the brothers for whom incarceration was just not to be tolerated . . .

TOOK FRENCH LEAVE said the Arizona Sentinel of December 30, 1893, and went on:

Wednesday morning, while some forty prisoners from the penitentiary were assisting in hauling the steamer Gila out onto the ways, Z.H. Booth, sentenced to 12 years for horse stealing hid behind a gang of his comrades, and ripping off his prison garb under which he had a white shirt and a pair of blue overalls, got up and passed by the guards and escaped. He passed down the street to the Yuma Water and Light Co's. wood yard, jumped over a fence into an old corral and crossed over the railroad track to the old government corral where he hid for the day, and where late in the afternoon Mrs. Marable found him under hay in a manger, while she was looking for eggs. The guards and trailers followed his tracks to the railroad where they were destroyed by the constant travel. When he left the corral he took up a small gulch over the hill, down to the ditch, when he turned and came back and took the road for Gila City, following it and the railroad as his fancy took him. Nothing has been heard of the trailers who were after him since he reached a point just this side of that place. At Blaisdell, he took a few pieces of jerked beef that hung on the line. Frank Eastman and two Indian trailers are following him. A reward of $250 is offered for his arrest and return to prison.

It seems strange perhaps, today, to realize how little offended a great part of the citizenry was by the antics of the outlaws; in many cases, they were not entirely friendless any more. In the matter of the Booth brothers, the press complained that their wives and families, "through sickness and poverty," were suffering more than the criminals themselves, and that it would be a Christian act to give them their liberty, so that they could do something to relieve the suffering of their unfortunate families.

It didn't cut much ice with the prison authorities.

Then there was the case of one William Faught, or, as the press insisted on calling him, Bill Fott.

He was not your ordinary horseback outlaw, but since he fled from justice, refusing to present himself to the Court when so ordered, he qualifies. He was no uncouth roughrider set on robbing trains or stage coaches; he was a well-educated man with training in both architecture and bookkeeping, slight of build, lightweight, and clerically inclined. Born and educated in Kentucky, at the age of thirty-two he became one of the Verde Valley's outlaws, under very strange circumstances indeed. He was a very interesting man, not out of the mold at all. And the ramifications of his case were remarkable too, not least because the one witness, a Constable, who could have saved him from prison, chose, for reasons of his own, to remain silent for a while, and then sullenly denied that he had any part in the matter. It was probably a matter of personal animosity.

At the time of his major crime, murder, he had already been indicted on charges of forgery, committed in Phoenix only a few days after he had arrived there from the Northern parts of the territory. But since the prime witness for the prosecution had unaccountably disappeared, the case against him was dismissed, and he returned to his temporary home in Ash Fork.

He was a worthless sort of fellow, hated by everyone he came in contact with, and at the age of 32, he narrowly escaped a lynching which he probably richly deserved.

It was June in the year 1898, and his victim was a man named A.N. Carter, who also lived up in Ash Fork and was working on a spur line of the Santa Fe Railroad that was to run south to connect with Phoenix. Carter was married, with three children, and a good-natured sort of fellow, greatly liked by his fellow workers. On that fateful Saturday, he had ridden over to Seligman to visit friends, and was still there after nightfall, on the street, and alone. The moon was partly obscured by clouds.

Then began a series of quite incredible events, initiated by William Faught, who happened to be in Seligman too at this time...

First of all, he went to one of the local saloons, where he introduced himself as a Sheriff's Deputy. He said he was on the trail of a notorious outlaw, was himself unarmed, and felt that he really needed a gun to make the imminent arrest. He showed no badge, nor any other proof of authority, but non the less,, the gullible saloon-keeper believed him, and handed over his own gun - to a perfect stranger. Faught promised to return it within a short while, and left the saloon.

A little while later, he came across Carter, shot him in the back and killed him, walked back to the saloon where he had borrowed the gun and calmly returned it, and then. . .*Then he lay down on the floor of the saloon, and went to sleep.*

It was not long before news of the shooting reached the saloon, and a noisy, angry crowd gathered, the uproar apparently awakening Faught, who simply slipped out into the night and got away.

But it was not long, either, before the saloon-keeper realized that he had foolishly lent his gun to a murderer, and the hunt was on.

But the darkness had swallowed the fugitive up, of course, and little could be done except make plans for the morning, when, as it would be Sunday, almost every railroad worker in town and in Ash Fork would be free. Deputy Sheriff Munds of Yavapai County was sent for, and when he arrived late Sunday evening, he found that a group of three pursuers out of nearly a hundred who had been searching the forest had found the culprit, weak and exhausted, had bound him securely, and were in process of gathering together as many of their friends and Carter's as possible for a lynching.

Deputy Munds put a stop to this, not without some difficulty, formally arrested Faught, and sent him off under escort to Ash Fork for the preliminary examination.'

And there, the mounting mysteries were further compounded. . .

First of all, Faught claimed that he had been deputized by one Constable Adams to arrest Carter for interfering with him, Adams, while he was trying to serve garnishment papers on a player in a crap game that Carter was running. But, he said, when he approached Carter later and tried to arrest him, Carter violently resisted, whereupon the phony Deputy fired the single shot that killed him.

Witnesses? There was only one, a young girl who hesitantly said that she had merely seen someone shoot someone in the light of a moon that was not bright enough for her to identify either of them.

"Was anyone else there," the Judge asked, "who might be able to give evidence?"

She shook her head; there was no-one else on the street at that time.

But then, two "bystanders" appeared - railroad men and friends of the deceased - who stated bluntly that they had seen what happened, that Carter had done nothing at all to justify arrest, much less the shooting; that Faught had simply walked up to him, and had shot him dead.

It was the shooting in the back, of course, combined with Carter's popularity, that made so many of the railroad men anxious to see Faught hanged. But the examination was not over yet. . .

Constable Adams was sent for and questioned, and he merely told the Judge that he knew nothing whatsoever about this case, and therefore chose to remain silent. But after pressure was

The hanging of James
Parker - Prescott 1897:

(a) Awaiting the victim

(b) Parker, (center
stage) all dressed up in
a suit, is surrounded by
Sheriffs James Munds
and George Ruffner,
Father Kuetu, Shorty
Lacey, Joe Dillon,
Jeff Davis, and
Morris Goldwater.

(c) The noose and hood
is set so that his
sentence of hanging by
the neck until dead may
be carried out. (photos
courtesy of Sharlott
Hall Museum)

applied, he admitted that he knew both Carter and Faught, and swore that he believed Faught was actively trying, when they met, to seize the bank roll from that famous crap game. It just made no sense at all.

And in spite of the fact that Constable Adams did have the legal authority to deputize Faught, he flatly denied that he had ever done so.

It seems that the Court, like everyone else concerned, was thoroughly frustrated by just too many lies, too many evasions, and too many mysteries.

So, on the sixth day of June in 1898, William Faught, more commonly known as Bill Fott, was sentenced to serve tweny years in Yuma's Territorial Prison. There, as Prisoner #1390, he behaved himself surprisingly well, no charges of fighting, no charges of assault on the guards, no obstreperous behavior at all, and therefore never any leg-irons or long days in solitary confinement in the dreaded dark cells.

Twenty years? No.

Seven years and three months later, he was a free man again; on September 23rd, 1905, he was paroled by Governor Joseph H. Kibby, and he too disappeared, almost, from history.

Almost, but not quite.

Some said he had gone home to Kentucky, and had opened a flourishing restaurant, where he had made himself well-liked and was fast becoming a very rich man; some said the railroad men had killed him shortly after his release, a seven-year-old vendetta; and some said no, he had hanged himself somewhere.

But no-one was ever quite sure.

It was just one more of the William Faught mysteries.

He could never have been called your typical Verde Valley outlaw.

But some of them, though perhaps very few, really lived up to the public image of what an outlaw ought to be like - fast with his six-shooter, good with his horses, and very protective indeed of his own skin; an individualist who needed, and took, help from no living soul on the face of the earth.

Such a man was the outlaw Jim Parker...

We are in the 1880's now, and though for some years he had been a fairly honest, fairly law-abiding citizen, albeit a man who knew well that in these violent times expertise with a hand-gun had certain advantages, he did have his little weaknesses...

One of his early brushes with the law seems to have been at Joseph Reddeford Walker's Hassayampa Mines, which lay some five miles west of Yavapai County's Capital Seat, Prescott, hard by the casually-flowing headwaters of the river of that name. And it seems that the miners there were a rough lot; in Jerome, where the mining companies were constantly hiring, there were notices everywhere which stated flatly: "No Hassayampa miners need apply."

The word "Hassayampa," incidentally, is an Indian term meaning "Hidden Waters," (or, according to some authorities, "Beautiful Waters.") But the interesting aspect of this broken water-way is - if you drank from the river, you were instantly turned into a congenital liar, and would never again speak the truth for as long as you lived.

But we must admit that scientific confirmation of this extraordinary abnormality has been somewhat elusive.

However, in Hassayampa Camp, Jim Parker was an outsider passing through, and there was a fearsome quarrel at a card game, a quarrel at which one of three locals at the table was foolish enough to reach for his gun.

Parker, they say, calmly rose to his feet and left; but at the door he turned and fired three shots, wounding two of his recent companions, and then - he just walked out of the saloon.

Conscious of the fury he had left behind him - one man against forty or fifty angry miners after his blood - he rode off at speed for Fort Verde.

There, he abandoned his horse, which had become lamed, and stole two fresh replacements. The Hassayampa posse had called in the expert Navajo trackers, and bloodhounds too, and Parker's trail, though initially lost, was picked up again twenty-two miles to the north, which means somewhere in today's tourist Mecca of Oak Creek Canyon. He was moving through water there, to hide his tracks.

Convinced that he had shaken his pursuers off the trail, he moved further north, way up to the railway line at Peach Springs, where the passage of a Wells Fargo shipment of gold bullion on the new Atlantic and Pacific Railroad was more than his envious stomach could tolerate; it was just *begging* to be stolen, and Jim Parker teamed up with some of his buddies of like philosophy and held up the train, hoping to enrich themselves with more gold than they could comfortably carry away.

It was February 7th, 1897; and it just wasn't Parker's day.

Outlaws, like plumbers or lawyers, weren't always necessarily expert at what they did for a living. First of all, Parker leaped from under cover onto the wrong carriage, where there was no gold bullion at all. And then, against all previous intentions, someone got killed - a Wells Fargo guard had fired, and had shot one of the gang.

And very rapidly, a Sheriff's Posse caught up with him, eye-balled him down, and arrested him. A Yavapai County Judge had signed the warrant:

A complaint upon oath having been this day laid before me, J.M.N. Moore, a Justice of the Peace. . .the crime of train robbery. . .you are therefore commanded forthwith to arrest. . .James Parker, and bring him before me at Prescott. . .

And it was a Sheriff named George Ruffner, a law-man fearsome and famous in his own right for his dedication and stubborness, (as well as for his horsemanship and his expertise with a gun,) who scrawled across the warrant:

Office of the Sheriff of Yavapai County, Az.

I hereby certify that I have served the within warrant on the within named James Parker, by taking him into custody at Diamond Canyon...

He appears to have been a little uncertain of the date; his notation "the 17th day" was altered to read "the 15th day," but then, as though to put matters right once and for all, he wrote underneath:

Dated Feby 20th 1897,

G. C. Ruffner, Sheriff.

And poor James Parker was remanded, without bail, to Prescott Jail to await his trial.

Train robbery was not to be declared a capital offense under Arizona law until almost a year later; but a man had been shot to death in this hold-up, and the prospect of the noose must have been very clear in Parker's mind.

He was a small man, well under average height, but solidly built, and very strong, though his most noticeable feature, perhaps, was the very high forehead that is often believed to denote a certain intellectuality.

And waiting interminably in Prescott Jail, for an almost certainly disastrous trial, was not something he was prepared to put up with.

It took him a little over two months to set the scene, to ingratiate himself with the guards, to prove to them that he was a model prisoner with no thought of an escape attempt ever entering his mind...

And when he was good and ready, he struck.

When a jailor unlocked his cell to bring water, Parker knocked the man down, seized his shotgun, and ran, together with two of his buddies. An Assistant County Attorney tried to stop them, and was shot to death for his efforts; and now, Jim Parker was on the run once more, this time with a more certain murder charge hanging over his head. A very short while later, the three of them found themselves horses - one of which, it was said, belonged to Sheriff Ruffner himself - and headed northeast towards Parker's old hunting grounds.

And it was there, in the lower reaches of Canyon Diablo, not very far from the railroad line of the Atlantic and Pacific where this escapade had really begun, but more than a hundred miles from Prescott's jail, that the very determined posse, led by none other than Yavapai County Deputy Munds of the William Faught case, found James Parker, given away by that old cliche - the rising smoke from a morning campfire, and hauled him back to Prescott jail.

This time, there was no further escape. James Parker was sentenced to death, and on the black-painted gallows he behaved like the old-fashioned gentleman he had always been, perhaps, at heart.

He took time out to examine carefully the murderous contraption that was to take his life...

Maybe it was all just showing-off. But maybe he wanted to make sure of the heavy knot that would be placed just so under his ear to ensure the instant breaking of his neck, and so avoid the usual slow and horrible strangulation.

This was two years before, at the hanging of one George Smiley, a railroad worker who had killed his foreman, the notorious Sheriff Frank J. Wattron had sent out invitations to the citizenry that postulated:

The latest improved methods of scientific strangulation will be employed, and everything possible will be done to make the surroundings cheerful, and the execution a success.

Two years early...But Sheriff Wattron's description must surely have reflected the mores of the times.

And was it perhaps this that persuaded Parker in his final minutes? We must not think that it was just vulgar bravado from a man with such a high, intellectual forehead.

It was all rather sad; his last request, accepted, was for Sheriff Ruffner to spring the trap that would hang him.

Why? In their younger years, these two, Parker and Ruffner, had been very, very close friends.

And perhaps that friendship was still there today.

Then there was James Pemberton, Case Number 751 in the Court of the Fourth Judicial District of the Territory of Arizona, in and for the County of Yavapai...

He was one of the Verde Valley outlaws who had decided to stay on in spite of the recent proliferation of the telepohone and the telegraph, which had somehow conspired together to make the outlaw's life a hazardous misery; he would commit his little larceny, say, somewhere near Strawberry, and would escape as fast as his horse would carry him to say, San Francisco Springs, way up North by the railroad line, a good sixty miles of very rough riding, only to discover that someone there had one of these infernal machines at his elbow, and that a Posse was ready horsed and waiting there for his wearied arrival...

It was a very frustrating situation, and most of Jim Pemberton's cohorts had already slipped over the border into Mexico, where the law was still the laughing-matter that it had once been in Arizona.

This was, after all, well after the turn of the Century that was supposed, (at least,) to make over the Territory into a civilized sort of place where even an outlaw could go about his business without too much harassment from the already burgeoning bureaucratic establishment...

It was, it fact, in October of the year 1906, and a little over a year after the murder for which he was being tried.

And there they all were, the famous and fatuous legal circumlocutions of the times:

...did, unlawfully, feloniously, wilfully, deliberately, premeditatedly, and with malice aforethought, make an assault in and upon the person of one George Giles, then and there being, with a certain deadly weapon, to-wit, a revolver, commonly called a six-shooter, then and there was loaded with gun-powder and leaden bullets, and by him the said J.N. Pemberton had and held in his hand, he, the said J.N. Pemberton, did then and there unlawfully, feloniously, wilfully, deliberately, premeditatedly, and with malice aforethought, shoot off and discharge at and upon the said George Giles, thereby and thus unlawfully, feloniously, willfully, deliberately, premeditatedly, and with malice aforethoght inflicting in and upon the person of him the said George Giles, one mortal wound, of which said mortal wound he the said George Giles did then and there die.

This extraordinary verbiage, it seems, wasn't quite enough. The Indictment went on, just to make sure of it:

And so, the said J.N. Pemberton, did, in the manner and form aforesaid, unlawfully, feloniously, willfully, deliberately, premeditatedly, and with malice aforethought, kill and murder the said George Giles, contrary to the form, force and effect of the Statute in such cases made and provided against the peace and dignity of the Territory of Arizona.

The Indictment was signed by one W.P. Geary, the District Attorney, and one cannot help wondering whether or not he regarded this kind of sounding brass as a legitimate part of his daily life.

Especially since, in all these years, the pseudo-language of the lawyers hasn't really changed that much.

But it truly does seem that Mr. Pemberton was indeed alleged to have murdered Mr. Giles, who was apparantly a U.S. Marshal, though this was known only by a very few people at the time.

The essence of the case was quite simple. Pemberton, it seems, was drunk in a saloon in Winslow, Arizona, which lies some eighty miles to the northeast of Camp Verde, and thirty miles over the Navajo County line. But his home territory was in Yavapai County, where all his friends were, and where he had narrowly escaped charges of horse-stealing on at least two occasions.

And so, very shrewdly, he petitioned for a change of venue, to Prescott, the Yavapai County Seat.

The petition was granted; but it really didn't help him very much.

The principal witness for the prosecution was one Caspar W. Naile, who, at the tender age of twenty-three, was a carpenter living in Winslow and was present at the time and the scene of the crime. His expenses for the trip to Prescott were paid for by the Government of the Territory - a total of $24.17.

And the defense attorney was trying his best to shake his testimony: Counsel demanded, in what was officially labelled as his Interrogatory:

"If you have stated that you saw a difficulty between said parties, then state what each of said parties did and said just prior to the difficulty."

Kindly notice that for Counsel for the Defense - murder had become a "difficulty." Nice thinking.

And Caspar answered:

"Mr. Pemberton was a little bit loud. He had had some dispute with the man running the wheel..."

(The man at the wheel was named Darling, Walter Darling; it surely must have made him the butt of very many rather witless jokes.)

"This man Giles stepped up to him," Caspar Naile went on, "and put his left hand on his shoulder, and says: "Now Pete, don't start any trouble in here." At that time, I did not know who the Night Marshal was, (but I afterwards found out,) but I saw that he had his right hand under his coat...He was in that position at the time he put his hand on Pemberton's shoulder and spoke to him. I don't remember the exact words he used, but Pemberton says: "I ain't starting anything, but nobody is not going to get the best of me." These are about the words he used."

The right hand under the coat is important here; and Counsel seized on it:

"State what the deceased did, if anything, to the defendant just before the shooting commenced. What demonstrations, if any, did the deceased make toward the defendant immediately preceeding the shooting? What was the defendant doing at said time?"

And Caspar Naile went on: "He stepped up to him and put his hand on his left shoulder and told him not to start anything. At the same time, I supposed he had his hand on his six-shooter, he was the Marshall and I did not pay much attention to that. The defendant was a little bit boisterous, he was having a dispute with the man running the wheel at the time. He was having a dispute over a bet."

But who fired the first shot? Counsel wanted to know.

And the witness answered: "I don't know; I think they fired about the same time. It looked to me as though they did fire at about the same time..."

And how many shots were fired?

"I could not tell, by the way they were fired," said the witness, "I never counted them...The shots were fired so fast that I could not tell how many of them there were."

But an examination of the guns soon after disclosed that each of them contained five empty shells in the chamber, and it seems incredible that Pemberton was unhurt; they were only a reported seven or eight feet apart at the time of the first shot.

Incredible, too, that no-one else was wounded:

"The house was full at the time," said Naile, "but the ones that was right at the wheel was this man Pemberton, who was gambling, Darling was running the wheel, and there was another man standing right there who had a beard, some stranger to me. My father, A.F. Naile, was standing near the bar talking to the

161

bartender, and there was a woman there, a piano-player. . .I had been around with Pemberton for about an hour before the shooting, and was standing there watching him at the time. . ."

"Who first drew his gun?" Counsel demanded to know, "the deceased or the defendant? Who made the first demonstration as if to draw a gun?"

"I could not tell," said Naile, "it looked like they drawed their guns at the same time. . ."

It was a classic case of the Western shoot-out, both the contestants obviously fanning the hammers of their six-shooters for this kind of speed, the crowd scooting for cover, and screams, perhaps, coming from the lady piano-player. . .

Wondering how Pemberton came out of this, at such close quarters, without so much as a scratch, it is easy to suppose that Marshal Giles must have been mortally wounded by the first shot, and lay there on the floor desperately firing as his adversary pumped four more unforgiving bullets into him.

It was the question of who drew first that was all important, a question that no-one could answer. And, correctly, the accused was given the benefit of the doubt: The charge was second-degree murder, presupposing that he just might have fired in self-defense, not knowing that Giles was an officer of the law.

And on December 4th, 1906, at 1:45 p.m., Clerk of the Court J.M. Watts filed the verdict:

We the jury find the defendant J.N. Pemberton guilty of Murder of the Second Degree.

Signed, *H.J. Suder, Foreman.*

Three short days later, Yavapai County Judge Richard E. Sloan passed down the sentence:

Twenty-five years in the Territorial Prison at Yuma.

The outlaws, in general, were not very nice people, but once in a while some redeeming quality seemed to shine through that thick veneer of peccability; and one such case was that of J.J. Smith, a farmer from the banks of the Verde River who became an outlaw, and in the course of time convict number 621 at Yuma Territorial Prison.

Though a native of Tennessee, he had come to Arizona's Yavapai County in the search for honest work, but he was just not physically capable of the hard work successful farming entailed; he was a slight and sickly man, weighing in at a mere hundred and fifty pounds, short and skinny, with dark eyes and hair but fair-complexioned. At the age of 24, he was without much education; his reading and writing were noted by the prison authorities as being only "fair," but his habits were described as "intemperate," which usually meant that he was addicted to what the clerks always wrote down as *tabacco,* using the now-obsolete but more nearly correct spelling. It was a habit which probably contributed to his painful pulmonary problems, which in turn must surely have made his chosen work intolerable.

Perhaps this was why he turned to robbery, though in this too, he was never very successful.

It was said that he once tried to hold up a stage coach, but turned to flee when the stage's driver derided him for his fragile appearance. It was said that he had, on occasion, even snatched the purses away from women, an offence that stunk to high heaven in those days, when women were called "the weaker sex," (perhaps somewhat hilariously,) and it was way beneath any man's dignity to lay a hand on them.

O Tempora! O Mores...!

He was caught, at last, and arrested, after *allegedly* taking part in John Halford's robbery of the Atlantic and Pacific train at Canyon Diablo, and they hit him hard; when Sheriff O'Neil brought him into Yuma, J.J. Smith had been sentenced to a rather severe thirty years, from the twenty-fourth of November, 1889.

There is no evidence that Smith went much out of his way to make friends with his guards, but there is plenty that suggests he quickly became liked not only by the prison staff but by his fellow convicts as well. Perhaps it was because, in these harsh surroundings where violence was often the order of the day, J.J. Smith went about his prison labors quietly and efficiently, giving aggravation to no man. It is certain - as proved by subsequent events - that they felt sorry for this poor, skinny little devil who was so often convulsed with dreadful fits of coughing that on occasion even brought up blood.

Were they, a century ago, less squeamish than we are today? Less cautious? Less sensible? Less knowledgeable?

The answers to these questions must be a resounding *yes.*

For J.J. Smith, suffering from the advanced stages of tuberculosis, was Yuma Territorial Prison's *baker.*

But it seems that no-one even thought of possible contagion, even though, at that time - and right up to the year 1909 - this disease was ranked as the number one killer of American males.

In the Smith story, it is essential to note the great probability, perhaps even the certainty, that he never took part in that train robbery his admitted friend John Halford had engineered.

What happened was that after the robbery, when a posse led by Yavapai County Sheriff Bucky O'Neil caught up with his quarry, Smith had joined up with Halford, who was travelling in the same direction.

But Smith was actually on his way to Nevada to look for work. But while John Halford was given twenty-five years, they gave an additional five to Smith because...

Because Smith broke away, and escaped.

He was free, in the clear as he made his way south, heading for Texas freedom and from punishment for a crime he had never committed.

But in his hard journey, he came across a young girl, her name lost in history, who was lost too, lost in the mountains.

And this is where J.J. Smith's common decency broke through that venal veneer:

Surely knowing the dreadful risk of recapture that he was facing, he guided her to a settlement he knew of, and as a result of his chivalry, walked straight into the arms of the waiting Deputies.

It is highly probable that this aspect of his capture was known to his fellow-felons and the staff as well, and they must have admired him for it.

This much we know:

He was pardoned three years and nine months later, by Governor Hughes, for two extraordinary and perhaps quite unconscionable reasons:

The first, according to prison records, was called "Doubt of Guilt."

The second said simply: "Consumption."

The prison physician had recommended his pardon, and all the prison officials joined in the application for clemency. And when the pardon came through, the convicts themselves, working for literal pennies a day, raised an incredible seventy dollars to speed J.J. Smith on his way.

They say that tears rolled down his cheeks as he walked down the hill to the Depot, conscious, perhaps, of all the unexpected affection he had left behind him, from men who, in common or garden toughness, prisoners and guards alike, lived a daily life in an orb that was quite beyond his understanding.

On the train, he was hit by a violent hemorrhage, that looked as though it was going to kill him.

For all of his young life, this had been a very severe problem for him, beset by the knowledge - if he ever tried to find out - that his sickness was almost always terminal; medical research had not yet found the answer.

But by chance, or perhaps by those unknown powers that guide our destinies, there was a doctor on board the train; and it seems that by his skilled ministrations he saved Mr. Smith's life.

And then...Then there was a very happy ending to this tale:

The Arizona Sentinel of September 30, 1893, carried a casual comment:

Collector Nugent saw J.J. Smith at Hermosillo, who was pardoned out of prison a short time since. He now has a restaurant at Nogales, where he is said to be doing a good business. The Collector says that Smith is looking exceedingly well, having improved greatly since his release...

Please join us in hoping that J.J. Smith lived happily ever after.

And sometimes, the outlaws had little quirks of their own:

It's hard, perhaps, to imagine a prisoner sentenced to life in the hell-hole of Yuma Territorial Prison, actually *refusing* a parole that could have sprung him at once.

But in the case of the native-born Frenchman Charles Rose, this is precisely what happened.

By avocation, he was a miner, but not very successful at it. At the age of 42, he had spent some years in the area of Horse Thief Basin in the Bradshaw Mountains, where silver had already brought a great deal of wealth to the more fortunate settlers, but it seems that he had an aversion to working areas where the good lodes were known to be and were therefore somewhat over-run. He chose instead to scout the valley for pieces of ore that had broken off from the mother lode and had been washed down by the rains, and then dig frantically in the hills above the points where he found them.

It was a policy that never paid off and Army friends advised him to try his hand at ranching up in the Verde River Valley.

He decided instead to go to Jerome and look for work in the copper mines, but he never quite made it; en route, he was approached by two Mexicans, armed with rifles, who threatened to kill him unless he handed his burros over to them.

Very sensibly under the circumstances, he let them drive his animals off, and then, he bided his time for a while, knowing exactly what he had to do; incredibly, they had not thought to search him for weapons, and he still had his revolver.

He followed the bandits carefully, caught up with them at the foot of the mountain, and shot them both dead.

He recovered his burros and their loads, and casually went on his way. . .

But a few hours later, he spotted a Posse riding hard on the trail, and concealed himself among the rocks, suspecting that they were after him, which they were not; it seems that having lost the trail they were following - that of a solitary horse-thief - they were riding back to Camp Verde to pick up some Indian trackers.

And trying to hide was the worst thing Charles Rose could possibly have done. He was spotted at once, questioned and then released.

But a day or two later, word of the shooting reached the camp, and the Deputies remembered their recent encounter; and on his way up the trail to Jerome, poor Charles Rose was soon picked up.

He was whisked off to Prescott for trial, made almost no attempt at all to defend himself, and accepted without complaint an extraordinarily sever sentence - thirty years in the Territorial Prison at Yuma.

There, it seems that he was a model prisoner, well-behaved, causing no trouble, and simply not making any fuss about the obvious injustice that had been done to him. And he stayed there for three long years before someone came to his rescue. . .

A journalist from the Arizona Daily Journal-Miner visited the prison, and learned that some of the wardens themselves were circulating a petition asking that a parole be granted to this man, regarded as one of the most intelligent convicts there. And three days later, his newspaper - written mostly for the huge mining community in the area - lashed out at the Press' enemy of the moment, the Arizona bureaucracy:

A petition is being generally circulated and signed asking for the paroling of Charles Rose, who is serving a life sentence in Yuma for the killing of a couple of Mexicans in the Bradshaws some four years ago. Mr. Rose is said to be in very poor health and many of his friends, who are substantial residents of this section are very earnest in asking for executive clemency. This crime was committed while protecting his personal property from thievery, and in resorting to desperate methods, (he) killed outright two Mexicans who it is said had also threatened his life. If a burglar enters at night the home of anyone and is shot down, no-one but the victim of that folly is to blame; but under the elastic conception of Arizona criminal matters if a miner in the hills in broad daylight has to shoot and kill two men who not only threaten his personal safety, but drive away his burros, he receives a life sentence. Rose is an industrious miner, bore a good name, and should be given his freedom at once.

This was on October 3rd, 1901, and only four days later, Governor Murphy, on the recommendation of Judge Sloan, granted Charles Rose a parole.

But, said the Journal-Miner, somewhat surprised:

Charles Rose...declines to accept the freedom granted by such action. He says that he believes the reproach of a paroled convict will be greater than that of an imprisoned one; that he would rather remain in the penitentiary making a record for good behavior, so that if he should ever be pardoned he can emerge into full citizenship at once. Another reason why he objects to parole is that he is a professional prospector, and without citizenship he would be debarred from making locations of mining claims...

One can imagine the consternation among the prison staff when a convict flatly refused to leave the reputed hell-hole of Yuma.

The Journal-Miner's anger was well-founded, and the point of the "elastic conception of Arizona criminal matters" was well taken:

About the same time of Charles Rose's offense, a would-be murderer named William Binkley tried to kill the wife who had left him by dynamiting the Prescott saloon in which she was a singer. Tried and found guilty, he was sentenced to ten years in Yuma.

However, after some eighteen months, his sentence was commuted to two years, and a few months later Governor McCord gave him a full pardon.

And the Press erupted again.

"CAN'T BE FAIR:" headlined the report of the pardon in the Arizona Sentinel, and the Prescott Courier wrote angrily:

It is this sort of thing which makes law-abiding people sick at heart. Binkley placed dynamite under a crowded resort, blew up the building in hopes of thus assassinating his wife regardless of the fact that ever so many people might be killed. A more diabolical act could scarcely be conceived of. The building was wrecked, set on fire, and that a dozen or more people were not killed was simply miraculous. The perpetrator of such a monstrous act is now turned loose upon society after less than two years imprisonment. . .

William Binkley went happily free. But Charles Rose, against his will, had to be forcibly ejected.

Not all of the Verde Valley's outlaws who finished up in Yuma were in the model prisoner mode as presented by Charles Rose.

And sometimes the prison records are very indicative of the violence inherent in the life of the outlaw. Scars and bullet-wounds were duly noted down by the Prison clerk:

"Stout build, scar across left forearm, scar under left eye, left third finger missing. . ."

And again: *"Two scars on left leg below knee, bullet wound at right hip, bullet wound at left instep."*

And then: *"Forehead, low: condition of teeth, bad; eyebrows heavy, walks with an ambling gait. . ."*

All these comments suggested lives governed by fights; and they didn't always stop fighting even under the harsh discipline of Yuma.

Take the case of convict Number 1300, a young Texan relocated to the Verde Valley, a man who had a natural disinclination for the work ethic, and just hated the sight of everyone around him.

He was fast with his gun, too; and proud of it.

The record read:

Name:	L.C. Miller
Sentence:	Life from 6/25/1897
Crime:	Murder 1st Degree
County:	Yavapai
Age:	27
Habits:	Intemperate
Can Read:	Yes
Can Write:	Yes

And so it all went on. And then came the Behavior Record:

Record:

Jan. 20, 1898:	Solitary 17 days for refusing to work and attempting to escape.
Apr. 8, 1898:	Solitary 1 day for fighting.
Jan. 15, 1899:	Solitary 13 days for possessing citizen clothing.
Apr. 11, 1899:	Escaped.
Apr. 18, 1899:	Recaptured.
Apr. 18, 1899:	Solitary 7 days attempting to escape.
May 8, 1902:	Sentence commuted to 20 years from June 25, 1897.
July 17, 1907:	Paroled by Governor Kibby.
June 2, 1909:	Returned to prison from Cochise County 2nd Spring Term as #3020.

Miller was not a very popular man, as far as outlaws go. When he was brought from Camp Verde to Yuma by Sheriff Ruffner and Deputies Munds and Bosha of Yavapai County, at the end of June, 1897, the Arizonan Republican wrote:

The officers were well armed with revolvers, and Winchesters, and sawed-off shotguns. . .Several acquaintances of Miller called at the jail to see him in the afternoon. They were not moved by any kindly regard for him; the only regret that followed him to Yuma was that he was not hanged instead. He is the most thoroughly despised criminal that has ever been led away to punishment. He is said to have the inclination of a desperado and the heart of a rabbit. He was undergoing a strange position between exaltation and misery. Exaltation that he escaped the gallows and misery in that his punishment will be life long, for it is not probable that any future governor of Arizona will have the hardihood to run against the record of the Court in which are inscribed the words of Judge Hawkins in passing sentence: "I hope that Arizona may never be cursed with a chief executive who will show you clemency."

Well, herein lay the reason for the scorn in which Arizona law was held.

In spite of Judge Hawkins' admonition, we have seen that after a mere five years, Miller's life sentence was commuted to 20 years; and that five years later, he was paroled by Governor Kibby.

We have also seen that less than two years later, he was back in jail again, a natural born recidivist, deserving of nothing but permanent confinement, and still giving everyone in sight a very bad time. The Republican was right.

This was a very worthless creature.

And it seems that a pardon, generally, was there just for the asking.

William Stiren, who had teamed up with John Halford, reported on earlier, to rob the A&P Railroad, is a case in point. He was an outlaw of some notoriety in his own right; on two separate occasions he had held up Wells Fargo stages, alone, without even the usual supporting gun in the bushes back there.

On one of those notable forays, he carried off so much gold, even though he had hidden most of it for future recovery, that when he found a fast-riding posse on his trail, he was forced to drop all the remaining loot in order to save his skin.

It is perhaps sad to relate that another lone rider, no doubt astonished at his good fortune, found the hidden gold, some eighty thousand dollards of it, dragged it for more than four miles at the end of a rope, almost wore out his horse with the effort, hid it again and sensibly rode off to find a wagon; and at last wheeled it off for his own pleasures to some place which was never discovered.

This much was found out by the Posse and their Indians who had followed his tracks, losing them hopelessly some three miles to the east of the abandoned Mormon settlement of Mazatzal City, which lay on the East Fork of the Verde River, hard by Deadman Canyon.

But there were some very smart guys on the side of the law too; finding signs of the original hiding-place, they set up an ambush there, waiting for Stiren to return and carry off his booty.

But they had absolutely no luck at all . . .

It is almost certain that Stiren did return, but he was no fool. (For the most part, the outlaws were very much what would be called today "street wise," and not so easily outwitted by the forces of law and order.)

Later, the Posse discovered tracks indicating that Stiren had circled their ambush for more than a full day, looking for them, finding them, and watching them before giving up completely and just riding off into the sunset; for home. He never knew that his gold had been carted off by some upstart lone rider, whose identity was never, ever discovered.

And it is at least possible that today, this stranger's great-grandchildren, in complete ignorance of the source of their inherited riches, are still living it up along the banks of the Verde River.

Good luck to them; effort should always be rewarded.

But William Stiren was caught at last, to become just Number 594 in Yuma, sentenced to twenty-five years.

In the prison, he soon became a trusty for his good behavior, and was employed as the prison blacksmith, which meant that his life was bound up with shoeing horses; he was apparently very good at it.

The Arizona Sentinel of November 6, 1897, said that he was employed as the prison electrician; not true.

They also said that on his release, he had served thirteen years and three months of his twenty-five year sentence.

Not true either; he was given an unconditional pardon by Governor McCord on November 1st, 1897, after serving eight years and three months.

No reason for the early release was ever recorded.

And to take another case - a young Yavapai County outlaw named Joseph S. Owen, 21 years old and Number 214 in Yuma, received a mere four years for robbing the Wells Fargo Express Stage, even though holding up stage-coaches was widely regarded as one of the most heinous of offenses at the time.

And he too was pardoned, by then-governor Tritle, after serving only fifteen months of his sentence.

Again, no reason was given; it was all part of the pattern.

But a rare once in a while, a pardon turned out to be quite unnecessary:

Take the case of one A.A. Stewart, a laborer from the Turkey Creek District, twenty-seven years old when he turned outlaw and was seized almost at once after what might well have been his first serious attempt at his new profession.

It seems that he thought robbing a train was really quite a simple matter; all you had to do was find a suitable incline that would slow the engine down, leap aboard, wave your six-shooter about, and demand that the passengers hand over their valuables, all of which he did.

But then, things got to be not so simple any more.

One of the passengers aboard this A&P train was a miner named J.S. Bartlett, and he was apparently a big and powerful man; it turned out that he was also impatient of the kind of trouble Stewart was offering. When the budding outlaw stuck a gun in his face, he knocked it away, dealt poor Stewart a stunning blow to the side of the head that rendered him at least semi-conscious for a moment or two, during which time he fired two quite useless shots, then picked him up bodily and just threw him off the train.

News traveled fast even in those days, and Stewart, limping from a sprained ankle, was picked up a day-and-a-half later when he staggered into the Peach Springs railroad watering-station, exhausted, somewhat dehydrated, and quite at the end of his tether.

And in no time at all, he was tried for Assault with Intent to Commit Murder, found guilty, and slung into the Territorial Prison for fifteen years from June 30th, 1898.

It was those two useless shots, not even aimed, perhaps not even fired with any understanding of what he was doing, that put him in prision; it was this that made it intent to commit murder, even though the shooting was probably a matter of reflex action. But in prison...

There, he boasted of being an outlaw, trying to earn himself some notoriety among his fellow convicts and the staff, to such an extent that four months later the Prison Record read:

Oct. 26, 1898, Adjudged Insane and transferred to

The next record read:

Nov. 10, 1899, Returned from Insane Asylum.

And then, he was back to his vigorous young self; he was described in his record as "Habits - Intemperate," justified by:

Mar. 1, 1899, Solitary 4 days for insult to an officer.

Apr. 15, 1899, Solitary 10 days for fighting.

Oct. 27, 1899, Solitary 22 days for refusing to obey officer and ? (sic)

And then, at last:

Aug. 26, 1899, Solitary for ? (sic) days for digging hole in cell.

A.A. Stewart, obviously, had had it up to here with Yuma, and it may be that, all along, he was not quite the looney they all seem to have taken him for.

What is certain was that he was intent upon escape. And escape he did.

A few months later, the report read:

From Asst. Supt.   Report -
He was confined in the new yard and between the hours of 8 and 10 o'clock p.m. he is supposed to have made his escape over the wall by

means of a rope ladder, under Guard Stand #2. Same was reported at 6 o'clock on the morning of the 12th, and searching parties started at once and keep up without success. Guards H.H. McPhaul and Flynn were discharged because of his escape.

Nothing except rumor was ever heard about A.A. Stewart thereafter, but the major rumor was that he had gone, first to New Mexico where he had found that the law was far more formidable than it was in Arizona; and then, had gone over into Mexico itself.

If so, it was perhaps a foolish move.

Outlawry was very rife there. But the Mexicans, in those days, seldom took the trouble to bring their outlaws to trial; more usually, they just shot them dead out of hand.

And given Stewart's proven intemperate temper, he just might not have lasted for very long down there.

Once in a while, the relative peace and quiet of the Verde Valley was shattered by the intrusion of what might be called an alien outlaw, which is to say one who just had no right at all to be there, and why didn't he stay in his own territory where he belonged?

Especially if he happened to be as ruthless and nasty a man as the notorious Tom Ketchum, murderer, cattle rustler, horse thief, train robber, and a general nuisance to everyone in sight.

Outlaw Ketchum was commonly called "Black Jack," just like a character out of Robert Louis Stevenson. But this was a misnomer which led to a lot of confusion all round; the real Black Jack was the far more famous Texan outlaw named Black Jack Christian, who never came near our Verde Valley in all of his scurrillous life.

Logical reasons for murder are sometimes hard to discover, and this is true of at least one of the two murders Tom Ketchum committed in Camp Verde, and the matter was complicated by the fact that for some seven weeks, no-one knew who the murderer was. He was just "a mysterious gunman."

Tom Ketchum, at this time, had let it be widely known that he was in the Sacremento Mountains, 200 miles away, while he was actually sneaking unseen over the border of Arizona and into the Verde Valley. And there, he committed what Mr. Jeff Burton, in his splendid and meticulously researched book "Dynamite and Six-Shooter," has reported as one of the most outrageous crimes enacted in the Southwest of the 1890's.

It seems that one R.M. "Mack" Rogers, and one Clinton D. Wingfield, had formed a partnership to buy and operate the Camp Verde Military Provisions Store. (In those days, it was called "A Sutler's Store," a nice old-fashioned term derived from the Dutch (of all things) *Zoetelaar,* meaning a Camp Follower, which in turn meant mostly the ladies the Army needed for what is today called R & R, or Rest and Recreation.)

It may be that Mack Rogers had offended the considerable and tightly-cohesive outlaw population in general by giving evidence against one of the their number, a horse-thief named Oscar Wade, back in the spring of 1899, as we know he had done. But it was quite certain that all kinds of undesirables were now after Mack Rogers' guts.

(Wade was acquitted; but from the stand he swore to get even with Rogers. He apparently never attempted to carry out his threat; but there were many others of very similar persuasion, and the danger to Mack Rogers was always there.)

Was Tom Ketchum a friend of Wade's? He was a very secretive man, known for keeping his thoughts to himself, and we will never know. And he had come a very long way to do what he felt he had to do.

It was early nightfall on July the 2nd, 1899, when the soft-shoed, unknown killer moved onto the porch where Rogers was chatting with two of his friends.

For a few moments, there was the casual exchange of chit-chat; and then, it seems that the light of recognition must have struck Mack Rogers, recognition from some previous encounter, perhaps, that has never been explained.

In any event, he ran to get his gun from the other room, but the mysterious intruder's shot got him in the back and killed him.

Clinton Wingfield, in the bedroom and working on his papers, heard the shot and foolishly rushed out to see what was happening; he found himself face to face with the gunman, and in a possibly instinctive reaction, the intruder fired, sending bullet at very close range through Wingfield's stomach and severing his spine. It was a mortal wound; two hours later, Clinton Wingfield was dead, killer unknown. (The reason for his killing might well have been, instead, a sensible desire to get rid of the only witness who could identify him.)

A Posse was formed instantly to track down this phantom, murderous intruder, but by all accounts it was a very inept body of men put together too hastily and too carelessly for any kind of disciplined efficiency. But the initial tracking was made relatively simple for them because the murderer had been riding an unshod horse; they still managed to lose the tracks some days later, till they had the sense, at last to call in our old friend Deputy Munds, who followed the trail clear up to the Mogollon Rim, and on to the New Mexico line where it just disappeared.

It meant that Tom Ketchum was home again, to continue his nefarious work where he belonged.

And continue it, he did.

Until, that is to say, he took part in a ferocious train robbery near Folsom, New Mexico, got himself wounded in the right arm, (which was subsequently amputated,) and found himself at last under arrest, tried, and sentenced to the rope.

The rope...

There is a considerable amount of obscurity about what truly happened to it.

We know that the recommended length for a man of Tom Ketchum's size and weight (considerable,) was five-and-a-half feet; we know that *someone* thought that this was not enough and increased it to seven feet; we also know that *someone* had the same thought and added another nine inches...

We can suspect that when they tested the contraption the day before the execution they left the heavy bag at the end of the rope overnight, which caused the rope to stiffen, almost like wire.

And finally, we are sure that *someone* soaped the rope to make the knot slip more easily; we have to remember that this was strangulation, not the breaking of the neck's vertebrae.

Meanwhile, it became evident that the Camp Verde murderer was indeed Tom Ketchum, and Arizona was demanding his extradition, which was refused by Governor Miguel Antonio Otero, because he distrusted the Law as applied in Arizona, and wanted to be sure that Tom Ketchum really would be hanged.

And hanged he truly was. Indeed.

It was Friday, April 26, 1901, some twenty-one months after the Camp Verde murders, that Tom Ketchum, 37 years old, his one

Tom Ketchum

arm chained to his side, was marched out into what Jeff Burton has described so succinctly as "an atmosphere of a macabre and somewhat muted carnival."

It was in the courthouse yard in Clayton, New Mexico, and it was nearly a quarter past one on a bright and gusty afternoon. They had tried to exclude the public, but...

People were jostling each other for good viewing-points and laughing derisively when Sheriff Garcia swung his axe to cut the rope to spring the trap-door - and missed.

His second try was successful. The body dropped, and the rope...

The rope tore Tom Ketchum's head clean off.

Sheriff Garcia's young son Fructuoso, forbidden by his father to watch the execution, had found himself a large knot-hole in the fence, and was watching. He saw the empty rope spring back up, heard someone - thinking that the execution had failed - shout: "Hang him again! Get another rope for that son of a bitch..."

The severed head was saved from rolling away by the black hood, fastened back and front to his clothing with horse-blanket pins, and once the initial shock was over, the answer to the difficulty must have seemed very apparant; the Doctor, who was there to feel the hanged man's pulse and make it all official by pronouncing him good and dead, was called forward, and he graciously agreed to sew the head back on again with a length of cotton thread.

And all authorities seem to agree that it was done very neatly indeed.

Then, a little over two hours later, a white-painted coffin was trundled up to carry the poor body off to a very lonely, and almost un-marked grave, a few miles north of the town.

The terribly bungled hanging was the talk of the whole Southwest, quite understandably, and it may have been that it contributed, as a formidable deterrent, to the noticeable decrease in outlawry itself that came with the turn of the century.

Together, of course, with the proliferation of the telephone, the rapid communication which was making the outlaw's lives so much more hazardous, even in the remote recesses of the glorious canyons we all know so well.

Whatever the various causes, there is no doubt that the early nineteen hundreds saw a remarkable decline in the activities of the conventional outlaw.

Those who had not been killed or incarcerated - many to await the demonstrated horror of the noose - were slipping one by one over the border into Mexico, some of them even to South America, where, perhaps, they could find once again the overt lawlessness they craved.

As we have said before... In 1910, the term 'outlawry' itself... was declared legally obsolete.

Tom Ketchum (sometimes erroneously referred to as ''Black Jack''), sneaked into the Verde Valley, murdered two enemies, and sneaked back out again. (National Archives)

FAR WEST STAGE LINE
NOTICE TO PASSENGERS

Adherence to the following Rules will insure a pleasant trip for All.

1. Abstinence from liquor is requested, but if you must drink, share the bottle. To do otherwise makes you appear selfish and un-neighborly.

2. If Ladies are present, Gentlemen are urged to forego smoking cigars and pipes as the odor of same is repugnant to the Gentle Sex. Chewing tobacco is permitted, but spit WITH the wind, not against it.

3. Gentlemen must refrain from the use of rough language in the presence of Ladies and Children.

4. Buffalo robes are provided for your comfort during cold weather. Hogging robes will not be tolerated and the offender will be made to ride with the Driver.

5. Don't snore loudly while sleeping or use your fellow passenger's shoulder for a pillow; he (or she) may not understand and friction may result.

6. Firearms may be kept on your person for use in emergencies. Do not fire them for pleasure or shoot at wild animals as the sound riles the horses.

7. In the event of runaway horses, remain calm. Leaping from the coach in panic will leave you injured, at the mercy of the elements, hostile Indians and hungry Coyotes.

8. Forbidden topics of discussion are Stagecoach robberies and Indian uprisings.

9. Gents guilty of unchivalrous behavior toward Lady Passengers will be put off the Stage. It's a long walk back. A word to the Wise is sufficient.

BIOGRAPHY

Aliza *(Editor)* and Alan Caillou

Alan Caillou was born in England in 1914, studied acting, and then went to Palestine in 1934. In 1939, he joined British Intelligence, operating behind the lines in Libya and Tunisia. After capture by the Italians and repeated escapes, he reached the British Lines and joined the Partisans in Yugoslavia and Italy until the end of the war in Europe.

He then went to Ethiopia as Chief of Police, Reserved Areas, then to Somalia, where he was constantly on safari among a dozen mutually-warring tribes - and almost every known species of African game.

In 1952, a civilian again, he went to Canada for five years, acting and writing, and then to the United States, still following those duel professions. He has written 52 books, seven screen-plays, and innumerable T.V. shows. He is now a permanent resident of Sedona, Arizona.

Aliza Lyle-Smythe-Caillou, of Latvian-Russian parentage, grew up in Haifa, Israel. After graduating from high school, she studied languages (six), and ancient history in London, England.

In May of 1939, she married Alan Caillou in Haifa, and four months later, at the outbreak of World War II, they both joined the British Forces in Cairo, Egypt. While her husband was a young officer sent to the Western Desert, she was assigned to the Topographical Branch of the Middle East Intelligence Corps in Cairo. Two years later, she was appointed Personal Assistant to the Political Intelligence Officer in Asmara, Eritrea, (now a province of Ethiopia,) and then in 1944, was sent to the Psychological Warfare Branch in Bari, Italy. After the war, the couple lived in East Africa, and in 1952 came to the Western Hemisphere. In 1987, the Caillous settled down in Sedona with their daughter Nadia and their four dogs.

Jim Roberts. Courtesy of Jerome Historical Society.

Jim Robert's grave at Valley View Cemetery, Clarkdale, Arizona. Photo by Bennie Blake.

Main Street at Jerome. Jim Roberts, right, c. 1903. Courtesy of Jerome Historical Society.

Chapter Seven
WATCHERS OF THE PEACE
Lawman Of The Verde Valley
By Bennie Blake

eeping order in a frontier town depended upon the courage and gunslinging skill of its peace officers, and not on any basic respect for law and order. Cowboys in town on a binge, the intruder carving up the face of a prostitute, and the average citizen alike knew that the lawman's six-shooter stood for peace. The peace officer, however, lived in a peculiar world in which firearms, his ultimate weapon, were available to everyone. In such a powder-keg, the man who wore the badge needed extraordinary skill with the gun he wore. So it was in Arizona's Verde Valley.

A strange melting-pot of individuals from around the globe pushed into the valley in the late 1800's and early 1900's. Many settled into canyons and gulches near today's Cleopatra Hill at Jerome, happy to have a job in the mines. Others settled into Camp Verde's pastoral scene. Many of these newcomers had emigrated to get away from trouble at home but had brought their troubled minds with them. Suddenly freed from the constraints of law and order, they exploded into violence: murder, knifing, mutilation, ambush, theft, mayhem, to mention a few. Camp Verde, though not a violent town, nevertheless required constant vigilance from the man with a gun.

Early lawmen came from Arizona, New Mexico, Missouri, Oregon and other points north, south, east or west. They came in all sizes and shapes. They were called marshall, sheriff, under-sheriff, deputy or watchman. But these men had several things in common. They possessed a rocklike tenacity when on the trail of an outlaw. And they had pledged their lives and some died for this pledge to keeping the peace in Yavapai County, Arizona Territory, whether it was in a tinderbox mining town like Jerome or the sometimes sleepy outlying settlements like Camp Verde, which could explode into violence on any otherwise peaceful afternoon.

Tombstone, down south in the territory, had Bat Masterson and Wyatt Earp, but the Verde Valley had her Jim Roberts, last of the old time shootin' sheriffs; Fred Hawkins, the lawman with cold eyes that looked right through a man; Johnny Hudgens, the law officer with ice-water in his veins; Charles Benjamin Rudd, Camp Verde's double-draw deputy; and Johnny Munds, Yavapai County's bloodhound of a sheriff. There were many others.

Along with their other duties, these lawmen trailed outlaws after shootings, knifings, strangulation, beatings, and robberies. They locked up offenders after mutilations committed with knives and, in one case, carbolic acid. They even stalked peeping Toms, stray dogs, chicken thieves, or cowboys out "hurrahing," riding into town shooting up windmills and other interesting targets.

In their time they tracked a number of the most dangerous criminals of their time through some of the wildest sections of the American West. Individually, each was a resolute lawman bent on tracking down violators of the law. Collectively, they penetrated deep into Arizona history and made a decisive imprint on frontier justice. But for them, the Verde Valley would, indeed, have been a bloodier ground.

By any measure, these men are unsung heroes. They were keepers of the peace, doing their duty as they saw it. Today, looking back in history in the annals of the lawmen, some say that Jim Roberts is the most memorable of them all.

James Franklin Roberts
Last of the Old Time Shootin' Sheriffs

Wrapped in their patchwork of hills and canyons on Mingus Mountain, early Jeromites watched their town explode into a disorderly growth that would require more than a kindly village constable to keep it safe. Jerome, sometimes called the wickedest city in America, needed and got deputy James Franklin Roberts. Vigilant and decisive, he watched over the town, its gulches and canyons, its home, its red-light districts and saloon, where people celebrated, especially on payday.

Roberts was born in 1859 in Bevier, Missouri, where early in life he learned survival skills in a frontier town. He knew good horseflesh when he saw it. He wore a bristly mustache and his blond hair close-cropped and parted on the side. Only his penetrating eyes and square, determine jawline betrayed that this easy-going demeanor masked a man as tough and unwavering as any outlaw in the territory.

What happened to bring Jim Roberts west, no one knows, but as a young man he rode into one of the wildest sections in the American West, eastern Arizona, near the head of Tonto Creek under the Mogollon Rim, later to be known as Pleasant Valley. It was a country wild enough and big enough to hold this adventuresome new arrival and all his plans.

But plans sometimes go awry, and so it was with Roberts. As he grew into his 20's, he built a cabin and spent his entire stake on a prize stallion and some mares, intending to get on with his business of breeding and raising horses with stamina and good bloodlines.

The Pleasant Valley War was smoldering, but Roberts apparently paid little attention to this feud between the Grahams and Tewksburys until he noticed that some of his horses were missing. Even that didn't draw him in until he found that his stallion and two mares from his breeding stock had been stolen. A. B. Peach, who was a native of Pleasant Valley, told that Roberts trailed the three rustlers, who were reported to be associated with the Grahams, rode to the top of the rim and killed them.

But his was not yet the end of Roberts' problems. Later, his cabin was burned, and seeing the ashes that had once been his home sent him over to the Tewksbury side. When the feud reached flash point, Roberts and his gun were ready. No one knows how many of the 29 dead fell to his gun, but 22 of the fallen were from the Graham side.

After the Pleasant Valley War was over, Roberts moved west once again, as his Anglo-Celtic forebears had done centuries before in England, Ireland and Scotland. This time in 1888 or 1889 he arrived in Congress, Arizona, a gold-mining town, where, in 1889 Sheriff William "Buckey" O'Neill appointed him deputy for the Congress area. In that booming mining town he met "Jennie," Pamela Virginia Kirkland, whose father, pioneer William Kirkland, had raised the first American flag over Tucson.

In his early thirties by this time, Roberts decided to bring Jennie along when, in 1891, new sheriff J. R. Lowry reappointed him deputy and transferred him to Jerome. The two young people went to Prescott and were married on November 17, and friends said they entered a waiting carriage and left that day for their first home, in Jerome.

At his new post, Roberts soon became known as a tough but fair lawman who got his man most of the tie and who had no patience with killers. Shortly after he came to Jerome, he was to show the locals his intolerance for outlaws, especially killers.

A favorite story is about Roberts and two men named Dud Crocker and Sid Chew. Crocker had been arrested for drunkenness and for starting a fight in a saloon. Since there was no jail in town at the time, he was chained to a wagon wheel along Hull Avenue to give him a chance to sober up. Later in the evening when a deputy came by to check on him, the officer paid little heed to the loitering Sid Chew across the street.

As the deputy walked out of sight, Chew, no longer loitering, quickly came across the street and unbolted the wagon wheel from the axle. Together the two men carried the wheel down the street to the blacksmith's shop, broke in and started to take off Crocker's chains. The blacksmith helper, who lived in the back, came in to see about the noise in the shop. Chew hit him and, as he fell, he hit his head on an anvil. Next morning he was found dead.

Free of the wagon wheel, the two men went by the rooming house where they lived, to gather up some belongings and head down the hill, away from Jerome. By this time the deputy on duty at the time had heard of the escape and had run to the boarding house to look for them. In the darkness of the street, the deputy was an easy target, but he was able to put one bullet into Chew's thigh before he himself fell dead from a bullet wound.

At a stable on the road down to the valley, Crocker and Chew at gunpoint forced the stablehand to saddle two horses, then hurried on down the hill.

Roberts, who had gone home to get some sleep earlier in the evening, was not to be long in following. But first, he stopped by to saddle his sure-footed white mule, his favorite riding animal in the rough country around Jerome, especially at night. He led a smaller mule, carrying a pack saddle.

Roberts' skill at tracking and his ability to outthink his quarry were to pay off on that day as they had so many times in the past. He learned at the stable that Crocker and Chew had ridden toward Camp Verde and, hoping to outthink them, reasoned they would probably ride in the Verde River to avoid being tracked and then bypass the town at night. Roberts himself took the road, determined to get there first.

Next morning, after checking in at Camp Verde and finding out no riders had passed though, he went back and soon spotted a wisp of smoke rising from the watermoties along the river. As he crept close, he spotted the men and told them to drop their guns. They ignored his orders and ran for cover, firing as they ran. Roberts was not one to rush as he aimed his gun, especially when his adversaries were killers. He took careful aim and shot Crocker through the head. When Chew ran toward him, spraying bullets, Roberts dropped him, too.

That same afternoon, the deputy rode into town with the two killers folded over the pack mule. He delivered the bodies to the undertaker and wired the sheriff in Prescott to send another deputy.

Not all enemies of the Roberts family were outlaws, however. The year 1903 was to challenge all the strength Jim and Jennie Roberts could muster. An epidemic of scarlet fever hit Jerome, and the disease took the lives of three of their four children: James, six; Myrtle, nine months; and Nellie, three years old. In 1904 the Roberts left Jerome with Hugh, their one remaining child, not to return until 1927. William, another son, was born to Jim and Jennie Roberts. He became a narcotics agent in Phoenix.

One tale of Roberts' work in Jerome clings in the memory of the oldest of old-timers:

It has to do with an escapade of a young Mexican named Chappo. No one seems to remember his real name. Chappo carried a chip on his shoulder. His trouble started in a poker game in which a town barber raked in too many chips. Chappo accused him of using a stacked deck, and his accusation was the more ready as the barber had given him a haircut he didn't like. Chappo pulled a knife on him, only to find himself beaned by a beer bottle.

Chappo went to his lodging and got a gun, and waited for the barber. He shot him dead in front of the Connor Hotel.

"Tell Jim Roberts if he comes after me I'll kill him too!" he yelled, as he ran up the road toward the mine.

From the city hall Roberts saw Chappo depart. When told what the killer had said, he said mildly, "Well, I reckon I'd better go and get him."

He went to the livery barn and threw a saddle on his white mule, his favorite mount when travelling among the rocks of the Black Hills. He didn't have any doubt which way the killer would go; usually when thinking of escape a man went out in the direction he came in, seeking to reach the more thickly populated cities of Prescott or Phoenix. The grade of the little narrow gauge line which ran into Jerome was the best walking, hiding places along the line were numerous, and there was always a chance of jumping a train heading for Jerome Junction, in Chino Valley.

Jim rode his mule to the railroad grade, and set out along it. His quiet manner and sleepy look were deceiving, for as he ambled along his gray eyes flickered ahead and to the sides, looking for sign of his quarry.

He had travelled not more than three miles when he saw a movement among some jagged rocks above the grade, and saw a head and an arm with a gun in it. His own gun hand came out so suddenly and smoothly he hardly seemed to be moving, and at the blast of the old forty-five a bullet struck the rock near the killer's head. As the man ducked behind the rock Jim slid from his saddle and using rocks as cover began a slow and deliberate advance toward the man he had come to get.

"Go back, Jim," Chappo yelled. "You come here and I'll kill you."

Dodging from rock to rock, the killer tried to get in position to make good his word, but he found Jim Roberts an elusive target. When Chappo tried a shot, Jim wasn't where he had been. Slowly and implacably the marshall closed in on the killer, who was rapidly growing desperate.

Jim found it necessary to get closer to cross a little more space. He made the move almost nonchalantly. The killer thought he saw his chance, and suddenly exposed his head and shoulders, bringing the gun to bear.

"I kill you now" Chappo shouted. Those were his last words, for Jim's lure had brought about the situation he had counted on. Chappo got away one shot, but it missed. The Marshall's shot didn't.

A citizen reported that one day, coming down the mountain, he had met the lawman:

I asked him if he had found his man. "Yes," he said. "I found him." "Why didn't you bring him in?" "Oh," said Roberts, "He's coming along behind me." And he was right. Two men followed Roberts into town bearing the body of the fugitive on a stretcher."

This last of the old-time shootin' sheriffs, as some called him, served as a peace officer for 45 years, as a deputy sheriff, constable, town marshall, and in later years a deputized watchman.

Herb Young remembered that he "never heard of Roberts having any vices . . . He was honest. He was said to like children, so let's assume he had a tender heart."

On at least one occasion he did show compassion and almost tenderness for his young deputy:

One night three men escaped to the outskirts of town after killing a man over a card game. They sent a challenge to Roberts and his young deputy to come and get them.

As Roberts and his deputy approached the desperados, the grim-jawed lawman told his protege, "You take the one in the middle and I'll get the other two." When the youngster began to tremble, Roberts told him in a kind but firm tone, "Get out of the way, Sonny, and I'll take 'em all."

Moments later all three killers were down.

Living in the Verde Valley there are still some people who, as children, knew "Uncle Jim" Roberts in his later years. They talk about him with a faraway look in the eye and a certain sense of awe. Some remember him as quiet and soft-spoken; others recall that he always gave them candy; but all like to tell about the great Clarkdale bank robbery in 1928.

In 1927 Jim Roberts had come back to Clarkdale as deputized watchman for the United Verde Power Company, a subsidiary of United Verde Copper Company. Over the following months, townspeople grew accustomed to seeing the 70-year-old watchman making his rounds each day.

On the morning of June 21, 1928, some may have even wondered why Roberts reversed the usual pattern on his beat. The old lawman himself said that, for some reason that he couldn't understand, he had gone in the opposite direction on that particular day. The result was that he was just one block from the bank when two bank robbers, Willard Forrester and Earl Nelson, were holding their guns on three bank employees and several customers and filling a bag with $40,000 of bank money. One customer, a Chinese cook, had taken off his shoes in preparation for his death. As the robbers burst from the door and leaped into an open car, David Saunders, the bank manager, sprinted out of the bank, firing as he ran.

One of the robbers then made one fatal mistake. Nelson, who was in the passenger seat, fired at Jim Roberts as the getaway car sped around the corner.

Later, at the inquest, Roberts said, "About five shots were fired at me." And he continued to say that, as the bullets hit, chips from the cement sidewalk and from the wall behind his head flew about him. He pulled his gun from his pocket - he never wore a holster

- took careful aim at Forrester, who was driving the car, and sent a slug into his brain. Teenagers from nearby Clarkdale high school looked on while Roberts snapped the handcuffs on Nelson, who had been subdued by bystanders.

Since both the bank manager and Roberts were firing guns, there was at first some question about who had actually killed Nelson, but the lawman got credit for the hit.

The getaway car was well equipped to get the robbers on down the road without any pursuers. Forrester and Nelson were carrying an arsenal of weapons, kegs of roofing nails, and cans of cayenne pepper to discourage any people, cars and dogs that might try to follow.

Jim Roberts was late coming home for lunch that day and the biscuits had gotten cold. When he walked in the door his wife asked what kept him. True to character clear up to the end, old Jim just looked at her and replied in his calm manner, "Oh nothing. There was just a little trouble downtown." That was all he ever said to her concerning the incident.

Thwarting a bank robbery at 70 years of age brought fame enough to last the lawman for the rest of his life. Six years later, on January 8, 1934, as Jim Roberts was walking his beat, he had a heart attack and died a short time later with his boots on, some said. But those who knew him well said, No, he died with is shoes on. According to them, Uncle Jim Roberts never did like boots.

FRED HAWKINS
The Lawman with the Cold Eyes

Fred Hawkins well knew the tinderbox instability of a frontier mining town when he came to Jerome in 1899, as deputy to Marshall Frank Ferguson. He came to town from Tombstone, where history had been written in names like Earp, Clanton and Doc Holliday.

That same year Jerome became incorporated; building was booming in town; citizens were marvelling at the construction of the "absolutely fireproof" Fashion Saloon; a smallpox epidemic broke out; Madame Jennie Banter's place caught fire; and the fireproof Fashion Saloon was gutted by flames.

Fred Hawkins stayed in Jerome in various law enforcement jobs for 20 years. By the time he left, the town had outlived the frontier stage, as had the state of Arizona. Jerome had struggled with labor problems and an uprising, perhaps led by remnants of Pancho Villa's army in Mexico.

Although there is no known photograph, features of this deputy marshall would remain vivid to any who had seen him. "He had the coldest eyes I have ever seen in any man. He didn't look at you exactly - he looked right through you. I had the feeling that whatever was behind me, he could see it."

Hawkins was an all-round athlete, lean and sinewy. His hair was reddish, a little darker than his mustache, which drooped slightly at both corners of his mouth. Hours of saddle-time in Arizona's sun and wind had weather-beaten his skin.

The Hawkins' house still stands in Jerome, on the hillside that looks across the Verde Valley toward the San Francisco peaks at Flagstaff, and he used it for more than just living in. "Standing on the front porch . . . Hawkins would sweep his telescope over the surrounding panorama of desert hills until spotting a lone campfire, perhaps many miles away. Mounting his horse, he would start out in the direction of the fire and several days later, would return with his prisoners, sometimes two or three of them."

Fred Hawkins was a tough lawman, but he could be kind and even chivalrous. A traveling troupe was once to appear at Jerome's opera house in the Masonic Hall. The troupe didn't arrive, except for Elsie Weis, a young singer and pianist from back east who, because of illness, was not traveling with the rest of the group.

When Elsie arrived, she discovered that she was alone and stranded in a tough mining town, with no troupe, no job and no home. But good fortune often comes from misfortune, and so it was with the young singer. Fred Hawkins found her a room in a respectable boarding house, and a job at the Fashion Saloon after leveling a cold, blue eye at the proprietor. Being a lady of good breeding, she hesitated to sing and play the piano in a saloon, but Hawkins was regularly on hand to escort her home at night. By the time she had saved enough money to buy a ticket home, the young couple had other plans, and in 1903 she became Mrs. Fred Hawkins. They later adopted a child, and Elsie taught music to Jerome children. Old-timers say she played a mean honky-tonk tune on the piano.

In enforcing the law, Hawkins "didn't kill unless he had to. He would disarm a man if he could, wound him if that would subdue him, or kill him if he must." On at least one occasion, after trailing his quarry, Hawkins walked back to town leading his horse, the dead man across his saddle.

Once, a shooting broke out in the Hogback neighborhood, and one man was severely wounded. The assailant got a bullet in the shoulder from Hawkins' gun. One year later, after serving his prison term, the man returned to Jerome and proclaimed that he was out to get Hawkins. But the deputy had other plans. He found the braggart in a back room of the Wigwam Saloon and ordered him to throw out his gun. Bullets whizzed by instead, and Hawkins answered with two shots, one to the head, the other to the heart.

Drinking booze and gambling often sparked brawling and gunplay. One such day Hawkins was called to Shea's place, a saloon hosting a brawl involving more than a dozen men. The officer had become skillful at improvising a system of justice when the need arose. Alone on this particular day, he deputized two men on the

Fred Hawkins' house in Jerome, above the Hogback. Courtesy of Jerome State Park.

Deportation during the Wobblies strike, 1917. Courtesy of Jerome State Park.

spot, and the three of them herded eleven men off to jail. Harrington, the proprietor, was one of the gang.

After becoming marshall in 1904 when Jim Roberts went to Calumet, Hawkins, like his predecessor, became known as an officer either to be challenged or avoided altogether, preferably the latter. Right away he tangled with a man on a rampage.

On January 28, 1904, the JEROME MINING NEWS reported, "Hawkins was called early Tuesday evening. Miguel Medina had broken down the door of a home and threatened a family. Hawkins and two others went to get him. He made a run at Hawkins with a knife." Fred Hawkins told it like this: "I saw it and shot once; he was within arm's length right close to me. I had to protect myself, and quickly, too."

To add to Hawkins' problems, a tong war of sorts had been building among Chinese residents of Jerome, and it began to heat up significantly at 4:40 in the morning of April 24, 1909, when "a tremendous blast shook the business section of Jerome, smashing windows all over the downtown area. The target area was the rear end of the roof of the Charley Hong restaurant, which occupied the site back of the Fashion Saloon now known as the English Kitchen. A large hole was blown in the roof over the kitchen, which was left in shambles. A Chinese cook escaped death by the lucky chance of having moved forward just before the blast."

Some of the locals said it was the beginning of a tong war and that rival Chinese were plotting revenge against Charley Hong, owner of the English Kitchen. The tong war theory was further fueled when Jim Lung, still another Chinese restaurant operator, was found beaten to death.

Fred Hawkins, town marshall and his assistant Charley King had no clues on which to begin an investigation. But they were patient men, and quietly proceeded (sic) to run down all rumors. It took them six weeks to find an answer to their questions, then they arrested a man, C. Lopez, a United Verde employee. Lopez, it was charged, had had a quarrel with the Chinese cook, stole some dynamite, and attempted to send his enemy on a swift journey to an oriental heaven. Lopez was taken to Prescott where in short order he was indicted by grand jury, tried, found guilty, and sentenced to ten years in the territorial penitentiary.

In August of 1910, night watchman Charles E. King was ambushed and killed. As the word spread, anger and grief simmered among citizens throughout the territory. As a replacement, a new deputy, Johnny Hudgens, came to Jerome as Hawkins' assistant.

During the next few years the world, the country and Arizona Territory were changing. Local citizens saw perhaps the greatest changes since the mines had opened. Arizona was a vanishing frontier and Jerome, a frontier town in its last stages. May of 1917, brought labor unrest at the mines. In July the Industrial Workers of the World (Wobblies) called a strike, but Jerome Miners Union refused to go along. A rash of these strikes had broken out almost

Ya Chin Shen, last Chinese retauranteur in Jerome, ran English Kitchen until c. 1970. Courtesy of Jerome Historical Society.

simultaneously across the state, and mine operators saw this unrest as a massive attempt to interfere with the war effort and perhaps their own profits and control.

On the morning of July 10, 1917, the vigilantes, about half the men in town, had rounded up approximately 100 strikers and others and loaded more than 60 into cattle cars to be shipped west. It was a new kind of duty for Deputy Marshall Hawkins to oversee labor agitators herded aboard a freight train for deportation.

But labor unrest was not to be the last or the biggest problem confronting Jerome and Fred Hawkins. Settled into the hills of Mingus Mountain, Jerome was a long way from the front in World War I, but the town was not to be left long in peace. The United States government developed a sudden and intense interest in the mining community and its production of copper, so necessary for the war effort. Furthermore, rumors were extant that pro-German sympathizers were moving into Jerome. Then, some said General Crowder's "work or fight" order, associated with the draft, sparked what has come to be called the Mexican Uprising.

Fred Hawkins, then policeman under Chief of Police Joe Crowley, had seen and heard some suspicious happenings in town. But he hadn't found the reasons. There was enough unrest, however, that Hawkins and others decided to purchase all arms and ammunition in the valley. Too late, they found that the cupboards in the stores were bare, and rumors were that Mexicans had been buying.

Hawkins, furthermore, did not know that Porfirio Hernandez, reported to be a follower of Pancho Villa, had met with others at a house in Deception Gulch to talk about an uprising. But out of the mouths of the young, it has been said, comes the truth. An 11-year-old girl overheard and went to a teacher to tell her about the plot. The teacher then told Fred Hawkins, who put the story together with other rumblings he had heard in town and took her seriously. Time for the uprising was some night soon. The exact date turned out to be July 16, 1918.

Hernandez's plan was to organize a force of men and then to wipe out town officers and mine guards. They then planned to rob the banks of Jerome, Clarkdale and Clemenceau and seize the powder magazines of the Jerome mine and the two smelter towns, then blow the mines and smelters.

Hawkins notified Robert Tally, head of the United Verde mining operations. Tally, still smarting from the recent strikes, believed this to be a serious threat.

As news of the uprising spread, citizens armed and protected almost every house in Clarkdale, Clemenceau and Jerome. As additional reinforcement, armed men lined the roofs of all downtown businesses.

The grapevine on the Mexican side was operating, also. Hernandez and his men knew that the plot had been discovered, and most of them backed out. Five of Hernandez's loyalists set fire to the depot at the mine and killed a guard. When John Hudgens, Hawkins' assistant, arrived on the scene, they knew him to be a man with ice water in his veins and they escaped into the enveloping darkness.

To complicate an already confused drama, Hawkins received word that a series of bombs, set off in town, would announce the beginning of the uprising. The hidden bombs were discovered, however, and removed.

Alerted by Hawkins, an impressive group of law enforcement officers had moved into Jerome for this performance. Among them were Jim Lowry and John Munds, two former sheriffs of Yavapai County; Bob Robbins, later to become sheriff; and Henry Carlson, United States Marshall.

Meanwhile, Hernandez and his remaining men had gathered below town in the gulch, ready to move into town. On the way at Clemenceau they met C.R. Wright, watchman, and James Lowry, deputized guard of United Verde Extension smelter, and three time sheriff of Yavapai County. Lowry's experience, however, was not to carry him safely through the night. In the ensuing gun-battle Porfirio Hernandez wounded Wright and shot and killed Lowry.

Coming up Hull Avenue and onto Main Street in Jerome, the rebels came into the gun-sights of Deputy Marshall Fred Hawkins, who called to them from a doorway. At Hawkins' call, armed men stationed along the rooftops opened fire, and Hernandez's revolutionaries scattered. The Mexican Uprising ended abruptly.

No one has been able to reconstruct accurately the events of that night. One thing, however, is certain. In the darkness, that evening was a collage of disorder and mass confusion. Jerome's Mexican population found themselves on both sides of the uprising. When it was over, James Lowry, age 65, was dead. Harry Carlson, Deputy U. S. Marshall, was wounded in the thigh. Chief of Police Crowley had a scalp wound. And Wright had a bullet wound in his left forearm.

The end of this drama was yet to be told. Hernandez had escaped, along with others, and hundreds of enraged local citizens, some deputized, were scouring hills and canyons through the valley. Ending Hernandez's terrorist reign would fall to one man, Deputy Sheriff and rancher Frank Dickinson. It was a battle with six-shooters at a distance of six feet. Dickinson, unscathed, lived to tell it like this:

I had been able to get a good description of the fugitive from the circular sent to me by the Yavapai County Sheriff's Office. I was positive of the man's identity when I first met up with him. I saw him first at 11:30 on Friday morning. He lied to me from where he came from. He began to talk about wanting a horse. I was satisfied he was the man wanted for murder and in order to get his attention off me for a second I pointed over his shoulder and asked him if that was a wolf or coyote in the distance.

As he turned to look I jumped off my horse gun in hand and faced him. I was armed with a .38 Colt. I commanded him to throw up his hands. He did not comply but drew his gun a .32 Savage automatic, the same gun that killed Jim Lowry. He began firing. I fired at the same time. My bullet struck him squarely in the chest. As he fell to the ground he shot at me four times. All of his shots went wild. I knew he was dead. I then headed on to Camp Verde to notify the Officers.''

Frontier lawmen like Fred Hawkins were said to possess unshakable courage and a keen sense of right and wrong, but sometimes even these convictions got them in trouble. Soon after the Mexican Uprising, Hawkins was to feel an injustice that would cause him to unbuckle his gunbelt as a peace officer - for good. Not having forgotten his chivalry, he arrested an employee of the United Verde, who had reportedly molested a woman. Robert Tally, who managed the mine, disapproved of this harassment of male employees. He fired Hawkins.

James Douglas at the United Verde Extension, who well knew Hawkins' good record, gave him a job. Later the former lawman supervised an oil drilling operation for a group of Jerome businessmen. On a business trip to California, he was subjected to exposure, which brought on pneumonia and caused his death. He died in 1924 in Long Beach. James Douglas gave the widow a house in Jerome, but he specified she was never to know who gave the gift. She was told the gift was "in tribute to a fine officer, a man who had done his best to keep the peace in Jerome."

Elsie B. Hawkins died December 30, 1931. She is buried in the Valley View Cemetery at Clarkdale.

JOHN W. HUDGENS
The Lawman with Ice-Water in his Veins

John W. Hudgens knew all about ambush when he first rode into Jerome in 1910 as deputy sheriff. He came to fill a dead man's shoes after his predecessor, night officer Charles E. King, had been killed from ambush. Except for his alertness, John Hudgens would have suffered the same fate.

A deceiving feature about this lawman was his youthful look, accentuated by a shock of curly hair that sometimes escaped from under his hat and lay across his forehead. That youthful look may have accounted for his being called "Johnny" and may, in the beginning of his time in Jerome, have caused those on the other side of the law not to take him seriously and live to regret it.

Outlaws around the Verde Valley soon learned that Hudgens was a man to be viewed with considerable awe. Some local citizens who knew him said there was nothing of the boy about him when he was on the trail of a killer. Then, his eye was cold and steady, and his aim was sure.

Johnny Hudgens was born in New Mexico and got his training as a police officer in Nevada. He served as police chief at Ely

Johnny Hudgens, c. 1915. Courtesy Jerome Historical Society.

Curly Wilson, left, and Johnny Hudgens, c. 1915. Courtesy of Jerome Historical Society.

until a health problem brought him to Arizona.

As a deputy sheriff under Sheriff George Ruffner, Hudgens caught the public eye by single-handedly taking a dangerous criminal. When Fred Hawkins' deputy Charles King was killed in ambush in 1910, Ruffner assigned Hudgens to Jerome to replace him.

Immediately upon Hudgens' arrival, Hawkins tried to prepare him for the worst, and Johnny wasn't surprised when, right away, he got a note warning him to get off the police force or get what King got. The intrepid lawman, however, was not one to be frightened away.

But Johnny Hudgens was just about to be tested. One night a boy came to him, asking for help. There was a problem in the gulch, he said. A Mexican in a drunken orgy was disturbing the peace down at the rooming house. When the lawman arrived, a man came out from under the porch, and the woman who ran the place identified him as Pedro Jiminez, the one causing the trouble. Jiminez pulled a .38 revolver, but Hudgens outdrew him and shot him in the abdomen. The JEROME NEWS reported that the assailant was in the Jerome hospital, suffering from a dangerous wound but was expected to recover.

A day or so later, the deputy got another note warning him to "Get out of town." In a few days on Main Street, Hudgens ran into the mine foreman coming out of the hardware store, where he had just seen four men buying .45 pistols. It was a warning, and it was all the deputy needed. He strode down the street, took his position and riveted his steel-blue eyes to the front of the store.

As the four men filed out with their new and just-loaded guns drawn, Hudgens opened fire with his own Colt automatic and six-shooter. Three of the would-be ambushers were dead on the spot, but the fourth escaped through a saloon and off down the hill. Hudgens went, too, on the heels of his quarry, who turned and tried to dissuade his pursuer with more bullets. Hudgens, however, alert to surprise, dropped his attacker in the street with a bullet to the head.

As winter turned to spring in the Verde Valley, May Day was drawing near. It was a day that, in America, customarily brought maypoles, little girls in party dresses and other signs of spring. May 1, 1912, however, brought tragedy to a Jerome family in the sensational murder of Walter Vogel, just turned 21. Vogel was an athlete, honest and ambitious, the locals said, and had entered the business world on his own. But Walter Vogel was in the wrong place on the morning of May 1, 1912.

On that day a man called David Schreiber, a local citizen thought to be demented from use of alcohol, entered Vogel's Saloon. It was later reported that Schreiber owned a building (present site of Paul and Jerry's Saloon) and had come to collect the rent owed by the Kentucky Saloon, next door to Vogel's. It was closed, and Schreiber, thinking he was in the Kentucky Saloon, entered the bar next door.

He demanded rent from Vogel, who said he didn't owe him any rent. Schreiber then pulled his gun and shot Vogel below the breastbone. Walter Vogel died about noon that day.

Meanwhile, Hudgens was called to the scene and, after a little time, considerable effort, and more than the usual number bullets, dispatched the murderer beyond the realm of doing any further harm.

At the coroner's inquest on May 1 on the death of Dave Schreiber, Johnny Hudgens was duly sworn and gave this testimony:

My name is John W. Hudgens. I reside in Jerome, Yavapai County, Arizona. I am a Deputy Sheriff of this County, also Deputy Marshall of the Town of Jerome, and am on duty in the night time. On the morning of May 1, 1912, I had gone home about six o'clock in the morning, and was just going to bed, when someone called me and said Walter Vogel had been shot, and they wanted me to come up town as soon as I could. I at once put on what clothes I had taken off and started back up town as fast as I could. At the livery stable I saw Mr. Ewing about to get onto a saddle horse, and I asked him to let me take the horse, as a man had just been shot. He gave me the horse, and I went to Vogel's Saloon as fast as I could. There they told me that Dave Schreiber had shot Walter . . . I asked the party where Schreiber was and they told me he had gone up towards the Montana Hotel where he lived, and that Walter had been taken to the hospital.

I at once started and rode up to the foot of the steps that lead up to the hotel. There I met Mr. Anderson and asked him to go with me up to the hotel, and he said he would. On the way up the steps I told him I was looking for a man who had shot Walter Vogel, and the man had a gun and to help me look for him and be very careful for he might shoot.

We went into the hotel, but I did not see anyone that looked like Schreiber. I knew him by sight, but had forgotten his name at the time, so I went to the telephone and called up Dick Barassa, Vogel's partner, and got his name and wrote it on a piece of paper and asked the clerk if he was in the room. He said he would go up and see. I told him to be careful, for he (Schreiber) had just shot a man downtown and might take a shot at him.

The clerk went up and came back and said he was not in his room. I said he must be here and I will look around and see if I can find him. I started out through the front door to the porch. I saw a man walking across the porch, but did not recognize him as being the man I was looking for. He was just in front of the door, walking by as I opened it, his left side towards me and his arms down by his side.

As I opened the door he whirled half around, and I saw he had a gun in his hand. As he whirled he raised his hand and shot, hit me in the left shoulder, and seemed to knock me to my knees. I then drew my gun as quick as I could, it was an automatic, and in the first attempt I did not push the safety down far enough to allow it to work, and while I was doing this, he shot me again.

I then got the gun to working and I shot at him. I thought he fell at the first shot, but I must have shot more than once. He kept shooting, and I emptied my gun, and drew another. He rolled over and kept shooting, and so did I until the guns were empty. I did not know how badly I was shot, but I thought my shoulder was broken. The smoke was so thick I could not see very well. We were not more than 4 or 5 feet apart, I think. After the smoke cleared away, I saw Schreiber on the porch floor with the gun in his hand.

I spoke to a party standing there, and asked him to take the gun away from him (Schreiber). He (the bystander) at once threw the gun over towards me and I picked it up, and told some persons who had come, to look after him (Schreiber) as I was going to the hospital.

Schreiber and Vogel died at noon that day, about the same time. Vogel's business partner later reported that young Vogel said just before he died, "Poor old Dave, he was crazy. He was not responsible."

Johnny Hudgens recovered from his flesh wound and continued for some years to work at keeping the peace in Jerome. Those years brought changes for the town. The frontier period was coming to an end. Along with the rest of the nation, Jerome was moving into the years of World War I, and Uncle Sam was becoming vitally interested in goings on in the town as the wartime demand for copper skyrocketed.

When World War I ended, local citizens celebrated along with the rest of the world. Then life quieted down in Jerome. On St. Patrick's Day, 1920, the VERDE COPPER NEWS carried this news item: "Mr. and Mrs. Johnny Hudgens are to be congratulated on the arrival of a fine baby girl this morning. Johnny doesn't know a soul in town today, and it's to be hoped he names her Patricia."

He did, of course - Mary Patricia. She was born ahead of time and weighed in at two pounds and ten ounces, but when the wee lass's weight dropped to slightly more than two pounds, Jerome had an incubator baby all its own.

Mary Patricia's house was "made of pine, had a hinged glass cover and kept a constant temperature of 94 degrees, by three electric bulbs, any one of which can be switched off" to control the temperature. Ventilation was by two holes at the head and foot of the box. "Mary Patricia," the paper continues, "lies on a pillow raised above the electric lights. She was fed diluted goats milk and was reported to be thriving in her glass-roofed house." Mortuary records show no death of this St. Patrick's Day lass.

Perhaps Mary Patricia received a special kind of care. Her mother, who was a graduate nurse, worked for Dr. Riley Shrum in Jerome.

Early in the 1920's the Hudgens' family went to Los Angeles, where Johnny was chief of patrol of Westwood. They then returned to Jerome, where he took up mining. During World War II he worked in a shipyard in Portland, Oregon.

Johnny Hudgens died in 1946 at the age of 66, in Prescott after a heart attack. Mrs. Hudgens survived him.

Remembering her husband in later years, L. Hudgens said that,

Otto's Place, Main Street, now Antique Museum. Walter Vogel, second from left. Courtesy of Jerome Historical Society.

before he came to Jerome, two of his men in Nevada were shot."
He never kept clippings of his bad times in his work, said it was
hard enough to live through them, and some of them were rough."

From the beginning Johnny Hudgens knew that his time as a
police officer in Jerome would be rough. But he stayed, and he
gave it his best. For this lawman, the record is clear: Hudgens faced
an ambush more than once, but he at no time ran away from it,
nor was he a man ever to depart from justice.

CHARLES BENJAMIN RUDD
Camp Verde's Double-Draw Deputy

Winter's snow still blanketed hills at Prescott early in January,
1865, when a group of pioneers left on foot, bound for some point
east. There, they hoped to find rich soil and a moderate climate
for raising their families, their livestock and their crops. An extra
horse carried blankets, cooking utensils and provisions enough for
ten days.

On the way the small caravan passed by the King Woolsey ranch
twenty-five miles from Prescott and picked up the Chaves Trail
to the head of Copper Canyon. From there, they followed an
Indian trail down to the Verde River. In the valley, green shoots
from an early spring thrust through soil along the river banks, and
native grasses signalled the presence of good soil and water.

Those early settlers well knew the area had long ago attracted
more dwellers than themselves. They soon found moccasin tracks
in the soft soil and, knowing the danger from Apaches, they
looked for a place safe from Indian attack.

Settled in between the river and Clear Fork (the Clear Creek
region), they dug a well and a ditch, then built a dam, cleared the
land and planted barley, corn, wheat, potatoes, beans and melons.

Meanwhile, the Apaches were watching. Seeing such crops
growing within their homeland so close to their homes, marauding
bands began to raid fields and steal the settlers' livestock. Under
Indian siege, the newcomers knew they needed help, and it came,
as 1st Lieutenant Antonio Abeytia and eighteen footsoldiers, of 1st
Cavalry, New Mexico Volunteers, a doctor and four broken-down
mules left Ft. Whipple at Prescott with orders to protect the settlers.
In August, 1865, they established a simple outpost called Camp
on the Rio Verde.

Early in 1871 the camp, then called Camp Lincoln, moved to
the present site of Fort Verde State Park.

Years of skirmishes followed between the Indians and the military
until 1882, the year of The Battle of Big Dry Wash, the last major
battle with Apaches on Arizona soil. April 10, 1890, orders came
to close Fort Verde, and one year later, officers and their men
mounted and rode out through the white hills and abiding dust of
the Verde Valley's arid countryside.

Eilza Katherine and William Mann Rudd. Courtesy of Eldon Rudd.

Eldon Rudd on horse with father, Charles Benjamin Rudd, c. 1922. Courtesy of Eldon Rudd.

Seventeen years, more or less, would elapse before the growing settlement would greet a man whom old timers still reminisce about, Deputy Sheriff Charles Benjamin Rudd. Some old-timers at Camp Verde sit up a little straighter and pound a fist into the hand as they recall, "Sheriff Rudd! Why, he was the only law we had, this side of Jerome and Clarkdale."

Camp Verde's new deputy was just what the town needed. He was a horseman, good with a gun, and kind. Lean and square-shouldered, he wore a .45 Colt and a .38 Smith and Wesson and carried a .30-.30 rifle in a scabbard on his saddle. When he drew, he always drew two guns, and he knew how to use them. He served the Camp Verde area as deputy sheriff and deputized watchman from the early 1900's to the early 1920's. On the streets there and in quiet living-rooms of old houses, he is still affectionately called "Sheriff Rudd."

Charles Benjamin Rudd was born in the Ozark Mountains in Fayetteville, Arkansas, on January 1, 1864, the fourth of the eleven children of William Mann and Eliza Rudd. By the age of twelve, he had watched a wagon train being put together for the trip west. He had seen his father, who had been west before, elected as captain to get the wagons safely across the plains.

It was a hazardous trip of four months, and many in the caravan turned around and went home. The Rudds, however, arrived in Springerville, Arizona Territory, in 1876.

There, William Mann Rudd was to offer his ingenuity and capacity for hard work as Apache County was divided from Yavapai. With a shortage of professional men, he was elected as the first county attorney. He studied Blackstone's Law Book and became a lawyer. He was also "a self-styled pill-roller, the only doctor in the northern territory of Arizona. He rode out, delivered babies, issued pills, and pulled teeth." His grandson, Eldon Rudd, U.S. Congress, 1976-87, has his forceps.

During the Springerville years and before, the Rudds held classes at home to educate their large family. A daughter Ida and two or three others became teachers in Arizona.

Growing to maturity, Charles Benjamin Rudd became a cattleman and spent much of his life on a horse. Having a good ear for language, he became fluent in Spanish and remained so for the rest of his life. Easing his six-foot-four frame into the saddle, he sometimes made trips into Mexico to buy scrub beef and drive them back across the border for sale in Kansas City. During those years he married a woman from Mexico and became alienated from his family. The couple had three children.

Many years are lost between Rudd's early manhood in Springerville and his mid-forties when he first rode into Camp Verde. He had been separated from his wife, and she was later murdered. Some who knew him in the Camp Verde years thought he might have acted as a nurse somewhere. They recalled that he helped

John and Vera Cruse Rudd, c. 1916. Courtesy of Eldon Rudd.

From left, Vera Cruse Rudd, Edna Rudd, Charles Benjamin Rudd holding Eleanor, and John Cruse Rudd, at Camp Verde, c. 1916. Courtesy of Eldon Rudd.

to take care of victims of the influenza epidemic in 1918. Others said that Charles Rudd had been through some very hard times.

Wherever Rudd was in those intervening years, he rode alone into Camp Verde in 1907 or '08 to enforce the law. There, after the death of his estranged wife, he married Edna Cruse, who was twenty-eight years younger and had three children of her own. Her father, William Price, had homesteaded the area near Flagstaff, now known as Lake Mary. He later also homesteaded an area near Camp Verde.

Charles and Edna Rudd had three children: Eleanor, Albert and Eldon.

Those Camp Verde years brought both pranks and serious business for the deputy. Early, Rudd came to be known as a lawman to be respected. He could get his six-shooters in a hurry, and he was a "no-nonsense kind of guy."

In a saloon one day while he was on duty, two men decided to have a little fun and to see how fast Rudd was with a gun. Not knowing the lawman always carried two guns, they eased up behind him and pulled his .45 Colt out of the half-holster Rudd always wore for a quick draw. But the deputy's steel-blue eyes were watching in the mirror over the bar. He allowed them to get the other gun before he wheeled and put a couple of shots into the floor. Rudd said, "Don't ever do that again." The man replied, "You don't need to tell me that!"

But there were light times for the Rudd family. They became a welcome sight on Sunday mornings as they hitched up a surrey-for-three, enough room for part of the family, and drove to church. Evenings often found Rudd patrolling dances for young people. He always carried a lantern, and if it was raining, he held it under his raincoat to keep the rain from breaking the hot globe. The boys would sometimes ask him if he wanted to wrestle, and would retort, "O.K. Jump on, and if I don't shake you off, I'll give you a free ride."

Around 1920 Deputy Rudd rode out with some other lawmen to check on a disturbance among Indians in the Fossil Creek country. He was investigating a possible murder. A strong odor and two cowboys camping in the area led him to the decayed body. Deputy Rudd rode to Irving to settle the dispute, held an inquest, arrested several suspects and headed back for town.

It was winter, 1920. Jess Goddard, cowboy and cattleman, and Ross Fuller, state employee out hunting predatory animals were stalking a mountain lion, and staying nights at the old Hackberry cabin, halfway between Camp Verde and Fossil Creek. For several days the going had been slow. The trail was cold, and tracking was difficult. The lion had killed a deer, a calf and a filly.

The trackers had three dogs: Rowdy, a veteran hunter and two of his pups. One morning the dogs picked up the trail and stopped the growling lion on a ledge of rock. Rowdy ran to take charge

Camp Verde Home Guard, day of bank robbery, 1917. Courtesy of Dave Hopkins.

The Honorable Eldon Rudd, Member, U.S. Congress, 1976-87 (Arizona). Courtesy of Eldon Rudd.

and put the pups out of danger, but the lion grabbed him and pulled him in for the kill. Ross jerked his .30-.30 and killed the lion without seeming to have aimed. He observed, "If I hadn't shot him, he'd have killed Rowdy."

Having in mind feeding the dogs after the hunt, the two had skinned the lion and brought some of the meat back to camp.

Next day Deputy Sheriff Rudd came by, on the way back from Irving with some prisoners and other lawmen. The lion trackers were worried because they didn't have enough food for the whole party of men. True to the western way, they left the latchstring out for their visitors, and chuck that day was sliced-up lion meat with gravy and biscuits, fixed in Dutch ovens. After lunch they told Rudd what he'd had for lunch, and he was angry. "I ate it, and I liked it," he said, "but I sure wouldn't have eaten it if I'd known what it was."

Among the highlights of those years in law enforcement is Camp Verde's only bank robbery in 1917, at the Camp Verde State Bank on Main Street. Three teenagers, Frank Godard and two friends, were sitting by the barbershop next door to the bank the morning of the robbery. They noticed a man with a rifle under his overcoat with the gun-barrel sticking out at the bottom. They didn't think anything about it at the time; everybody carried a gun. Then they saw him go into the bank. David S. Butler, the bank manager who was from the East, customarily locked the bank during lunch-hour and strolled across the street to the boarding house for lunch. Later on this day, disgruntled citizens began to murmur to themselves that the banker had not returned from lunch on time.

On this particular day, however, the banker had never made it to lunch, and suddenly, while some locals were milling around, he ran at full speed in front of the Wingfield Store and up to the bank. He was scratched, dirty, out of breath, and so frightened that he had soaked himself.

Piece together, the story was that the robber had been skulking about near the bank for a part of the morning and had gone in around noon, when few people would be there. He had drawn a gun on Butler and made him empty the safe. The robber then walked him at gunpoint up the hill to the southwest, (where the Glory Hole is in Camp Verde) where a horse was tied, and told him to sit there until he and his horse were out of sight.

When news of the bank robbery spread, the town came alive. Deputy Rudd was out harvesting that day, and someone went to get him. Rudd loped his horse all the way up to the bank, and the teenagers noticed that his horse had "the heaves. He was clackin' and coughin'."

With a fresh mount Deputy Rudd led a four- or five-man posse through the hills toward Prescott, searching for the bank robber. Camp Verde's homeguard and half the town turned out to watch them ride out. Jack Blome, teacher at Camp Verde, rode with the pose. They tracked the robber to Grief Hill, where he had been camped, and there the posse split, and one part went toward Brown Spring and the other toward Prescott. Every trail, however, led to a dead end. Some say the robber went down toward Squaw Peak and crossed a sheeptrail and the sheep obliterated the tracks. Others recall that a rainstorm washed away any tracks the robber had made. He was never caught. Mr. Butler, the banker, promptly went back east and was never heard of again in these parts.

Charles Benjamin Rudd was a man who would tolerate very little nonsense, and he was unyielding about some things, among them cards and alcohol. He would allow neither in his house. But he was a good story-teller. Evenings often found the children sitting on the floor, listening. Once upon a time, when he was a little boy he had a rose garden, so one story began. One day he put his hand through one of the bushes into a bird's nest, and a rattlesnake bit him. Treatment then was to put whisky inside and outside the patient, and this time, the patient got sick, from both the snakebite and the whisky. Rudd said it taught him two things: to stay away from alcohol and never to put his hand into a bird's nest.

In the early 1920's the Rudd family departed Camp Verde for Long Park near Flagstaff, where Harley Price, Edna's brother, had homesteaded. They later moved to Sedona, where Eldon Rudd went to school in a one-room schoolhouse where Brewer School is today.

Memories remain of those few years before Charles Rudd's death. Vera (Cruse) Broughton recalls swimming in Oak Creek and scaling Sedona's spectacular red rocks when children were free to explore anywhere they chose.

One day a son of Rudd's by his former marriage drove into town in a new Model-T. "He was handsome, and all the girls were after him. He stayed for a couple of weeks, and when he left, he gave the new car to his father. It was the first car we had." The young man rode away on a horse, a gift from Rudd.

During those years in Sedona, at about the age of six, Eldon Rudd first felt the hard metal of a gun in his hand as his father, kneeling behind him and covering his small hand with his own, taught him how to fire a gun. But the father taught his son more than how to shoot. He instilled an awe and respect for the power of firearms.

Eldon Rudd grew up to a career with the FBI, most of it in Latin America. He was a carrier-based fighter pilot with the Marines in World War II. From there he went to Washington, D. C., as a member of Congress. The Honorable Eldon Rudd, like his father, is fluent in Spanish, and also wears a lean, square-shouldered, six-foot-four look. He married Anna L. Merritt, of Cuero, Texas. They have two daughters. The Rudds live in Scottsdale.

Albert Rudd died in infancy on February 9, 1919. He is buried at Clear Creek Cemetery at Camp Verde. Eleanor Rudd Gremsgard lives in Oregon.

Ruth Elizabeth Cruse died in 1908 at the age of six months. She is buried in Flagstaff. John Cruse Rudd died in Cornville, Arizona, April 26, 1980. He is buried in the Valley View Cemetery at Clarkdale.

Vera Cruse Rudd married Ernest Glenn Broughton, a contractor. Now a widow, she lives in Cottonwood.

Charles Benjamin Rudd died at the age of 65, on January 15, 1929 in Sedona after a brief illness. He is buried in Cook's Cemetery (Grasshopper Flat), just around the bend and up the hill, west of downtown Sedona.

JOHN L. MUNDS

Yavapai County's Bloodhound of a Sheriff

John L. Munds' appearance belied his toughness. As a lawman in Yavapai County, he had the look of a youngster about him; yet he pursued some of the most dangerous outlaws of his time. But he was more than a lawman. Trained in business, he managed his own and his father's stock and made investments in mining. As a cattleman, he took care of his father's herd of horses and cattle, as well as his own.

John L. Munds, youngest of three children, was born in 1868, in Rosebud, Oregon. In 1875, William and Sarah Munds, with their children, loaded up two covered wagons, rounded up their herd of 110 cattle and fifteen loose horses and departed Rosebud, bound for Arizona. In 1876, they saw their first early spring in the Verde Valley.

Today several northern Arizona landmarks bear the family name: Munds Trail, northeast of Sedona; Munds Park, named for Munds Ranch, 20 miles south of Flagstaff; and Munds Mountain, a dominant landmark east of Sedona.

Ten years after John Munds arrived in the Verde Valley, his life was changed forever. Out on the range one day, Frances Willard loped, sidesaddle, into his life on her high-spirited gray horse, Fred. It was an encounter from which Munds would never recover nor did he want to.

Frances Willard was born on June 10, 1866, granddaughter of Alexander Hamilton Willard, a traveller with the Lewis and Clark expedition. She was destined to make history. As a young girl, riding a horse to school, she yearned for even more knowledge and, unlike most young women of her time, later journeyed far away to Maine to get an education. She became a pioneer school teacher in Arizona.

As an advocate of women's suffrage, she cut a wide swat across Arizona and the nation. As a state senator Frances Munds won this acclamation from the Senate, issued after her death: ". . . the life of Frances Willard Munds was a brilliant page in the history of Arizona."

Francis Willard Munds,
c. 1915. Courtesy of Jerome
Historical Society.

Johnny Munds, Yavapai
County Sheriff, 1899. Photo by
Dr. Lee Hawkins. Courtesy of
Jerome Historical Society.

Two years after Frances and John met, William Munds began to talk about sending his son away for a two-year business course in Stockton, California. Frances urged John to go, assured him that she loved him and would wait. And, being a strong-minded young woman, she decided to teach while he was away.

In November, after she was settled at her new post in Pine, she planned a trip to Prescott to renew her teaching certificate. John was soon to leave for school in California. As a farewell, he rode to Pine and led her horse from Cottonwood, to ride part-way back with her on her journey to Prescott. The two made the trip across part of Arizona Territory's wildest places along the Fossil Creek trail on horseback to Camp Verde. From there, Frances continued on to Prescott in a buckboard with friends, and John left the next day for Stockton.

By the time John finished business school, more than two years later, Frances had taught at Pine, Stoddard, Mayer and briefly at Jerome.

As soon as Munds arrived back in the Verde Valley, wedding plans began. The couple were to be married in Frances mother's home (Mary Willard) in Cottonwood. The Reverend Windes, being the only minister in the district, was to conduct the ceremony. Typical of Frances, she had seen to arrangements far in advance.

On the day of the wedding, two o'clock, the scheduled time, came and went. All guests were in place. The minister was not. Wallace Willard, Frances' cousin, mounted his horse and pronounced, "I'll bring that minister here, dead or alive."

Heavy rains had brought the Verde River up to flood stage. Willard, who was later to become a Rough Rider in the Spanish American War, was not about to let a flood stop his cousin's wedding. He swam his horse across the torrent and rode to Windes' house. Being a bold horseman, Willard saddled up for the minister and fitted a rope around the horse's head like a hackamore, to keep the head above water. He told the minister to get on his horse and to hold on tight, then took a few dallies around his saddle-horn and plunged once again into the muddy waters. Both horses fought the swollen current and, with riders soaked but safe, clattered up the embankment on the other side.

Windes walked in among the waiting guests, whiter than Frances' wedding gown, shaking and near collapse. Even so, Frances and John were married at 8:00 P.M. The Reverend Windes, having recovered before the reception was over, had a wonderful time.

The new Munds family lived at the Spring Creek Ranch (between Sedona and Cottonwood) for a while, and, in late spring, 1890, moved to the Willard Springs Ranch (near Munds Park).

About that time a horse thief was trying his skill and good fortune in the Oak Creek-Mogollon Mountain area. One day John, looking like a carefree teenager, saw a man on a horse near the corral. "Watch the gate, kid, while I catch a horse," the stranger said. Pulling his rifle from the scabbard on his saddle, John said, "Hold it, Mister. Those are my horses." The man then made one fatal mistake and went for his gun, but John shot first. The dead man was Jimmy Wilson, the wanted horse thief.

In January 1895, Sheriff Ruffner appointed John Munds as deputy sheriff of Yavapai County. From that time on, perhaps because he still bore the look of a youngster, people of Yavapai County called him Johnny.

Meanwhile, an outlaw named Fleming "Jim" Parker had drifted into Arizona Territory in the early 1890's. One of Munds' most spectacular chases began after Parker escaped from the Prescott jail in the courthouse with two desperate outlaws. Parker, Munds learned, had galloped away on Sheriff Ruffner's white horse Sure Shot, known for his speed and endurance.

Ex-sheriff Jim Lowry, Sheriff Ruffner, and deputies Munds and Yoeman trailed the outlaws toward the northeast and believed they were headed for Bill Williams Mountain where Parker had friends.

Planning ahead, Sheriff Ruffner sent Munds and Yoeman back to Prescott to gather a posse, camping equipment, food and horses and then to take the train from Prescott to Williams. He hoped they could intercept Parker there.

After setting up camp near Williams, Munds and his posse rode out to look for signs of Parker. A sheepherder said that a man on a white horse had robbed him the day before, of his rifle, ammunition and food.

The herder, looking puzzled, said he had noticed something strange about the horse: his shoes were on backwards. When the horse came into camp, the shoes pointed in the direction they had come in from. The posse examined the tracks and discovered that the herder was correct. Following the trail, they came upon a small pile of nails, and from there the horse's hooves were unshod.

Along the southern side of Bill Williams Mountain, another sheepherder had seen a man ride in on a white horse, but the rider had taken off the bridle and let the horse go. As soon as he could, Munds sent a telegram to Ruffner to tell him his horse was free. The sheriff replied that he would send someone to look for him, but he was certain Sure Shot was already on his way home.

In the meantime, news of Parker and the reward offered for his capture followed him out to Tuba City and points north, where S. S. Preston, from Preston's Trading Post, and six Indians dogged his trail and surrounded him. Parker still had Ruffner's saddle and bridle.

Sure Shot, heading for home as Ruffner had predicted, showed up at Jerome Junction, not much worse for his horse-napping. After that, when he wore Sheriff Ruffner's saddle, it was with a bullet hole in the back from Deputy Yoeman's gun.

At his hanging in June, 1898, Parker examined the scaffold, shook hands with the sheriff and deputies, and said he had no hard feelings. Remembering his boyhood when he and George Ruffner had been friends, Parker asked the sheriff to adjust the straps and pull the lever, because he wanted to be hanged by a friend. As the hood was adjusted, he asked who was doing it and said he wanted Sheriff Ruffner to do it. Ruffner carried out his wishes, and, being not only sheriff but undertaker, drove the hearse to the cemetery for Parker's burial.

Johnny Munds' fame spread. In 1898, he was nominated for Yavapai County Sheriff on the Democratic ticket and elected in November.

Less than one year after Munds' election, a stranger strode into Camp Verde late in the afternoon on July 2, 1899. Townspeople had held a meeting that day to get ready for a picnic and dance on the Fourth of July. Young girls and their mothers were sewing new dresses and planning special dishes to fix for the picnic. That stranger's coming, however, would cancel any festive events for that holiday and for some time in that part of the Verde Valley.

The late afternoon visitor sauntered into the Wingfield Store and shot owners Mack Rodgers, thirty-eight, and Clint Wingfield, twenty-eight. It was a crime without apparent provocation or motive. He did not attempt to rob the store.

The assailant then hurried back to his horse and rode out across an irrigation ditch into the enveloping dusk. Mack Rodgers was killed instantly, but Clint Wingfield lived for several hours. Both were buried on July Fourth in the Clear Creek Cemetery near Camp Verde.

Camp Verde had no telephones at that time, so Harvey Hance saddled Clint Wingfield's horse and rode to Prescott to notify Sheriff Munds. After the sheriff rode into Camp Verde, he got together a posse, including some Indians to help with the tracking. Munds knew they were pursuing a dangerous killer riding an unshod horse, and he knew from measurements, the size of the killer's boots and of the horse's hooves. The hard ground and flat rock that covered much of the mountainous area made tracking difficult. And the possemen were riding through rough country, where even the most intrepid riders sometimes dismounted and led their horses.

Riding toward Long Valley, Munds met Ed Wingfield and Clint's brother Frank and asked them to join the posse. Together, they rode toward Payson, where Munds learned from a storekeeper that a man named Charlie Bishop had been camped near the Mogollon Rim all summer. Payson citizens, he said, view him with suspicion - and for good reason. He carried a .45 six-shooter in his right front pants pocket and a .30-.40 rifle in a scabbard on his saddle. He wore a canvas belt with a double row of cartridges for his rifle and a .45. From the storekeeper Munds got a complete description of Bishop, his clothing, horses and the brands they bore.

Next morning the posse found Bishop's camp and also arrested two men camped in a secluded spot near the rim of East Clear

Creek Canyon. After they admitted to knowing Bishop, Munds dispatched the two to the Flagstaff jail in the custody of the Wingfields.

For almost a month, a posse trailed the suspect in an area bounded on the west by Camp Verde, the north by Flagstaff, the south by Payson and the east by the territorial line at New Mexico. The posse was never sure it was after the right man, or even the same man. It was chasing an elusive quarry, who, on at least one occasion, had help with a getaway horse.

Sheriff Munds, having gathered a description, determined to get additional help. With the Wingfields he sent a bulletin to Flagstaff to be for publication in every newspaper in New Mexico and Arizona Territory:

$2750 Reward for the arrest or capture of a murderer, who goes by the name of Charlie Bishop, who murdered Mack Rodgers and Clint Wingfield at Camp Verde, Yavapai County, Arizona, July 1, 1899.

The following description of the murderer, his wearing apparel and his outfit:

Age - 32-36 years. Weight - about 175 pounds.

Height - 5 feet 10 inches - Well built - Dark complexion - Dark-brown hair, eyes, mustache and beard - quick nervous action.

Wears black hat, brown shirt, dark pants and cut away coat, wears canvas belt with a double row of cartridges. Colt .45 in his right front pocket of pants without a scabbard, wears spurs with long shank made of a file.

Carries a .30-.40 rifle in a scabbard on saddle, that has a double cinch, with hand cinch off. Limber bit bridle with rope reins, carries a gallon canteen and large field glasses. Sheriff has possession of his horses.

If arrested, I will go and get him from any jail in the United States or Mexico:

> *Signed:*
> *Johnny L. Munds - Prescott, Arizona*
> *Sheriff of Yavapai County.*

Searching unnumbered canyons, mesas and hiding places along the Mogollon Rim, the posse had dwindled to only a few. The horses were tired; their riders were more tired. Munds dismissed the posse and boarded a stage at Luna Valley, determined to pursue the fugitive into New Mexico Territory. At the border he took a train to Albuquerque, arrived on July 28 and sent telegrams to Frances and to his undersheriff, A.A. Johns.

Johns wired back immediately that a man answering Bishop's description had attempted to rob a train near Folsom, N.M. The bandit's right arm, almost shot off at the elbow during the holdup, had been amputated. The outlaw was in Santa Fe, New Mexico Penitentiary Hospital with gangrene, not expected to live. He had admitted that he was Tom E. Ketchum.

Through the years historians have confused Tom Ketchum and an outlaw named B. J. Christian, to such an extent that Ketchum has been erroneously credited with several of Christian's robberies. Ketchum saw himself as heir to the title "Black Jack," but he didn't like the nickname, which reporters began to call him in 1897. Although his close associates never called him that, the sobriquet stuck, and he is so called to this day.

Governor Murphy of Arizona Territory signed extradition papers but U. S. Marshall Foraker at the pen at Santa Fe, refused to accept them.

Munds then hopped a train to Santa Fe to see Tom Ketchum. The prisoner did not confess to the Camp Verde murders. The sheriff then went back to Prescott and tried extradition once again.

On April 27, 1901, a telegram reached Sheriff Munds. Ketchum had been tried and convicted of attempted bank robbery. He had been hanged at Clayton, New Mexico Territory, on April 25, 1901.

This mystery was never solved. Charlie Bishop, whom the posse had chased along the Mogollon Rim, was innocent of the killings, even though he may have, unwittingly or not, provided the murderer with a mount. Black Jack himself denied ever killing anyone. Accused of violating a unique law of the territory, he was brought to trial on the capital charge of "assaulting a railway train." And he was convicted.

Before the hanging, Black Jack had his favorite meal of fried chicken and pie. His last request was for a fiddler to come and play for him. whereupon, he mounted the thirteen steps to the platform. Attendants bound him and secured the noose around his neck. When he was ready for hanging, a black hood, firmly fastened in place with horse blanket pins, shrouded his head and shoulders.

Sheriff Salome Garcia was to cut the rope, but having had a few belts, he missed it and had to try again. This time his hatchet severed the rope, the trap door fell, and Black Jack plummeted through. His body jerked once, then plunged to the ground. Blood spurted through the black hood.

Spectators surged forward, aghast and confused. They had bought tickets to see, for them, the biggest event of the year, the hanging of Black Jack Ketchum, and they were not seeing it. When Dr. Slack took off the black hood, they could understand why the outlaw was not hanging. His head had been jerked from his body. As disappointed spectators turned away to go home, the doctor reached into his bag, took out a needle and suture and sewed the head back on. No mourners followed the body to the cemetery.

Even the most strenuous occupations have another side, and life at last goes on at a slower pace. And so it was with the Mund's family. In 1899, William Munds, Johnny's father, was elected the firsty mayor when Jerome incorporated. In the early spring of 1890, John Munds made a trip to the Verde Valley. The Prescott Courier reported:

...7,000 sheep which were being lambed at the north end of Jerome mountains are in a most pitiful condition. The sheep men were buying

water from the railroad company at 75 cents a barrel. The sheep, probably crazy for more water, as they stampeded for the Verde River 12 miles distant, and scattered all over the country, leaving the helpless little lambs scattered here, there and everywhere. The sheep men were gathering them up and toting to water on burros. The sheriff (Munds) says it was too pitiful to see the little weaklings, standing alone, bleating for their mothers. He picked one up and carried it to a place of safety.

John Munds went back to his cattle business in 1904, into mining at Chloride in 1912, and operated a mine at Oatman, Arizona 1914-15. In 1918, he was appointed special deputy for the United Verde Extension Company at Clemenceau and stayed for many years. Frances Munds came there to be with her husband.

Frances and Johnny had three children: William Harold, Sarah (Sally) and Mary Frances.

Frances Willard Munds died in Prescott, December 16, 1948. She is buried there in the Mountain View Cemetery. John Munds died in Prescott, March 2, 1952. He is buried beside his wife.

KILLED IN THE LINE OF DUTY

James G. Hawkins was a teenager when he left Missouri on a wagon train with his parents in April, 1875. With the same group, Nancy and Samuel Cotton Dickinson were traveling with their daughter May. Family history of the journey across the plains shows that the biggest problems on the trip were a constant threat of Indian attack and shortage of water. The wagon train reached Camp Verde, Arizona, in August, 1875.

After a few years of growing up and getting to know each other, James Hawkins and May Dickinson were married. They had two children, Charlie and Minnie.

James Hawkins was the brother of Lee Hawkins, first dentist in Jerome and owner of the town's first automobile.

In 1891, James became a Jerome policeman, but was killed three months later at the age of 30, while bringing a prisoner under arrest. The coroner's jury ruled that the death was from a gunshot wound. Dr. Myron Carrier examined the body.

May Hawkins died from pneumonia near the time of her husband's death, while both of their children were quite young. Grandparents Nancy and Samuel Cotton Dickinson raised the two children.

When Charles grew up, he became a cowboy and left Arizona to live in California. Minnie married Maurice C. Smith, and they eventually settled on a cattle ranch in Williams, Arizona. They had three children: Eugene, Cecil and Agnes.

Charles Emmerson King was born in Meridan, Illinois, in 1863. He had lived in Montana for much of his life as a cattle and horse man. King lived for two years in Alaska before coming to Jerome as a police officer.

For eight years before his death he had served the town as night policeman. Charles King was said to be the most loved and most hated of all Jerome's police officers - loved by the law-abiding and hated by the lawless.

King, 47, was killed from ambush by N.B. Chavez, an ex-convict, newly arrived in Jerome. At 9:00 p.m. on August 27, 1910, King heard shots fired from the red-light district in downtown. He hurried to tht part of town and was asking a young Mexican girl about the cause of the shooting when two more shots rang out. One bullet hit the girl in the thigh; the other slammed into King's back.

Surgeons removed the bullet, but four days after the ambush, King died. On the day of the funeral, every business in Jerome was closed from 1:00 to 5:00 p.m. The town fire department took over arrangements for the funeral.

Charles Emmerson King left a wife and two children. He was buried in the city cemetery in Jerome, but the remains were moved the following year to Rosedale Cemetery in Los Angeles.

James Lowry's was a name long known and respected in Yavapai County. He had lived in the county for 35-40 years, and in earlier years he was in the cattle business in Mayer. In 1886 he was elected sheriff ans sereved two terms. He later won re-election, but retired in 1908. In 1917 he came to Jerome as watchman for The United Verde Extension.

Lowry, 65, was described as "a plain, blunt man who made friends readily and kept them forever."[28]

The officer was killed July 17, 1918, when he attempted to stop an uprising among Jerome's Mexican population. At the bandstand in Clemenceau, below Jerome, Porfirio Hernandez, leader of the Mexican Uprising, shot Lowry as the revolutionaries congregated to march on Jerome. Lowry fell with at least three bullets in the abdomen. Friends picked him up, but he died within a minute or so, probably before he got to the hospital.

Mrs. Lowry, who was a semi-invalid in later years, had been in Los Angeles much of the time in recent years. Just before the uprising she had written to her husband to tell him she was well enough to meet him in Prescott for a visit. Just ten minutes before he was killed, Lowry had gotten permission to be off work for one week to spend the time with his wife.

Dave Rees, popular Jerome policeman, was born in Prescott February 1, 1880. He had been on the police force for sixteen years when, in 1933, he was found dead near the Nevada Cafe in Jerome. He had been shot in the abdomen. The sheriff of Yavapai County offered a reward of $500 for information about the killing, and the town of Jerome added $500. The killer was never found.

Dave Rees left a wife and children. One daughter graduated from high school soon after his death.

James Gabriel Hawkins (1861-1891),
Az. Courtesy of Jerome Historical Society.
Constable, killed in line of duty, Jerome,

The lawman's family insisted that the killer was after another man and had killed Rees by mistake. What actually happened to Dave Rees, why and at whose hand still comprises one of the mysteries in the annals of lawmen of Arizona's Verde Valley.

"All the world's a stage," Shakespeare wrote, "And all the men and women merely players." Arizona's Verde Valley makes up only a small portion of that world stage where many lawmen have entered, taken their place at center and moved on. Some had a shoot-first mentality; others used reason before guns; and some died before the drama was over.

In the long and colorful history of law enforcement in the West, perhaps no period is as dramatic as the late eighteenth and early nineteenth centuries.

Gold and silver, cattle and oil...any one alone was enough to lure men westward in the hopes of striking it rich. Many went west to work. Many others also followed the trek toward the cow-towns, the mining settlements, the railroad construciton sites, and the territory beyond the restraints of civilization. They went, not to work, but the prey upon those who did.

A code of sorts grew out of this frontier atmosphere. Shooting an unarmed man was wrong as was shooting a man in the back, Two men shooting it out was considered perfectly acceptable. It was the established way to settle disputes. The loser was not able to appeal his case in most instances...at least not to any earthly judge. His remains were planted in a six-by-three grave in some boothill.[29]

It was a frontier ethic, and it had to be handled accordingly. Today, however, a new breed of lawman, in the wings only decades ago, is on stage. G.C. "Buck" Buchanan, present Sheriff of Yavapai County, has said, "...we are continually faced with increased service demands brought about by growth and change in social values. Meeting the demands of the 90's is indeed a challenge, but one accepted with dedication and purpose."[30]

While the early sheriffs, their deputies, and lawmen who watched over the peace often relied on their gunslinging skills to do their jobs, the modern law officer is likely to be concerned with how a rapidly changing world affects his one unchanging focus of keeping the peace.

According to Sheriff Buchanan, education is a major tool today in law enforcement. In an article, *The Role of Sheriff: Past-Present-Future,* the late Truman Walrod said, "The sheriff of today appears practically a fetishist when it comes to education."[31]

Looking back in time into the annals of the lawmen, we see a succession of players on Shakespeare's stage - Jim Roberts, Fred Hawkins, Johnny Hudgens, Charles Benjmin Rudd, Johnny Munds and those who gave their lives. But in the limelight today is a lawman who lives and works in a rapidly changing world, but is focused on that one unchanging function: to be watcher of the peace.

BIOGRAPHY

Bennie Blake teaches English, Creative Writing and History on the Community Faculty at Yavapai College, Prescott, Arizona. She is also a free lance writer. She is the author of numerous articles published in newspapers and periodicals. She has also edited many literary works, including fiction, nonfiction, and poetry, as well as masters' theses and doctoral dissertations.

She lives in Sedona on Oak Creek with her husband, Stanley, and French Poodle Nick. Her favorite recreation is hiking and exploring wilderness and forest areas in and around Sedona's red rocks.

ACKNOWLEDGEMENTS

I extend my deepest thanks to Nancy Smith, Archivist at Jerome Historical Society, for helping me countless times to explore the riches of the Society's archives and to add the missing links needed to put these chapters together; Greg Weldon at Jerome State Park, whose skill at photography made possible some photographs that I thought were impossible to find; Lori Davisson, Research Librarian at Arizona Historical Society, whose research on Arizona lawmen revealed a heretofore hidden treasure; to the other writers who have worked on this book for their hard work and good humor; and my husband, Stanley, for his patience and many trips to the store for frozen pizza.

Chapter Eight
WOMEN OF THE BACK STREETS
Jerome's Ladies Of The Night
By Bennie Blake

n the West in the nineteenth century, there was a loneliness so deep that a man could become vulnerable to any ploy, any means of exploitation by those who were out to get his money. He might resort to gambling, finding a prostitute, booze or even opium. Jerome, Arizona, had all of these - in abundance.

In an early mining town in America, a female was as rare a sight as an elephant, it was said. Indeed, tales of the West abound with anecdotes about the woman-hungry man. Just a glimpse of a lady's underwear hanging on the line was so inspiring to these early miners that one lonely but enterprising bachelor acquired some ladies' lingerie and charged a fee just to look at it, and an additional fee just to touch its lacy borders.

In one rough gold-mining town a miner spied a young woman with her baby in arms and asked if he might hold the child for just one moment. She handed over the infant, and the miner held the child close, then gave back the bundle and thrust a portion of his gold into the mother's palm.

Many of these stories suggest that it was more than the sex drive that brought about this deep desire for the gentle taming that women brought to these isolated pockets on the frontier. There was a disease called loneliness, and many an emigrant from his home in the East sought a cure in the early saloons or on or under a blanket with one of the ladies of the evening.

Even before buildings were constructed in Jerome, an advance guard of ladies of easy virtue arrived and "lived in tents or pitched their blankets behind trees and therefore earned the name of blanket whore."

Following closely behind was their more enlightened sister, the madam. During the 1890's in Jerome, these often enterprising newcomers established a red-light district, sometimes called the tenderoin, in the middle of the business section.

The term "red-light district" originated in Dodge City from a custom among uninhibited railroaders of leaving their red brakemen's lanterns hanging outside the door of their girl of the evening to discourage intruders.

The most successful madams were waling contradictions. They had to be charming to customers but ruthless in business; skillful at public relations but discrete; and tough but motherly. Each madam managed a staff that was volatile by nature. In a growing mining town like Jerome, she dealt with often irascible customers, freshly scrubbed, freshly shaved, with hours of boredom to work off from a 12-hour shift underground in the mines. It was a time of unrest, of searching, of gnawing loneliness that could easily lead to an insane violence.

A memorable madam in Jerome was Jennie Banters (aka Bauters), who came to town in the early 1890's. A smart businesswoman, she was at one time reputed to be the richest woman in Arizona Territory. Among Jennie's other qualities was the gift of enterprise. After having been burned out for the third time in Jerome's frequent fires, she began in 1899 to put up a building of brick on Hull Avenue, where Sullivan Hotel and Copper are now. Her Main Street business was the first one in town to have a sidewalk in front. Earlier that year, her place caught on fire, and it is said, "she rushed to the firehouse and offered free passes to the boys if they would save her establishment. It was said "the men rose to superhuman efforts that day and Jennie's place was saved."

Like many other madams, Jennie was known to be big-hearted, helpful and especially tender-hearted toward the miner and prospector who might be down on his luck.

BELGIAN JENNIE, said C. A. Brown, who lived in Jerome from 1896 to 1900, of all the honky-tonks deserves to have her name spelled out in capitals. Her place of business was built like any other rooming house of that period. Large reception room across the front with a wide front door, glazed and with a concealing lace curtain over the glass.

As was told to me. On entering, one was met by a trim maid in spangled short skirt and a revealing bodice. Net stockings, whose topes were hidden up underneath her waistline. She would take the customer's hat and coat and brush the snow or dust off with a little whisk broom bearing around its handle a big bow of vivid pink ribbon. The ribbon matched the one in her hair.

The back wall of the reception room was pierced with a door where a rich velvet drape hid from prying eyes a softly-lighted hallway giving to private rooms on either side. It was told to me, that one whispered a name to the maid, and was either ushered in behind the concealing drapes, or was told to wait as "Midgie" or another was "busy" and please be seated.

Easy chairs partly hidden behind folding screens gave the caller a sense of being "Special" as he drank his double-priced whiskey in partial seclusion. Jennie herself, might darken the cubicle with her well-stacked figure, and pass the time of day, and even ask about the waiting one's health. If Midge was too long "busy," Jennie would buy the visitor a drink and parlay her take with him buying another to keep even with his gracious Madam hostess while his desire for Midge, or Midgie, increased as his blood rushed to inflame his needs.

Believed to be Jennie Banters at Jennie's Place, Main Street, Jerome, c. 1898. Courtesy of Jerome Historical Society.

Jennie's Place, Main Street, 1898. Now site of Sullivan Hotel/Copper Shop/Nellie Bly. Courtesy of Jerome Historical Society.

Plenty of time was of the essence at Jennie's place.

But Jennie's place was not the only bordello in town. "Next to the Jerome Hotel there was a house called the O.K. Rooming House. While most girls charged $1.00 if the miner couldn't speak English and $2.00 if he could, the girls at O.K. Rooming House could charge $5.00 because they were better class. They also sold beer for $1.00 and sandwiches."

But some of the miners couldn't, or wouldn't, pay $5.00, so they went to Lily's. Even though her business thrived, Lily was a very lonely woman who would go alone to the last picture show of the evening. The men poked fun at some of the girls but not at Lily. The author of this tale does not say where Lily's place was.

One of the madams, the Cuban Queen, named Anne Johnson, one old-timer remembered, was tall and dark and chose her girls for their sultry beauty. Some were believed to be mulatto. The house, also called the Cuban Queen, was the only one in town that had gambling.

After Jennie Banters' business was running smoothly and Jerome's fires had diminished for a time, she departed for Goldroad, another mining community south of Kingman. There she unwisely took up with a man, C. C. Leigh, believed to be addicted to opium. By the year 1905, she had tired of him and his opium habit and told him to get out. The Mojave County Miner later printed the details of that Sunday morning, September 3:

Saturday Evening Leigh had hung around the saloon conducted by the woman and had apparently not gone to bed. Early in the morning he and others took a drink at the bar and in a conversation he stated that he intended to get a certain sum of money if he died for it. Shortly Leigh went to Jennie's room and kicked open the door. He was armed with a gun and the woman attempted to escape. The first shot was fired at her in the room and as she ran toward the street Leigh followed shooting as he went. Three shots were fired, all taking effect. At the third shot she fell partly in the road and partly on the stony ground close to the wagon rut. Leigh went back into a cellar under Jennie's room for the purpose of reloading the gun and immediately returned to the spot where the woman's body lay. Observing that she was not yet dead he moved her head so that he could get a better shot and then deliberately fired the pistol. He then placed the gun to his own breast and after selecting the right spot fired, producing but a slight wound. He then laid himself out on the ground by Jennie's body as though he expected death to come right away. He carefully placed his hat over his face to shield it from the sun. A crowd then gathered about and Constable Fred Brown came up and took Leigh to the lockup. When the brute was shooting, the woman begged pitifully to be spared but the man was bent on destroying her life and refused to listen to her appeals.

On January 18, 1907, Clement C. Leigh was hanged at 2:00 P.M. for the murder of Jennie Banters.

Jennie was not the first of her profession to be murdered in this manner. A prostitute name Bohemia was slain in Jerome in 1894, also by her boyfriend.

Life went on, however, for citizens of Jerome. But changes were brewing. At one moment in Jerome's early days, someone, perhaps a leather-skinned woman and wife of a miner, had peered into the future and had seen a town where wives could have church suppers and children could go to school and grow up in a peaceful place. It was a dream, and part of that dream would come true. But first, prostitutes, gamblers, opium users and bootleggers would have their day in Jerome.

The year 1899 was an important one. The town became incorporated, and bordellos, saloons and gambling houses thrived. So did the girls, who added a bit of spice to everyday life on Cleopatra Hill.

One beautiful young prostitute twirling a green umbrella and wearing a French gown strolled leisurely up Main Street. Across the way in a bar, which is now Paul and Jerry's, a burro, a nightly visitor to the saloon, begged for beer from the miners. On this night, the burro had more beer than usual and staggered across the street toward the young girl. He took a big bite of her umbrella which, spectators said, must have resembled grass. The girl tried to pull her umbrella free, but the unruly burro clamped his iron jaws shut. Hearing the sound of raucous laughter from Main Street, Jerome's miners poured out of saloons to watch a spectacle that was, for them, a unique and hilarious attraction a tug-of-war between an inebriated burro and a prostitute.

C. A. Brown, who as a teenager was always watching for similar spectacles, described one Fourth of July in Jerome, when he saw:

a gayly decorated and glorified spring-wagon. The driver of the rig was in uniform with cockade and feather nodding to one and all. His livery was of the House Colors of his employer-ess who rode with him in the elevated seat. The ornate vehicle four-seater. One quite forgot the driver with his tasseled whip and plumed hat. They became but dim background scenery for the twelve lovely girls. They were resplendently robed in Fashion's best. A jealous zephyr grudgingly bore to our flaring nostrils all the perfume of the flowers of the world.

Tiny parasols, gay indeed, were twirled by soft hands, protected by white gloves reaching to their manicured armpits. The girls waved, they pirouetted, they smiled, they smelled wonderful. They, that is, some of them shook my grimily extended hand. The older one who must have been their step-mama, introduced each of the girls in turn. Flora, Vici, Tommy, Kitten, Edna, Pearlie, Gwen, Frankie, Jo-Anne, Maudie and Trudy. It was the last one Trudy, that pressed a bon-bon in my hand. Trudy wore a silken scarf loosely around her lovely neck. The scarf was just as blue as her wide large eyes. The scarf embellishments to feminine beauty were called "fascinaters." Trudy didn't really need it. She would have looked lovely with just a string of knuckle-bones around her velvety throat. When I opened the bonbon, there was a little note, "I hope you come to see me."

Although townspeople were divided over many issues, prostitutes in particular, they could unite before their common enemy, fire. Most had seen some of these conflagrations, and together they rejoiced to see new buildings, some built of brick, going up where old ones had been gutted or completely destroyed. Among these was the Elite Club House. The *Jerome Mining News* reported on January 9, 1899, that the Elite had reopened, having a separate wine room, a main room with various games, roulette, craps, poker and faro, and in the back, an orchestra and, back of that, a section with private boxes for those who wish to dine in seclusion.

The *Jerome Mining News* concluded with the highest accolade for the proprietor:

Mr. Lanham deserves great praise for his nerve in fitting up such an elaborate resort in Jerome as well as his energy in quieting all signs of disturbance during the entire evening, in spite of the exhilarating surroundings, not a man was killed or even fatally wounded. We bespeak for the Elite a liberal patronage, as its elegant furnishings and gentlemanly attendants certainly deserve.

In 1903 the Fashion Saloon expanded to eleven games: faro, craps, roulette, monte, stud poker, Chinese lottery and others. On April 20, the *Jerome Mining News* reported that the new saloon and gambling house was "the largest and most complete establishment of its kind in the Southwest, if not on the continent."

Even the finest of these saloons, however, did nothing to enhance the family image that many citizens carried of Jerome. They contended that liquor, prostitution and gambling often sparked violence, and, in addition, there was opium, readily available to those who knew where to find it.

"One might always detect a customer of a Chinese laundry," said C. A. Brown, explaining that the Chinese always slept and cooked their opium under the ironing boards. "The opium thrown in for free by the Chinese shirt-washers was with me always. I had noticed that no girl seemed to be 'crazy' to let her lovely head rest on my manly bosom."

In March of 1904 the *Jerome Mining News* reported a death from opium:

He Smoked Hop and Is Now Dead

A few days ago the sheriff's officer arrested a Mexican by the name of Jose Armarillos, and on Saturday the officer said the fine had been paid and requested that he be discharged, which was done. He (Armarillos) became so elated over his escape from jail that he immediately began to celebrate the event. He drank all kinds of mixtures until they lost their charm for him, and he went down to Chinatown. He went and purchased $1.00 worth of hop and went up to a little shack on Granite Street, which is used for that purpose, and proceded to invoke the blessing of a hop dream. The dream seemed pretty good to him and he kept it up until he got so much that it caused heart failure and he died this morning about ten o'clock.

The Elite Saloon, 1898 on Hull Avenue. Now an empty lot. Courtesy of Jerome Historical Society.

Fashion Saloon, 1899. Now Mine Museum. Courtesy of Jerome Historical Society.

In spite of death and arrests, opium use persisted, and officers kept up their watch for dens, said to be operating among the Chinese. Newspapers reported that officer Fred Hawkins, with the help of other lawmen, raided dens and arrested smokers. As the years passed, opium use diminished and, like the Chinese population, dwindled. But it did not cease. Along with opium, marijuana, although less publicized, was in use in town. One old-timer recalls that plants were growing in the gulch and that citizens sometimes traveled to Mexico and brought marijuana back. Police records show arrests during the 1920's and '30's for marijuana use.

Lawman Fred Hawkins had little time for loafing in those days. He responded to a call in February, 1904 to investigate a Jack-the-Ripper assault on Fannie Howard, a girl from one of the houses. For these girls, violent attack was always a danger. A newcomer to town, L. W. Watson, had slashed her face so badly that ninety-one stitches were required to put her face together again. The February 18 issue of the *Jerome Mining News* reported that the pair had been visiting some of the saloons and had returned to Fannie's room.

Fannie Howard reported that at 6 a.m. she was awakened by Watson grasping her throat, while flourishing a knife.

He started to use the knife, the first cut running from the ear to the point of her chin. Slash after slash he inflicted. She pleaded with him to call a doctor. He demanded his money back. In places the cheeks were laid open, exposing the teeth. Watson demanded to know why he was taken into custody.

Police believe they have made an important capture. The cutting is similar to ones inflicted upon "fast women" in Tucson, Phoenix, and Los Angeles. It may be the same man.

Struggling to rid their town of this kind of violence and the vices that triggered it, citizens continued to fight. In 1905 Deputy Fred Hawkins reported to the town council that he had displaced all the girls from their customary places of business. Agitation against gambling grew, also, and the town passed an ordinance against any gambling after January 1, 1906.

Gamblers, however, certain that this ordinance would devastate their business, continued operations and declared the ordinance illegal. The county attorney agreed, and the sheriff issued county licenses for the Jerome operations to continue.

That same year the council heard a complaint that the women of easy virtue, cheered on by the gamblers' victories, had returned to their familiar haunts. The council decided in September to allow the prostitutes to stay in business, but they had to register and be examined weekly. The town health officer was to conduct the examinations for a fee.

In the year 1913, the reformers won a victory when the town of Jerome passed an ordinance restricting houses of ill fame to certain blocks in the downtown section, with Hull Road running down through the middle of the red-light district. Citizens showed vestiges of humor when the alleyway from Main Street to Hull Avenue came to be called Husbands' Alley, which no doubt served certain promiscuous spouses in time of need.

Having won the most recent skirmish against the prostitutes, townspeople then deployed their forces against the gamblers. The council drafted another ordinance, but gamblers still refused to close. J. B. Hoover, of the Fashion Saloon, publicly announced that he would not allow the ordinance to interfere with his business. He kept the games and was promptly arrested. He fought the case to the Territorial Supreme Court, where Chief Justice Sloan ruled that Jerome did not have the power to prohibit gambling and ruled the ordinance invalid.

The territorial legislature had passed an anti-gambling law in 1907, but, in spite of state and local laws, gambling continued in Jerome. In 1917, the council voted in an ordinance clamping down on card games behind closed doors. The next year Fred Hawkins attempted once again to check sporting games. In March he raided a game in the basement of the Arizona Pool Hall and arrested eight players, five of whom paid $100 fines each while three chose 30-day jail sentences. All card games were banished, and all slot machines removed.

The year 1919 saw similar arrests, with raids on the Palace and Fischer pool halls. Some individuals soon found that they could make an occasional sum by raiding crap games. During such a happening at the St. Elmo, there was a shooting, and the raiders got away with $800. In October, the council ordered a cleanup campaign extending to a strict ban on gambling. Eight gamblers were warned out of town, and two went to jail.

Meanwhile, townspeople against the prostitutes got some help from an unexpected source. During World War I, all red-light districts in Arizona closed. All soiled doves, 40 women, departed their Hull Avenue haunts, but as in the past, many drifted back. Various reports were that men from Jerome built houses for some of the girls and they didn't leave at all. Others appeared once again at the cribs behind the Sullivan Hotel, which in 1926 prompted John Sullivan to protest that all prostitutes must clear out of Hull Avenue.

A favorite tale of some of the locals has been passed along and is around today. In 1918, John Crowley, a handsome young man, had come to town as the new chief of police. One part of his job was to close the houses of prostitution. He did it, but only after considerable effort. On the following Fourth of July, people of the town had planned a dual celebration for Independence Day and the ending of World War I. During the festivities, the police chief noticed three girls in French gowns marching in the parade. Overhearing the protests of spectators, he walked toward one of the girls who was pushing her way through the crowd. As he neared her, the other two young women grabbed the chief's arms, and not wanting to spoil the holiday mood, he marched arm-in-arm with the two prostitutes while Fourth of July revelers cheered.

In October, 1922, the council ordered a cleanup campaign with a strict ban on prostitution. Two "notorious" women were jailed, and several others left town.

During this period, the economy in Jerome was booming. Arizona was the highest producer of copper in the country. Miners had more money to spend.

Bootlegging, which had been born in 1915 with state prohibition, boomed, also. Moonshine was plentiful, and as always prohibition was not keeping thirsty Jeromites from wetting their whistles. In 1916, they could buy a quart of bootleg for $5.00. In 1917, after the United States entered World War I, making and selling bootleg whiskey was one of the most prosperous industries in the country.

Despite its prosperity, the bootlegging industry kicked off another cycle of violence in the valley. National prohibition entered the scene on January 16, 1920, and federal marshalls and local officers together began to raid stills and confiscate equipment. Costa Katch, a bootlegger, was murdered. W. R. "Goat" Morgan was murdered in what was believed to be a bootlegger's dispute.

During the 1920's bootlegging became East Jerome's principal industry. Two stills, the largest one in the valley and the largest in Yavapai County were raided in East Jerome. Stills, however, were not confined to that area. They were spread about the valley, in mine tunnels, water tunnels, outhouses and basements, in places safe from discovery. One was even secluded in the 600-foot tunnel between Peck's Lake and the Verde River at Clarkdale. One Verde Valley rancher reported, "There was a still in every bush."

Bootlegging kept revenuers busy and created humor for some people in the valley. One resident had a dog named Prohi, and it was said the canine could smell a revenuer a mile away.

Quantity of bootleg whiskey in the valley was constant and large, but quality was variable, old-timers say. Some moonshine was very good, some very bad; and a few people died. One kind of bootleg made in the valley was powerful. It was called white mule, and, if it was good, it sold in 1922 for $25 a gallon.

Officers continued to raid. In August 1924, they confiscated fifty stills, and revenue from fines skyrocketed. The largest still captured in Arizona during those times was at Cherry Creek in 1928 - a 450-gallon capacity. That same year Joe Hall, the Bootleg King of Arizona, was arrested with 300 gallons of whisky in his Cottonwood home. In 1929, Hall was sentenced to one year in prison and fined $1,000.

The valley's saga of the bootlegger ended with the repeal of prohibition in 1933. Legalized liquor returned, and almost overnight the white-aproned bartender replaced the wary bootlegger. "Jerome probably barely felt the difference. The first place one could

Tom Cantrell, Chief of Police, 1930's into 1940's and unidentified prostitutes in front of Miner's Tavern, run by Joe Pecharich. Courtesy of Jerome Historical Society.

Jerome's travelling jail, has slid downhill 225 feet. Now located in old red-light district. Photo by Bennie Blake.

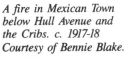

A fire in Mexican Town below Hull Avenue and the Cribs. c. 1917-18 Courtesy of Bennie Blake.

get draft beer was Fischer's Pool Hall, now Paul and Jerry's."

Prostitutes, closely supervised by police and health officers, were still in town for some time after most of the bootleggers had dismantled their stills. Mattie Leyel, who in later years was Head Nurse at Cottonwood hospital, came to work in Jerome in the 1920's. Part of her job was to help the health officer with regular examination of the prostitutes. In 1981 she remembered them well. "There was one that was a very pretty lady. She had a daughter that was around nine years old. She went into prostitution to keep the little girl in school."

Mattie Leyel recalled that prostitutes had their standards, too, and sometimes had occasion to check up on their clients. One day a man came into the hospital with a venereal disease, and somehow the madams found out about it. One of them came to the hospital and asked where he was, "I told her where he was. He had a screen around him, and she went in to see if he had been down to her place. She was relieved. Apparently he hadn't."

Lillian Douglas, the main madam during the late 1920's and 1930's and even into the 1940's, had a house which still stands just below the facade of the old Victory Market near the traveling jail. Lillian, old-timers say, ran a good house, but it wasn't easy. Police pulled her and her girls in every month for loitering, but her fines were less than the other madams' were. Revenue for the town of Jerome for vagrancy was $5.00 per head per month.

One resident of Jerome during the 1920's made deliveries for the drug store, and Lillian was one of their customers. At the time, he was in his teens, and he was never allowed to go to Lillian's alone and never beyond the outside of the front door. He remembers Lillian as being kind, dressed like any housewife, and not made up as he had expected a madam to be.

Lillian, nevertheless, knew her business. Being an enterprising madam, she regularly paraded her girls into the bars down by the Copper Star in the southern part of Main Street.

Some of the people who lived on Diaz Street below Lillian's got to know her and her girls, who sometimes came for dinner and on Christmas always brought presents to the neighbors' children.

On July 7, 1931, Lillian's house, the second floor, was the scene of one of Jerome's most chilling murders, when 30-year-old prostitute, Juanita Marie Dean, known as Sam, was strangled. Sam had come to Jerome by a circuitous route, going from Texas, through Colorado and to Arizona. Like many other prostitutes, she had a husband, a gambler named George, who apparently didn't come to Arizona with her.

Questions at the Coroner's Inquest produced little evidence of the why and the who of this murder. Sam, they said, was easy to get along with. Mrs. Palacios, who lived just across the stairway from where Sam was murdered, was the last person to see her alive, at 8:30 that Tuesday morning. The coroner's verdict was that the

Juanita Marie "Sammy" Dean, murdered July, 1931. Courtesy of Jerome Historical Society.

Lillian's, late 1970's. Now remodelled apartments. Courtesy of Jerome Historical Society.

House used by two prostitutes, c. 1920's and early 1930's. Still standing. Photo by Bennie Blake.

murder occurred between 8:30 a.m. and 2:00 p.m. The murderer would have passed within three or four feet of Mrs. Palacios, who was sitting on her front porch, but she could give no description of the man.

"Letters from Sam back home to Texas indicated that the mayor's son had wanted to marry her, and when she turned him down, he vowed to get even. The coroner's jury ruled death to be at the hands of an unknown assailant. There is no record that her boyfriend, a hard miner and fighter, was ever questioned about the murder." Sam's sister came from Texas and took the body home to Dallas for burial.

The 1930's passed with a succession of murders, knife battles, shootings, accidents in the mines, a peeping Tom's shooting, suicides, a bank robbery at Clemenceau, men out of work and depression.

During those years the madams and their girls continued to spice up life in the town. People who came to visit Jerome delighted in going to the Connor Hotel to see the ladies, dressed in their finest, as they came in for dinner. The prostitutes always had their own place to dine. They were quiet and never mingled with other diners. They sometimes gathered, also, at the New York Cafe to eat and to wait for customers. The Wigwam on Hull Avenue beside the cribs was always a place to buy booze and to rent a room when a man might take his lady of the evening for just a brief stay.

As the years moved along into World War II, houses were closing, and most of the prostitutes left Jerome. Some had suffered from occupational hazards: venereal disease, crude abortions, too much drink, overdose of laudanum or an assault by an enraged man. All, like the men, had suffered from the disease called loneliness. Most of the houses, too, had been destroyed. Jerome's earth tremors sent the Cuban Queen and the Monte Carlo sliding downhill and into obscurity in the 1930's. Lillian's house, nearby, escaped damage.

Many of the houses were torn down between 1948 and 1960. The section of the cribs that Jennie Banters built was torn down in 1972. One of the last reminders of the girls was the shells of the cribs, where only the walls of their small apartments still stood, windows and doors lost long ago. Only an open sky, pink wall-paper and rose borders remained. The entire structure disappeared one day in the mid 1980's when a bulldozer drew alongside and pushed over the last remnants in only a few minutes.

Only two buildings that housed prostitutes remain: Lillian's, which has been remodeled into an apartment house, beside the lonely facade of the old Victory Market; and a small, two-room structure next door, used by two of the girls in the 1920's and '30's.

Reformers in Jerome had won at least in part. Prostitution is still going on today. It can be found in other varied forms in any community in the West. The girls are with us still, but their job has

The cribs on Hull Avanue. Third story is portion of Sullivan Hotel. Courtesy of Jerome Historical Society.

Prostitutes at the cribs on Hull Avenue, c. 1920. Collection of Joe Lazaro.

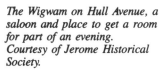

The Wigwam on Hull Avenue, a saloon and place to get a room for part of an evening. Courtesy of Jerome Historical Society.

been partially taken over by the amateur.

Gamblers still deal the cards. The last slot machines left Jerome between 1940 and 1945. They had been around for years and, at $5.00 per machine per month, had generated a sizeable revenue for the town.

Other narcotics have joined opium. One citizen was arrested in 1935 for possession of cannabis. Bail was set at $500.

Any need for the bootlegger passed long ago in 1933, with repeal of prohibition.

Jerome almost died in the early 1950's. It was even called a ghost town, but it refused to have an epitaph. Red-blooded, never-to-be-forgotten characters lived there and forged a town known across the country and in other parts of the world. These characters suffered, and they died. But they still live in memory, in tales of old-timers, in books . . . and in Jerome.

Go there some quiet evening and walk along the backstreets. If you are imaginative, you will see the first soft snowflakes of an early winter settling on the sidewalks . . . A miner's booted footprint in the snow as he hurries into the saloon to warm his backside beside a pot-bellied stove.

You'll hear soft laughter carried on the evening breeze from where the old cribs were on Hull Avenue . . . A heavy footstep on an old board sidewalk . . . A door on Jerome's traveling jail clanging shut . . . Click of the trigger on a lawman's gun . . . and prostitute Sammie Dean's last lonely moan of anguish.

Chapter Nine
JEROME'S BILLION DOLLAR BOOM, BUSTLE AND BUST
1898 To The Present
By Nancy R. Smith

side from Fort Verde and the occasional ranch house, prospectors in the Black Hills of Arizona only had their burros, dogs and assorted animals for companionship. After the mining camp of Jerome became established, saloons and gambling resorts became favorite places of entertainment and socializing for these solitary hunters of fortune.

One day the old prospector known as Rim Rock, meandered into the saloon of Joe Seegar. Charlie Brown, an apprentice foundry worker for the United Verde, recalls the event in his HISTORY OF JEROME:

"Rim's poke holds a medium sized fortune in placer gold." Of course Joe was anxious to find out where Rim panned it. With seven free drinks under his sunburned belly skin, he loosened up -- I heard the whole yarn. 'One night there was a hell of a wind storm blew up and I filled my pockets with rocks to keep from blowin' away. Didn't do any good. Next morning I was cleanin' out my pockets, and durned if it wasn't mostly placer gold. I musta got blowed more than twenty miles. I was so shook up, I laid mostly dead for three days, when my dog Dusty come leadin' the burro into camp. Dusty had a fresh killed rabbit in his mouth. The burro had the canteen in his pack an' it was full. That was three months ago, and I've been looking for the place where I camped ever since. I had to come in for grub, and I'm goin' right back to look some more.' Whiskey makes a pretty good lie detector, so Joe poured old Rim seven more drinks. When old Rim came to, he didn't even know his name or where he was. [Joe] took the price of the drinks from Rim's poke. Where the gold came from remains a mystery to this day. Old Rim with his dog Dusty, and his burro disappeared and has never come back to Jerome, or any other place. Old Timers think he is somewhere in the mountains still looking for the place from where he was blown. Some folks think old Rim was lyin' about not knowing who he was when he came to. Joe Seeger thinks different, he declared that fourteen drinks of the booze he gave old Rim would make a mummy talk. He ought to know!"

In those days, hard-rock miners could be a loose and wild bunch. They needed a place to unwind, and, if possible, with understanding women. Mr. Brown tells of such a place located in Walnut, aka Deception Gulch:

"Below the Hog-back ridge of rocks there was a lovely little gulch. Trees and bushes and grass throve there. Sulfur fumes never reached its verduned slopes. It was sparsely settled, being without a road, and much too far for walking into town up the rocky paths. It was called Deception gulch. No one knew why. Its waters were cool, clear, and scant. Its slopes were ever green and blooming. After the war with Spain and "Remember the Main!" An enterprising man had saved his money made during the war, and built a road of fair grades to reach its depths. There he constructed a saloon and dance hall. It soon became the rendezvous for our wilder spirited youths, both men and girls. A mechanical piano was operated by a man who knew how to pedal it. Fist fights between ten cent dances were common. It reached its nadir of rowdyism when two contenders for a little Mexican girl's snuggles went outside to win or lose. A stalwart named Elmer, bit off his rival's ear. He won and spit out the morsel, and snuggled his sweetie-pie. The law which had kept hands off hitherto, decided things were getting out of hand at the Dewey Cafe. By popular acclaim the gulch got a new name CANNIBAL GULCH. Teeth and fingers had been lost in previous fights, but somehow, an ear struck the popular fancy as beyond fair fighting."

Since the ore body appeared capable of producing gold, silver and copper for an indeterminate number of years, the business men and women invested their money and energy into buildings which would last. One of the things they felt necessary to help insure their investments was incorporation as a town in the Territory of Arizona. This would allow tax monies to stay in the town and not go to be spent for roads, fire systems and other necessities somewhere else. As has been recorded many times, in the early days of tents and flimsy wood structures, the fire demon swept through major parts of Jerome at least 4 times in less than 12 years. Incorporation could lead to laws to prohibit wooden structures within the main commercial area. It would also allow the town to form a Jerome Volunteer Fire Department, and equip it to adequately fight fires.

The Town of Jerome was approved by the Yavapai County Board of Supervisors on March 8, 1899. The Common Council was set up, and William M. Munds, owner of the Jerome Meat Market, became Mayor. This Council established the government and instituted the first ordinances directed at the health and safety of the 5000 plus citizens reported to be in and around Jerome. Civic responsibility and duty became the major spare-time activity of many of the men. But not all of men of the town!

The Jerome Volunteer Fire Department organized their Chemical Company #1 on July 27, 1899. Tom Campbell, assistant Post Master (and later Governor of Arizona) was elected Chief, and Tom Page became Assistant Chief. On August 1st a Hose company was to be organized. There were eventually 3 companies in the Fire Department: Pronto Chemical, Victor Hose and Miller Hose. The

Jerome Volunteer Fire Department hose company racing team, c. 1910

Holiday on Main Street, c. 1910

United Verde's company hill and society rows, c. 1900

fire hose companies formed teams and competed amongst themselves and against other towns. Prescott was a favorite opponent. This was a popular racing event, especially on the Fourth of July.

Prior to the Chemical Company's formation, the Town had a fund-raising dance to buy a chemical engine for the city. The community was good for fund-raisers and loved to have dances. The Jerome band even had a ball to raise money for their instruments! It has been said that the most popular activity in this town throughout the years has been to drink beer and dance. The Fashion Saloon itself sold 150 kegs in 17 days one summer!

The Fire Department's Annual Ball, traditionally held around the 21st of February, was an excellent fund-raiser, and was often considered the social event of the season. The firemen had dress uniforms, maroon and silver and worn especially at the gala affair. Those men who did not wear uniforms wore evening clothes and gloves. The women got new dresses for the event and they danced with everyone.

Other distractions, designed to make Life more than just work, were the up-town saloons, such as the Fashion, the Senate, Shea's place, and the Manhattan. Intoxicants, card and board games, and light entertaiment were provided. In 1903 Jerome was able to boast having the "Largest and Most Complete Establishment of Its Kind in the Southwest, If Not On the Continent." The Fashion Saloon, now housing the Jerome Historical Society's Mine Museum, advertised its new addition. The JEROME MINING NEWS printed the story, from which the following excerpts are taken:

"This immense establishment now occupies a building with a frontage of 50 feet and a depth of 180 feet, with four floors ... nearly one-half acre of floor spaces on which to accommodate their business. Jerome B. Hoover and Arthur Cordiner, the owners of this establishment, came to Jerome 8 years ago, and purchased what was known as the Stoney lot and a frame building located thereon, being what was and is now conceded to be the best business location in the then camp and now city of Jerome. They made many improvements in the old building, and carried on a successful business there until Sept 11, 1898, when the great fire of that date destroyed their building and its contents, they saving only the stock of goods stored in a fire proof cellar on the hillside.."

Fire struck again on May 19, 1899.

"It was then that the business world appreciated that their motto, 'We Never Sleep,' carried on their stationary, was not meaningless, for before the fire had completed its work of destruction the wires were carrying messages ordering supplies with which to replace the loss, and within 18 months from the date of the fire the mortgage had been released..." The upper floor of the old Fashion is occupied by a bar, gambling tables, a business" office in the front and private card and social rooms in the rear ... A broad flight of stairs lead from this room to the German beer and lunch room below. "The new addition to The Fashion (now occupied by Paul and Jerry's Saloon) is entered either from the main street or through a large archway cut through the south wall of the concrete

building. . .The room has been entirely renovated and refurnished. The bar in this room is a half circle, the only one of its kind in the territory, and is of polished oak, the back bar being an original and elegant design. . .The basement in this part of the house is well lighted and has been fitted for use as a bowling alley. . .In the house there are 11 games of chance in operation, including faro, craps, roulette, monte, stud poker and a Chinese lottery. . .To successfully carry on this business over 30 people are employed, the payroll amounting to considerably over $50,000 per year."

News of sporting events and politics were communicated by wire to the Fashion and interested patrons. The length of the lease on the addition, the old Senate saloon, was 5 years with an option for renewal. The temperature of the town, the territory and soon the nation was to turn cold to gambling, booze and women in saloons. The Fashion never picked up the option after gambling became illegal in Jerome in 1906.

Most of the women of Jerome did not frequent such places. Those who did were usually singers, musicians and entertainers. Not to be confused with the "bad girls" who worked the brothels and back streets, these women were educated, refined, stylish, and cultured. They often married leading men of the community. The Company doctor, Dr. Charles Woods, married a French violinist, an ex-entertainer in a saloon. She also gave children of the community music lessons. At that time it was an insult for a woman of the "elite" to go out and get a job -- but singing was alright. Before she arrived in Jerome, the wife of one of the Company's Bosses heard that the only women in Jerome after the turn of the century were ex-saloon entertainers. She often went to card parties and socials wondering which of the ladies used to work in a saloon. The first "proper" invitation she received after coming to Jerome was engraved, and from the doctor's wife!

After the opening of the United Verde & Pacific Railway in 1894, the population quickly grew to include the wives and families of the Company Bosses and the "common" miners. The little narrow gauge ran six trains daily for the most part. People and goods traveled in and out of Jerome. Boarding and rooming houses were everywhere. The United Verde provided limited housing for its employees and their families. Downhill from the mine plant and smelter were wooden Queen Anne style houses for the Bosses. In later years this area was called Company Hill or Society Row.

Here the "Elite" lived. That is, those who did not own their own houses. The men held such jobs as General Manager, Chief Timekeeper, Chief Engineer, Underground Construction Foreman, and Smelter Superintendent. The women raised their children, managed the household, and often the servants, and involved themselves in church and other social activities.

In-house help was not just for those of the Company Hill. Other families were used to having help do household chores also. The nationalities of the servants varied. Glenellen Minty Ewell recalls Japanese and Chinese cooks. She also recalls how hard it could be to get help to stay. It seems they either could not stand the life in Jerome, or they got married and took care of their own houses, possibly taking in laundry.

One of Glenellen's most vivid memories was of Susie, the local Apache Indian woman who worked for the Minty family on the Hill. Susie lived on the Hogback where there was a little Apache camp of 3 or 4 wigwams. Glenellen relates:

"She was quite a character. She worked for us at times, her niece Maggie too. What a beautiful pianist she was! she was well educated at Carlyle Indian school. There she sat in her bright calicos at our Steinway piano, fingers rippling over the keys, playing a beautiful piece of music! This "wild" Apache!...Susie's husband was John Ketchum. He was one of General Crook's Scouts. "All Indian Squaws wore bright colored skirts, quite full, and under this were 3 or 4 full petticoats. I watched Susie disrobe once when she was to mop our kitchen. These garments neatly folded. Her black under slip was knee length; wore heavy black stockings. (Her) garments peeking through black slip were light color. She seemed to use several large safety pins! I still wonder how they kept so clean! Susie was a good worker and wouldn't use a mop -- floors weren't clean unless scrubbed. There were no gadgets then, like vacuum, etc. Just a broom; carpet sweepers came in later."

It has been said that the social standing of a person was established by where on Cleopatra Hill she lived. This is not necessarily so, as there were fine people living everywhere on the hill. There were, however, different neighborhoods. Company Hill or the Society Rows have been mentioned. South of that area high on Cleopatra was another privately-owned residential area. Here there were a number of multi-family homes, with residents of many different nationalities and professions. The southern residential areas were mostly known by the names of the mining claims they were on: Copper Chief, 16 to 1, Mountain View, and the Florencia. The "Hogbacks" were on the "arm" extending toward the valley. Sturdy concrete and brick houses were built on the Lower Hogback (Hampshire Ave.) by the United Verde Extension mining company for their geologists, warehouse foremen, doctors, comptrollers and such. The wives here also tended to have in-house help, play bridge, tennis, and socialize as much as possible.

The Mexican and/or Spanish people lived together in separate neighborhoods. They were known as El Palomar (below the Hotel Jerome), El Barrio Chicano (below the main commercial district), El Verde (downhill from the Powderbox Church), El Golcho (primarily the upper Gulch Road area known Blue Bend), and La Daisy (the town by the Douglas Mansion created for their workers). Family and church were the main focuses of social activites in these neighborhoods. In isolated communities such as Jerome, people must create their own entertainment when they do not wish to take

Jerome Opera Company presents "The Mikado," Feb. 27, 1906

Apache Indian house servant, c. 1905

The elite ladies socialize c. 1910

advantage of commercial ventures. Before the fires at the turn of the century there had been an Opera House located on the south edge of the commercial district. A finer one was to come.

The T.F. Miller Company, a mercantile store, was originally located in Jerome on the mine road above the Congregational church. Miller, a relative of William Clark, wanted to relocate closer to the commercial district and the growing residential areas. In 1898 a four story brick structure was started. It opened in 1899, and was to house not only the largest mercantile company in town, but also places for businesses on the ground level, a floor for lodge rooms, and a floor large enough for an Opera House facility, complete with stage. The Jerome newspaper of December 11, 1899, announced:

"The new Jerome Opera House will be formally opened next Tuesday and Wednesday evenings December 19 and 20, by America's greatest romantic actor, Paul Gilmore. Manager (Walter) Miller is to be congratulated upon securing such a first-class performance for his opening. Mr. Gilmore will produce Dumas' Immortal Romance, "The Musketeers" on Tuesday evening, and "Don Caesar" on Wednesday evening." "McCarty's Mishaps" was scheduled as the next production, and was billed as the "funniest farce comedy ever written." Another period favorite was the temperance play "Ten Nights in a Barroom."

Later talented local people formed the Jerome Opera Company, performing classics in full costume. The February 27, 1906 program for "The Mikado" gave the following officers and performers of the community: Mrs. C.A. Minty, musical director; R.A. Armstrong, business manager; A.H. Dawson, secretary-treasurer; honorary members Gen. & Mrs. R.H.G. Minty, Rev. & Mrs. H.G. Miller; performers Mrs. L.E. Arnott, Miss Vesta Docker, Misses Faull, Dorland, Fagerland, Johnson and Goodwin, Mrs. A.H. Lyons, Mr. and Mrs. C.V. Brockway, Mr. and Mrs. Mrs. W.C. Miller, E. Brockway, C. Havelin, J.J. Kuder, W.S. Owen, Dr. J.W. Coleman, C.V. Harris, T. Merrill, and Mr. J. Sharp. Mrs. Minty taught vocal and music to serious students, as well as performing warm duets with her husband for their family and friends.

The Opera House facility provided a place for masquerade balls, grand dances for all groups including the annual ball of the Fire Department, and dances for all the societies. Fairs were held to raise funds for churches and charities. And, of course, Jerome was on the Southwestern theater circuit which provided the finest professional performers available to small, isolated communities.

Charlie Brown recalls:

"One time when a Stock Company was giving a play in the Company Store hall, the biggest laugh to ever greet an actor's lines, occured when the Tough Moll was found weeping in her sordid bedroom by her heartless 'Man'. I see him yet! He came into the room with his hat on the back of his head, hands in his jacket pockets, shut the door with his rump, and decisively sneered. 'Well! Water - front Mag crying?' At that sublime

moment, just outside the open window, a burro raised his voice in lamentation of his cruel fate. Oh! It might have been his love-call. One event like that in a life time should be enough for any one. Two such, would be utterly incredible. What could the sobbing voice of a fallen woman do against the He-haw of a melancholy jack-ass."

An Arizona Canary! That is another name for the four legged garbage disposals left to wander nightly on the streets and through the yards of Jerome. Their owners, usually wood haulers, would round them up in the morning, well fed, and put them to another day's work. In later years the children would commandeer a burro for a ride to school or to a friend's house.

A Ladies' Social Union was formed by the women of the "Elite." Its objective was sociability. Calling on each other, attired in hobble skirts, gloves and leaving calling cards, became hard going considering the terrain in the upper part of town. It was decided to meet twice a month in particular homes. Later the gatherings were held at the Congregational church.

The Company Hill wives met often for card games such as 500, bridge and casino. Since the Victorian living room of the Company house was small, they often had to take down the beds, moving them outside with other extraneous furniture to make room for the 4 or 5 tables necessary for the afternoon's games. If and when the weather changed, there was a scurry to get the beds back inside.

Churches provided another location for social activities and fulfilled the need of religion in the now booming mining camp. The Baptists built the church later sold to the Congregationalists. The Catholics had their first edifice above Company Hill, but it burned in the 1898 fire. They soon built a brick church, the Church of the Holy Family, which still stands above town on the old mine road.

The Methodists chose another part of the hill on which to build their sanctuary. In 1899 they provided a Protestant church for the south side of Jerome, in another residential area. The congregation grew, needing a new building 20 years later. Of the various groups who worshiped in Jerome, the Methodist have maintained services to this date.

At first there were few Episcopalians in town. The Congregationalist church was the closer of the two Protestant churches to the homes of these families so they attended services there. In early 1898 General R.H.G. Minty, ex-Civil war leader and Auditor for the narrow gauge railway, started reading services to a group who called themselves the Christ Church. The next year a more "official" church was organized by the Bishop of Arizona. In later years they bought the old church from the Congregationalists. Still later, they built a fine edifice which remains today above the Town Park.

On Sunday afternoons it was customary to pack a picnic lunch and go for a walk on one of the many well-worn trails around

Jerome. A favorite was the hike up Hull's Canyon to Hull's mine, about 3 miles. On a particulary good day, the walk could continue on to Walnut Springs, meeting neighbors and friends there and along the way. Young people adventurously walked the tracks of the narrow gauge or climbed the giant rocks around the Gulch. Hiking was commonplace since automobiles, introduced to Jerome in 1903, were not. Motorcycles were seen more often on the narrow trails. Groups of cyclists would go for an outing, occasionally ending up in Camp Verde or the Montezuma Castle area.

Mercantile stores delivered groceries, which made life easier for many ladies trapped in period clothing. The order could be phoned in since telephones came to Jerome in 1899. Johnny Lyons' market used horses, and the T.F. Miller Company used mules and some saddle horses. The groceries were held in two large baskets, one on each side of the animal. A small child could fit into the 3'x2'x2' and balance an uneven load of goods. Light wagons were used on the wider roads.

The Jerome Gun Club was established, not only to provide a group to go hunting with, but to also provide a club where men could practice shooting clay pigeons. The shooting range was located across lower Main Street from the Methodist church, overlooking Bitter Creek Gulch. This group competed with ones from other towns. In 1899, a Thanksgiving Turkey shoot was held out at Jerome Junction. The target turkey was 26 cents a shot, at 200 yards with an open sight. First prize was $10 and second was $5. The poorest shot of the day got a quart of whiskey. One might wonder which was the better incentive in a camp such as Jerome.

Another source of relaxation for men was a sportsmen's club. Some upstanding citizens, including a bar owner, merchant, and gambler, arranged to "plant" 300 small bass in Peck's Lake. The lake was at that time free of weeds. It was a home for ducks as well as birds, such as doves and quail. Jean Allison, one of the early members, continued the practice of planting various species of fish at popular fishing holes in the Verde Valley and the Oak Creek area. Hunting and fishing were to remain excellent diversions.

Jerome people traveled by horse and wagon to Sycamore Canyon, Oak Creek and the rim country, often seeking cool shade in the hot summers. Some purchased cabins among the tall trees, using them as get-a-ways from the stressful conditions of an active mining life. Johnny Summers, operator of a hauling company located on Hull Ave., purchased property east of Packard's ranch near the entrance to Sycamore Canyon. It was called "Dragoon Canyon Park, Jerome's New Pleasure Resort." There was a spring and stream for fishing. Summers planned to make good roads and open it to the public. It was located 12- 16 miles from Jerome.

The sportsmen also organized the Jerome Boat and Gun club,

Deception Gulch watermelon party c. 1905

Delivering groceries to the Gulch c. 1905

building club and boat houses at Peck's Lake. Baseball games were also held on the flat land around Peck's Lake. Many families would gather for a day's outing.

Glenellen Minty recalls the wonderful picnics at Pecks Lake. Her father, Courtney, would drive the carriage with a team of bay mules. He would pick up family members Laura and Walter Miller, the Minty grandparents, and all the food, and off they would go down the hill. Glenellen would often sit between her father's knees, hold the reins and drive the mules. The ladies would spread out the robes under a shade tree while the men went fishing and the children played. Late in the afternoon they would load up the carriage and start the long trip uphill.

Another sport not thought highly of was badger fighting. An editorial item in the JEROME NEWS of March 5, 1910 is a tongue in cheek story:

"A badger fight was pulled off last night at the same old stand. It was the same old badger, too, and he had been well fed for the occasion. Aside from a dent in his ribs, the result of a hard fall in the last fight, he was in excellent shape. Ed Buehler, an experienced handler of badgers in his old home in the Hoosier state, pulled the chain. Charley Dunham [well-known local wall painter] will give the animal a fresh coat of paint and set it under his bed until another wise gazabo floats in."

The sport had flourished for years, and while this newspaper article brought frowns by fighters, the game continued in the valley for a number of years.

Athletic clubs were started, advocating boxing, and wrestling matches which were held in the Opera House. Jerome also had a football team which successfully challenged various towns. Other men's groups formed were the Knights of Pythias, the GAR, the Mingus Tribe of the Red Men, the Copper Lodge of the AOUW, Masons, Elks, Knights of Columbus, and the American Legion.

People in Jerome came from many nations. Jerome became a small melting pot of different nationalities and ethnic groups. Many formed lodges, or societies, to bond their lives to the old country and their heritage.

In April of 1899 members of the Hispanic community formed Jerome Lodge #13 of the Mutual Society of the Alianza Hispanio Americana Institute, whose headquarters were in Tucson. The local lodge was to remain an important factor in the lives of the Hispanic community into the 1950's. In 1915 the Liga Protectora Latina was formed as a funeral society. Another created later to help families of dead workers, was the Sociedad Regular Colectiva Funeraria y de Ohorro.

In 1901 the Croatian Fraternal Union, Jerome Lodge 138 was created by the natives of Croatia who had taken advantage of the opportunity to go to America to build new lives. The Croatians were known as strong, hard workers, willing to take on the most dangerous jobs above or below ground. In 1894 leading Croatians

Alianza Hispanio Americana float c. 1920

Rosemary DeCamp, movie and television actress

in Pennsylvania organized the society to help families in the event of an accident or death. The Jerome lodge was made up mainly of Croatians, with some Serbians and other Slavs. It went up as high as 130 members depending on the fluctuation of copper production.

In the 1930's the Italian community organized the Cristoforo Columbo Lodge to assist Italian residents in times of need.

The town as a whole celebrated three major holidays: the Cinco de Mayo, Fourth of July and September 16th. The townspeople decorated their homes and buildings with bunting and flags preparing for the occasion. On the Fourth of July local bands played in the bandstand in the center of town. Often Main Street was closed and games, races, greased pig contests, and the drilling contests were held. There were also horse races, sack races, egg races and a race up Cleopatra Hill to water tanks. In the afternoon was the Fire Department's hose cart races and at night there were fireworks.

Miners, like cowboys, often, on holidays, played work- related games, such as mucking races and drilling contests. The JEROME NEWS reported an accident during the September 16th celebration in 1911:

"James Kennedy, one of the drillers, received a blow on the head from a hammer, which accidently broke, and caused his death a few days later. Kennedy, who was drilling with Charley Shull (both expert drillers and held the championship of this district), was holding the drill when the hammer broke, on a downward stroke, and struck him a terriffic blow on the head. . .The force of the blow did not render Kennedy unconscious, in fact, did not affect him the least particle as he kept on drilling with his associate until the time limit and the team won the first prize of $140 cash. After dividing the prize Kennedy left for home and on his arrival there complained of severe pains in the head. He soon became unconscious. . .An operation (was) performed and the skull was found to be fractured. Mr. Kennedy lingered in an unconscious state until Monday, when life became extinct."

Accidents at play were oftentimes smaller examples of those at work. The Hispanic community planned for weeks for Cinco de Mayo and the September Independence Day celebration. They would hold dance benefits in the Opera House to raise the money for the parades and lavish floats. The prettiest Mexican girl was elected by a contest to reign over the festivities. She rode at the head of the parade, followed by beautiful floats, bands, Boy Scouts, and later World War I vets.

The parade course started at the curve next to the Mexican town, the Barrio Chicano. It proceeded down to the United Verde Extension Mine where it turned and took the road that went to the West end of the Hogback. There it started back up the hill onto Main St. The queen dismounted from the float and was escorted to a decorated platform which had been constructed right in front of the Opera House. In later years it was built, by the mining company, on Main Street in front of present-day Paul & Jerry's Saloon. Patriotic speeches began, given in Spanish. Music, food and games continued throughout the day, which climaxed with a ball at the Opera House until dawn.

Theaters and movies were also favorite sources of entertainment. Images, sounds and stories were placed on the screens of no less than six movie houses in Jerome's past. The earliest movies were shown in 1896. The machines were the old kind with flickering images of travelers in wagons struck on the railroad tracks, pushed to safety by heroes, and the big 'Chase' going on for mile after hilarious mile.

Early stage and movie shows were held at the Zaragosa Theater on upper Main Street, run by Santiago Tisnado. Spanish movies were shown as well as live performances of Zarzuelas, Spanish operettas. Zarzuelas were brought to Jerome by Manuel Areu. His son-in-law, Palemon Bablot, and company performed "vaudevilles" between films at the Lyric as well as the Zaragosa. The operetta consisted of spoken dialogue alternating with set musical pieces celebrating Spanish life, which was characterized by the romantic idealization of urban and rural life of middle and lower class Spaniards.

The Coliseum and the Electric Company theaters were also located on Main Street., playing silent films. The Coliseum was owned jointly by Bill Haskins and Phil Pecharich. When their partnership ended, Haskins opened a theater in the new town of Clarkdale. Pecharich expanded his entertainment empire of bars and restaurants to include the new Liberty Theater.

Construction was started on the Liberty Theater in April, 1918. Work did not go smoothly due to the Spanish influenza epidemic that year. It finally opened during the 1918-19 winter. The name, "Liberty", had been selected from those submitted by school children. It was patriotic considering the War To End All Wars was on. The Liberty originally had a concave nickelodeon-style front, with a ticket booth in the center. The entrance was on the east side, leading to the main floor or the balcony. The theater, which still stands on Jerome Ave., was built at a cost of approximately $80,000. This was reportedly recouped in the first year of operation. Advertisements from 1919 tell of two shows daily, 7:30 and 9:00. Admission was generally 30, 20 or 10 cents for main floor, balcony seats, or children, respectively. The instrument played at the Liberty Theater to accompany the silent movies had 90 stops, like bells, thunder, pistol shots, etc. The cue cards would come with the film. The piano player would get it the night before to coordinate the song to the scene. For a day's work the player often made $4.

In November of 1918 John D. Johnson bought the Joseph Thorbeck building, on Main Street. Johnson and his cousin had been running the Modern Cafe. They planned on extending the existing building to Hull Ave, making it about 137 feet deep. They also added another story. When they purchased the building, the Jerome Mercantile Co. was on the first floor and the Miners' Union was below the Main Street level. The cousins built an elaborate silent movie theater, opening in March of 1920. They noted that "talkies" were coming, and prepared to add sound equipment. The mortgage was held by the Bank of Jerome. It failed in the middle 1920's, leaving the Johnsons with many financial problems.

The novelty of sound films proved to be a death blow to the Liberty. Pecharich took advantage of the Bank of Jerome's failure and leased the Lyric Theater. He eventually bought it and changed the name to "Ritz". The Ritz opened with newly upholstered seats, on November 14, 1929. The Liberty was closed as a theater by early 1930. The first floor interior and facade were changed. Pecharich rented the street level as a cafe. The main theater room and balcony have remained pretty much the same ever since.

From time to time movie companies would take advantage of the wide open spaces and sensational scenery in the Verde Valley area. Movie star Rosemary DeCamp, who grew up in Jerome and whose father was General Manager, recalls scenes from her childhood in her book WIND 'EM UP:

"One year Harry Carey came to Jerome and made a picture called "East is East" about a tenderfoot easterner trying to make it, in old Arizona. Everyone in the town felt involved becaused they used some of the mining camp people in the crowd scenes.

"One night my folks bundled me up and took me down to the old mine shaft where the company was shooting. I was pretty young and sleepy, but I'll never forget the sizzling white lights shining down on the leading lady. She was sitting on a pile of rocks by the mouth of a tunnel. At first I thought she must be an Indian because of all the paint on her face, white and black, and her eyes were rimmed all around with blue. Her mouth was dark red. Her hair was pretty though, kind of fuzzy-blonde and long. The best part was the accordion music. They had a fellow there playing gypsy songs. It sounded so lovely in the warm night. My mother explained that the actress had to cry and the music was supposed to bring tears. Well, sure enough, as soon as the camera started grinding, that girl's eyes ran rivulets. Some of the paint ran, too. Then they would stop and mop her face, paint it some more, and do it all again. I finally fell asleep, but years later when I had to weep in front of the camera, I wished for that gypsy music.

"The best part of the Harry Carey episode was the 'take-off', my dad and some of the mine executives put together. It was called 'Yeast is Yeast' and was all about a moonshiner and his daughter being chased by the 'revenooers.' I don't know how it got filmed and processed, but the result was weird. It was all black and white, no grays, and very jerky. My mother said it made her seasick to look at it. . .kind of like some of the 'hand held' jobs we see today."

The Jerome newspaper, VERDE COPPER NEWS, wrote extensively about the "home grown, home written, home acted, and home filmed picture." E.E. Kunselman, a cameraman from Phoenix, was employed to film, develop, edit, and make subtitles for the movie. Many well known people of Jerome were drafted as actors. The filming started about 10 a.m. at the Jerome Transfer company barn by the Hotel Jerome. Miss Ann Housten, Scotty Mitchell, Matt Shea and other members of the troupe were made up at photographer Gottlieb's studio under the direction of Miss "Doc" Davis formerly of Universal. The VERDE COPPER NEWS tells the gist of the script:

"Scotty sold his elaborate cowpuncher outfit to Matt for $10, retaining only his trusty revolver, presumably because he wanted to find which end the bullet came out of. He kissed the burro, Isador, a fond good-by, and went away to spend the tenner."

"Yeast Is Yeast" was shown in Clarkdale but not heard of since.

During World War I, the mining town became a prosperous two-mine town where people's spirits were light and flirtatious. The United Verde Extension mining company had struck ore just in time for the war needs. There were more single professional people in town desirous of social activities. Teachers, usually young ladies fresh out of Arizona and other states' Normal Schools, were considered very important in the social activities in Jerome. There were also a number of young geologists and mining engineers from Yale, Carnegie Tech, Michigan, and Golden, Colorado mining schools, brought specifically to work on the open pit project at the United Verde.

Ellen Hopkins, school music teacher in 1916 and 1917, found living accommodations limited. She and a roommate were allowed to temporarily live in the Guild Hall of the Episcopal Church, which was located on the mine road. The young engineers and geologists would take the opportunity after work to stop in for tea with the eligible young women.

The new teachers were escorted by "old-timers" to the Opera House to attend the first dance of the school year. There they would meet, formally, the eligible young men working at the mine. Dance programs were filled within minutes, and arrangements were made for further get-togethers such as hikes, picnics and dances.

In August of 1917, while on a hike to Mescal canyon, two young Jerome ladies decided to refresh themselves by taking a dip in the stream. A monsoon-caused flood occurred, taking their belongings along with the water downhill. An ad in the classified section of the August 27th JEROME SUN read:

"REWARD: for the shoes and stockings and other wearing apparel belonging to two young ladies who were bathing in Mescal yesterday just prior to the flood. The owners are willing to pay good and substantial reward for the return of same as they are keepsakes."

The next days SUN ran the following ad:

"WANTED: to know what reward will be given the person who finds

the clothes which were lost in the flood in Mescal Canyon Sunday. Certain gentleman would be glad to attempt search if the reward is sufficient. Will the lady please furnish information, who lost the garments?''

And the day after:

"REWARD: The young ladies who lost their wearing apparel last Sunday in Mescal flood beg to say that pleasure is its own reward and the person who finds their clothing may have the pleasure of returning same to them.''

B. Brooks, writer of "Babbling Brooks in the Desert" column in the same issue of the SUN, ends the drama with this quip at two adventurous mining men in town:

"They say around town that Tom Finnerty and Louis Ferber are in on that reward for the clothes that were washed away. Some doubt if the clothes were washed away at all. Just keep your eye on Tom Finnerty and Louis Ferber.''

Owing to the town's prosperity, parties and dances became more lavish and frequent. There were 3 or 4 young men, calling themselves the Jolly Bachelors, who alone ran dances almost every other weekend. They saw a need and organized the events, hiring local bands to provide the music.

Another active group in town was the Business and Professional Women's Club. Helen Beck Droubay, who came as a new teacher, was a member and remembers some of the fun:

"Many of the married women in camp were ex-teachers or ex-nurses so there was a feeling of companionship and unity. . .The new teachers and nurses soon joined. The club members met once a month for dinner, business and bridge. The mining company paid a very good cook to prepare the dinner and it was held in the clubhouse the company provided.

"We had a Bride's Dinner every spring, not long after school was out. There were nearly always quite a few weddings at the end of the school year. A special dinner was prepared, and a special table was arranged for the engaged members. They were given a program of skits, dances and songs. We worked for a month or so making parodies on the popular songs of the day.

"One year, the Business and Professional Women's Club decided to give a masquerade ball with a pirate motif. The company sent their carpenters to Miller's Hall and they made port holes out of all the windows and painted old tires as life preservers and hung them in the hall. They even constructed a gang plank from the street to the entrance of the hall. We ladies collected barrels and old bottles as decorations. With everybody in costume, it seemed to release all inhibitions, and the affair turned into a bigger brawl than the ''Fireman's Brawl.'' One lady said to the school superintendent, 'Did you see how drunk Miss Burns was?' 'No, I didn't,' he answered. 'I guess I left my glasses home.'

Members of the group rented a room provided in Sauer's Telephone Company building on Clark St. They would have card games and other social activities. Card tables and chairs were furnished, but the silver, dishes, linen and food had to be brought in. Many other dances were held in this facility.

The Business Women's club opened an employment exchange at the club room to bring together, without expense, women who had work to be done and women who were anxious to secure employment. Competent and worthy applicants would be sent to prospective employers as all would be investigated by Miss Buckley, the Red Cross nurse. The club also had a student loan fund.

New men's and women's organizations were formed, adding to the enjoyment of the increasing population in Jerome and the Verde Valley. The Jerome Lodge No. 1361 of the Elks was formed in 1919. A town census was required before they could be organized. One was taken by the Town government. It showed a population of 8409 persons, in town. The Elks' peak membership came in April of 1926 when there were 451 members. When the United Verde mine closed, the lodge moved to Clarkdale and is still active there. The Elks also had a scholarship fund for Jerome students.

The Alexander Moisa Chapter of the American Legion held dances and benefits in the Opera House. It dissolved shortly after the United Verde closed in March of 1953.

In November of 1922 the Rotary Club of Jerome, forerunner of the Verde District Rotary Club, was organized. It was admitted to membership in Rotary International on Jan. 3, 1923. Good deeds by this group include student loans, a junior baseball team, free employment agency for boys and girls, child welfare efforts, Community chest and civic welfare, highway safety, and a golf tournament and picnic. The women sponsored the local Camp Fire Girls, Fourth of July fireworks, Home Defense, March of Dimes, Heart Fund, Rotary Fund, Civil Defense. The group was renamed the Verde District Club in 1951 in Clarkdale.

The Kiwanis of Clarkdale-Verde district was formed in June of 1925 at the Legion hall in Clarkdale, and still exists.

With automobiles becoming more economically possible, Jerome turned more and more to the Valley and its rims for outings. The road to Stoneman's Lake outside of Flagstaff was being put in first class condition. Stoneman's lake was a favorite outing place for people of the Verde district because of its excellent fishing. Valley rodeos began in May. Valley roundups were held at Spring Creek, White Flats for the Upper Oak Creek round up, and the T-Bar roundup at Camp Verde. The Clarkdale Country club opened a golf course in 1917. Later another 9 hole course was created and a clubhouse built. A bull fight was held in Clarkdale by the river. It was not well received, and that was probably why it was the only one noted in the local newspapers.

In May of 1922, the Federal Forest Service appropriated money for building the necessary roads to open the top of Mingus Mountain within the next year. From the summit of the Prescott-

Jerome highway, there extends to the east a broad mesa, more than 1000 acres, that is almost perfectly flat. The proposed improvements included golf links, tennis courts, baseball grounds, cottage buildings, and a fine clubhouse. The highway between Prescott and Jerome had been realigned and graded in 1920, offering a better route between the two towns. A road to the top of the San Francisco peaks was started, later laying open the mountain top for winter sports. Another favorite picnic spot was Montezuma's Castle, which was, at that time, a magnificent Indian ruin, not yet a National Monument.

The Verde Hot Springs Hotel company announced that it was building a hotel to be ready by November 1, 1928. It was located about 35 miles from Jerome. The curative properties of the Spring water had been known for years, and would be available for the guests of the hotel in baths and for drinking.

A permit to hold wrestling matches within the city limits was granted by the Town Council. In 1936 a Town Boxing Commission was established. Boxing, wrestling and baseball were always favorites among Jerome men, especially those who liked to gamble on the outcome. A well-known fight promoter opened a barber shop in Fischer's Pool Hall on Main Street. The American Legion formed the Verde District Athletic Club, planning on promoting fights. The fighters had names such as Battling Curly, T-Bone Firbo of Jerome and Kid Chow of Prescott. While a favorite with the men, women of the town had trouble seeing the attraction. A VERDE COPPER NEWS issue of April, 1920, printed a letter from one female spectator. We offer excerpts from "Bestial Brutality of Beefy Bruisers Brings Blush to Bessie's Brazen Brow":

"Dearest Anna: If you will promise honest to gawd not to tell ma or any of the home folks, specially Rev. mister Esop Hucklepenny, I am agoing to tell you a secret, and I rely on you as a lady not to tell anybody. Except maybe Geraldine and Helen and of course the boys. Now don't throw a fit I know you are a excitable nervous sort of girl not a bit like me always calm and cool like a horseradish. Well, I been to a prize fight! Last night there was a swell film in town, and I says to Frank, lets go and he says have you plum forgot there is a fight at the opera house and I am going. And what am I agoing to do all the evening I says and Frank uses a sware word and says all right I suppose you can come along but I should think you would rather stay home and read the Ladies Home Journal, he not realising about woman's rights and hunger strikes and everything. Well, we went and had seats right next to the ring and what do you think, Anna, there ain't any ring at all its a square platform with ropes tied around it all decorated with red while and blue real tasty like the handkerchief booth I and you had at the busy bee bazar. Only there wasn't any handkerchiefs at this affair, and when they began to get bloddy noese I reached mine up to one of them poor fellows, but he didn't have any pocket or handbag to put it in so he had to get along without it. But I am away ahead of where I am.

You can imagine how I felt, me teaching in Sunday school and past exalted junior sister of our chapter and everything, and there I was just like one of these here demmy mondanes or vamps or adverturesses, and me a respectable married woman. I had on my new crape desheen and a large leghorn hat faced with pink which always brings out the natural bloom I am forced to use on my cheeks since the flu and being married to Frank... Well Frank says going home you have seen three good clean fights Bess and I give you my word Anna I never saw such a dirty bloody crowd in my life as these boys were when they finished each other. But you know how men are Anna only of course you don't but it isnt your fault that you are nearsighted and wear a No. 46 and I always did say you had a grand character. Fondest love from your true friend Bessie.''

Jerome in its best days had a champion basketball team and leading baseball club. In May of 1925 the Northern Arizona Baseball League was organized. The United Verde supported baseball teams in Clarkdale as well as Jerome for a number of years. The sister cities became quite competitive. Once a professional player, Hal Chase was hired as trainer. A big controversy started because Chase had been banned from major league baseball for his involvement in the 1919 Black Sox scandal. The Jerome team's winning that Fall pacified the people who had objected to the hiring of Chase.

Later only one Verde Valley team was formed. The Copperheads were headquartered in Clarkdale. Jerome maintained its home team, the "Miners", which was in the minor league. Other teams were incorporated into a Twilight league made up of the National and American leagues. In the National were: Miller's, Miners Meat Mkt., Steamshovel, Selna's grocery. The American league consisted of Scott and McMillan, Service Drug, Speakezy club, and the Victory Grocery nine. Games were played on the Clark Field located on dump land out Perkinsville Road (now site of the Gold King Mine Museum), and the 300 level diamond near the swimming pool and tennis courts.

The United Verde company provided three swimming pools for Jerome. In 1922 the first, located 3 miles outside of town on the road to Prescott at Walnut Springs, was opened. During summer months many people packed lunches and walked out the road or the more adventurous hiked up Hull's canyon past the Verde Central mine to the cool, popular swimming hole.

In 1928 a large pool was opened on the 300 level. The area became so crowded that the company felt compelled to make arrangements to control the use of the pool. The headlines emphasized the separation of the "Races". It was announced in the August 10, 1928, VERDE COPPER NEWS that:

"...due to congested situation of new swimming pool at 300 level separate periods have been set aside for swimmers of the American and Mexican colonies. Beginning next Sunday night, the water will be changed and the Americans will be permitted to use the pool exclusively until Thursday noon, at which time another water change will be made and the Mexicans will have the use of the tank until Sunday night. This system will be followed throughout the summer. The United Verde Pool

at Walnut Springs will be conducted as usual with no special periods set aside for segregation of races.''

At the same time a pool in the Mexican neighborhood by Juarez and Conglomerate Streets was being built. It was advertised that a clubhouse was also being built. The opening made the newspaper:

''The pool is identical in construction to the American pool on the 300 level, the change room containing every modern convenience is provided in close proximity. The length of pool is 30x70 feet, depth 2-1/2 to 9-1/2.''

Alfredo Mayagoitia read Mr. Tally's message:

''Many of our oldest and most faithful employees, many of our best workmen, many of our valued friends, are members of the Mexican colony. We take pride in the fact that you are good citizens and are always ready to work and support any movement for the public good.''

The Mexican community continued to have organizations separate from the Anglos. The Gloria a Juarez No. 20, a Mexican Masonic lodge, was formally installed in 1928 at the Miller lodge rooms. It was named in commemoration of a Mexican hero. The Anglo Masonic Order joined with this new lodge in celebrations.

Mexican Boy Scouts troop was formed in February of 1928. In early 1926 a Boy Scouts camp at Peck's Lake, named Camp Taylor was created. Forty years later the Town of Clarkdale leased and turned it into a recreation & picnic spot. The Jerome Scout Troop No. 223, formed in 1917, attended state gatherings, often bringing home trophies from field days and round-ups.

The Hispanic people, adults and children provided much music for the people of Jerome from night serenading to organized bands and orchestras. Juan Ortiz and Alberto Castaneda promoted a youth band to continue their playing music during the summer. It was called the Reception Band because it practiced in Barragan's Reception Pool Hall on Jerome Ave. Mr. Tally agreed to sponsor the band.

Lily S. Hernandez reports in her paper LOS PIONEROS MEXICANOS:

''A professional musician, Anastasio Mercado, music professor in Mesticacan, Mexico, came to Jerome and organized another band with his countrymen, all were musicians in Mexico. This was called the ''Miner's Band''. . .The Miner's Band played in town on Wednesdays and the Reception Band played on Sundays. . .They set up across the street from Paul & Jerry's on (a special platform).''

They also performed at street festivals and dances. Another popular group was the Kopper Kids.

Hispanic social clubs were: El Club Orquidia, all girls; Santa Cecilia, catholic coed club; and El Club Deportivo for men only and including a Sports Director, Luis Najera, who had been a pro-boxer.

KCRJ was a 100 watt, 130 KC radio station which went on the air in Jerome on June 12, 1930. K-Charles-Robinson- Jerome was originated in the Charles Robinson Jewelry Store on Main Street.

Jack Lynch and William A. Clark, III by the airplane they died in, 1932

John's Place, a favorite watering hole, 1941

It was on from 8 a.m. to 6 p.m., providing records, news and announcements. A Spanish hour was established, which featured live music by local entertainers. A tower was constructed on the Hog back by the cemetery. Later the station was moved to a near-by house. Its programs were heard for miles around, and operated into the 1940's, under the ownership of the Stuarts of Prescott.

The sport of aviation gathered enthusiasm in the late 1920's. William A. Clark III, heir to the United Verde, was an advocate of flying, and of a major airport in the Verde Valley. His dream was for the valley to have an international airport. Clark and his friend, noted flight instructor, Jack Lynch, were killed in May of 1932 in a Sunday crash near the foothills. An airport in Clemenceau had been established in 1928, and a group of anxious aviators was formed.

Lois Ward, Prescott area aviatrix, tells the story of Manuel Guiterrez of the Jerome Victory Market. Manuel bought an Eagle Rock aircraft and got Ersel Garrison to try to teach him to fly. Evidently Manuel did not have the proper depth perception to land.

"One day while flying around the pattern, the instructor told him to use a patch of weeds as a reference point on the ground and that could guide him to a proper approach. It worked so well that Manuel was in-spired to fix a permanent aid to his navigation. He took a pickle barrel from his store, painted it, and hauled it out in his delivery truck to an appropriate spot beyond the end of the runway...as a white marker for reference...Everything went smoothly, his landings became classic...One of (his good buddies) moved the pickle barrel. Manuel had to execute a go-around. His approach was all wrong. Again he got instructions and learned to fly the new pattern. About the time he got the new approach perfected, one of the boys moved the barrel again. In his despair Manuel was heard to say 'son-of-a-gun! I just get the landing down pat and that barrel, it moved again!' Eventually he landed the aircraft in an arroyo at the end of the runway and smashed it."

Not all flights ended in disasters. Air shows and air carnivals were held at the small airport. Fund-raisers were held, offering short, scenic flights to be paid according to the passenger's weight. The pleasure of flying is still enjoyed in the Verde Valley.

Meanwhile, back on earth, the Jerome Public Library was taking a firm hold on the new quarters in the old hospital, remodeled as a library and clubhouse in 1928. By that time it contained between 6000 and 7000 well selected volumes. It had been moved from a small facility in the Hampton House to almost half of the ground floor in what has become known as the Clubhouse Hospital.

At the turn of the century there had been Clark's Revolving Library which provided citizens with some reading material. A number of town women petitioned the Town Council to look into getting a Carnegie Foundation library. The attempt to interest Carnegie in Jerome was unsuccessful.

The credit for starting a public library has been given to Mrs.

Val De Camp. She started the present library in a small store room in the Hampton House. The work was entirely volunteer at that time. Most of the books were donated by the townspeople, and were old.

The VERDE COPPER NEWS special Clubhouse issue gives credit to Mr. Val De Camp for getting the facility for the workers and other residents in the busy town. In the April, 1930 issue of THE MINING CONGRESS JOURNAL, "Recreation in the Verde District" by Noel Pegues, conservatively describes the Clubhouse in Jerome:

> *"The clubhouse has a large men's lounge containing pool and billiard tables, a soda fountain and card room, a ladies' lounge and card room, and a small ballroom which is used for dinners and dances."*

Miss Pegues' article gives a 1930 description of the recreation facilities provided for the workers and citizens of Jerome, Clarkdale, and the entire the Verde Valley, which had been provided by the United Verde Copper Company.:

> *"At Peck's Lake, around which the Verde Valley Golf Club course is laid, a public playground has been established. Swings, teeters, merry-go-rounds, and other paraphernalia for childish enjoyment have been installed. Similar equipment is provided in the public park on the 300 foot level in Jerome. Four swimming pools have been built and are operated and maintained by the copper company. At both Jerome and Clarkdale pools are provided for the Mexican population as well as the American. There are club houses at both towns for the Mexican employes, and these too are operated without profit by the company. Oak Creek Canyon, scenery, fine trout fishing, cottage resorts throughout the 12 mile canyon...Stoneman and Mormon lakes popular, bass and perch fishing, virgin pine forest, summer resort...Mingus Mountain, maintained by Forest Service and picnic benches, tables, fireplaces, etc., are provided by the company. The nine-hole golf course within a mile of Clarkdale...all grass fairways, and being built around Peck's Lake, has the only natural water hazards of any course in Arizona...beautiful club house, with men's and women's locker rooms, a large lounge, dining room and kitchen, dance pavilion, erected as a part of the William A. Clark Memorial ...both motor and row boats are housed at Peck's Lake, excellent course for the speedy crafts. There are four tennis courts in Jerome, located near the park and the swimming pool."*

During the lean Depression years at the beginning of the 1930's, these recreation areas became very important. The mining companies tried to employ as many men for part-time as possible. Families would go to the pools, playgrounds and tennis courts, socializing with others in the same situation. It was commonplace for midday or evening meals to be pot-lucks, each family contributing what it could. This is another part of Jerome's life found years later, in the 1950's and 1970's when times were again lean.

The Dynky Lynx Miniature Golf course was located in the Town
.Park area between the Bank of Jerome and Miller's Store in the

very early 1930's. The property was owned by the United Verde, but the golf course was managed by D.L. Bouse. Its popularity was intense but short lived in Jerome. Such prefabricated courses were a phenomenon of the Depression. They were all over the country. The miniature golf craze came back in the 1950's, but by that time the Dynky Lynx had disappeared, replaced by grass, trees and shrubbery.

This Town Park area has always been a spot of relaxation and recreation for residents and visitors. In early days, wood and barrel benches were set up around the gazebo, where people could listen to the music or watch the parade or games on Main Street. The Workers Progress Administration workers of the late 1930's built a strong stone wall to hold up Clark Street, laid out a grassy park, and constructed the large stone steps we see today. These steps make excellent seats for the Main Street show.

Another valley resort was called Geary Heights. Patrick Geary had homesteaded land between Clarkdale and Cottonwood. His daughter Helen, who was an entertainer in Jerome, around Arizona and other states, returned in the middle 1930's and created a dime-a-dance club. There was a bar, restaurant, and 50 feet by 60 feet dance floor in the main building. There were also cottages one could rent for private entertaining. The waitresses wore skirts to the knees and were reportedly school teachers. Music was provided by a juke box and local bands, but out of town bands often played. There were other dance halls and clubs in Cottonwood, Clemenceau and Clarkdale, but Geary Heights was perhaps one of the most extensive for its time.

School activities were of interest to parents and other citizens. School programs often provided the only evening's entertainment. Sports were of interest, and occasionally bet upon. Plays and musicals were held in the High School auditorium. One successful production held in the Jerome High School in 1935, was a program complete with drill team exhibition featuring a magnificent display of flags. After the presentation, there was a dance at the Opera House. Jesus Franco was the director, and Socorro Sahagun, the baton-leader.

Children usually find their own diversions from school and home life. At the turn of the century and the next decade or so, some children up on the hill were required to take dancing, art, piano, and sometimes voice lessons. Traveling carnivals and circuses, along with local fairs and water carnivals at the pools, were special attractions. An amusement area off Hull Avenue was run for a short time in the early 1920's. Some activities not previously mentioned are: the Aztec Roller Skating rink at Clemenceau, another later in Jerome at the old Gulch school, bowling alleys, special interest clubs such as the Jerome Junior Philatelic Club, and the indoor target range of the Verde Valley Rifle & Pistol Club, located under the Lyric/Ritz Theater, with the entrance on Hull Ave.

Looking south on Main Street, c. 1930

Dynky Lynx Miniature Golf Course, c. 1931

Mining activity was quiet at the United Verde for most of the 1930's. The United Verde Extension was on its way out of business because of a lack of profitable ore. Stores were closing uptown due, in part, to a lack of business, and, in part, to the large amount of ground movement occurring. A combination of underground mining activity, large dynamite and black powder blasts, and water and other liquids added to the ground, contributed to ground movement. Many homes were lost due to the unsettling land. The effects were the worst in the commercial district. Dozens of business structures were damaged and eventually demolished in the area East of Main Street. The Lyric/Ritz Theater, located on that side towards Town Hall, had moved substantially by 1935. It was reinforced in December, but continued to slide dramatically. One could watch a movie and see the sky through the cracks in the walls at the same time. The Town government took steps to close it as a public place. Two professional opinions as to the building's stability were given to the Town Council.

A letter from Lester A. Byron, Architect, Phoenix, dated March 2, 1936 made this analysis:

"I have examined the property known as the Ritz Theater, and operated and owned by Mr. Phil Pecharich, for the purpose of recommending to your honorable body such disposition as should be made of this building in the interests of public safety . . . (The) average slippage of bearing soil in this area is at the approximate rate of 1/2 inch down and 1/2 inch to East per month . . . (There has been) settlement in (the) pavement which was leveled late in 1935. Cracks in (the) East wall materially increased since last rain; (The) floor of (the) basement shows difference in elevation of 1'-8". . . In consideration of the above facts, the deplorable present condition of this structure, the rapid failure which has recently taken place, and finally in the interest of safeguarding public life, I recommend that this building be closed against occupancy of any nature and that it be torn down."

T. B. Stewart, Jr. was another builder who had been involved with the construction of schools and buildings in Jerome and Clarkdale, including the Douglas Mansion. Regarding the Lyric-Ritz Theater building stability he writes:

"In conclusion, I appreciate that Jerome offers some striking examples of the extent to which buildings may be racked and distorted without falling. In this case, too, while I believe the odds are all against it, this structure may stand for some little time yet. On the other hand, all indications and presumptions are to the contrary, and I must recommend against its further use for the present purpose."

Phil Pecharich agreed to tear the structure down. By June 15th of the same year he had opened the 700 seat new Ritz Theater on the corner of Jerome and Hull Avenues. It was built from plans by Del Webb. This last active theater in Jerome was closed about 1950 and demolished as an unnecessary building within a few years.

The United Verde Extension mine closed in 1938. Workers moved to other mining towns or to California, seeking new occupations. Jerome's population fell drastically. As the rumors that the United Verde mine (now owned by Phelps Dodge) was going to close soon circulated, other people took the opportunity to leave. Some remained, content to remain in the small town which had provided them with so much throughout the years. Card games, socials, dances and clubs continued with less members. The Clubhouse was still open, as were the upper floors of the Miller building. Before and during World War II, there were still many recreational facilities found in and near Jerome.

In 1945 Phelps Dodge closed the Clubhouse. Mrs. Annie G. Minhinnick, the librarian, left for the coast. Mrs. Charlotte Gardner was asked to take over the library which was being moved to a room on Main Street under Miller's store. The salary was meager, $75 each month with another $300 allocated for new books, magazines and papers. To one like Mrs. Gardner who loved books and reading, there was no question of what she would do.

The company officials approached her again in 1949, this time discussing the closing of the library. The company could no longer pay a librarian. Mrs. Gardner volunteered to take care of it for nothing but there was a rule against volunteers. She suggested the Star Club of the Diamond Chapter No. 7 of the Eastern Star take over responsibility for the library. They did and she stayed on until she left Jerome in 1952.

The books were put into storage until 1958. The Jerome Historical Society turned over the old Music Store building on Main Street to the Town of Jerome with the provision that it will be used as a public library. Repairs were made and the books were moved again. Through the efforts of the Community Service Organization, the Friends of the Library, county and local government funding, and the free rent and utilities provided by the Historical Society, the Jerome Public Library still offers the joys of reading, now in the basement of the old Fashion Saloon.

In March of 1953, Phelps Dodge ceased mining production at the United Verde mine. Social activity almost stopped. Since the Town of Jerome was still incorporated, there were still civic duties and responsibilities to be handled. The people who wished to stay and help formed the Jerome Historical Society in the attempt to preserve and perpetuate Jerome and her colorful mining history. The Society and the Town became the Chamber of Commerce and initiated an intense publicity campaign to tell about historical old Jerome. With the mining wages gone, the Tourist Dollar was needed as another source of income to keep the town alive. Social activity centered on this goal and the creation of a mine museum in the old Fashion Saloon. A number of mining artifacts were brought into town and placed at various locations for the interested visitors. Town members wrote publicity, distributed it and made countless black and white routed signs advertising America's Largest Ghost City.

Pot-lucks and fund raising dances were held. The dances did not make much, but the people were united in the effort to save Jerome. The annual reunion, originally scheduled for Halloween Night was started in 1953. This homecoming is still attended by hundreds of ex-Jeromites who come back in October.

Newcomers "discovered" Jerome. They took advantage of the cheap houses for sale, and fixed them up. The town slowly stabilized. The Community Service Organization was formed by concerned citizens in 1966. Their objective was to help the town government with community projects which could not be supported by tax monies. One of the important fundraisers created was the Annual Home Tour started in 1966. This event is still being carried on in May by the CSO and the Chamber of Commerce. Money from sales of the Jerome Copper Camp Cookbook, sponsored by this group, go to help the water and sewer systems.

In the late 1960's more and more people, wandering and looking for a quiet place to live, arrived in Jerome. At first the young people were not accepted because of their hair length, their clothes and their style of living. They, the "hippies" as they were called, found their own friends to socialize with. The Town fathers and mothers, and these young people stayed separate for many years. Private social gatherings were conducted in homes. Occasionally pot-luck dinners were held. Uptown the two bars, now called the Spirit Room and Paul & Jerry's, never lost a beat. As in the early days of Jerome, it was still a city of booze drinkers. Juke boxes provided music for the customers and the teenagers now danced in Rock and Roll. While visitors to the town swore there were only a handful of inhabitants, the population actually was counted at a little over 200 at its lowest.

By 1970 the population was approaching 300. The town was still quiet, with at least three separate groups of people in residence. The old-timers from Jerome's historic past were one group; a number of artists and writers, new to Jerome and generally in their 40's and 50's, were another; and the third, the long hairs who had lived mainly in the Gulch but were gradually moving into the apartment houses uptown. Each had their own sources of entertainment. The Valley provided many clubs, theaters and activities from bars to bowling. And, of course, there was television!

Concern for the deterioration of the historic buildings and civic affairs brought the three groups together in the 1970's. They learned to trust each other, united in the desire to keep Jerome on its feet. Pot-lucks became larger, drawing in representatives of the various groups. Music was live at the bars. The Verde Valley Art Association, a cultural center in Jerome since 1953, drew more of the different segments together with opening nights and new art shows. Many of the newcomers were art-oriented. New shops were opened and the Jerome Chamber of Commerce was reorganized. It has sponsored many arts and crafts fairs, antique shows and an annual

Hull Ave. entrance to Verde Valley Rifle & Pistol Club in rear of Lyric / Ritz Theater during demolition, 1936

Music Festival held at the mine's 300 level, in the effort to draw more appreciation and revenue for Jerome.

The Jerome Volunteer Fire Department still has an annual dance. Nowadays it is a masquerade dance on Halloween. There is also a barbecue fund-raiser towards the end of summer. They don't pull hose carts around much any more. The men and women now have been trained in every aspect of firefighting which might occur in this town. Weekly drills keep them on their toes.

Jerome was designated an official United States Bicentennial City on her 100th birthday in 1976. The Jerome Bicentennial and Restoration Commission was started. It was intent on the stabilization of the Victorian houses on the hill and the United Verde apartments. The Historical Society joined in this effort by obtaining a ten year lease from Phelps Dodge on the buildings.

The Jerome Historical Society has remained an important organization, dedicated to the preservation and dissemination of Jerome's colorful history. Through its efforts, and those of numerous friends of Jerome, the entire town was recognized for its historical significance to the state and country, when it was designated a National Historic Landmark in late 1966 by the U.S. Department of the Interior. The Douglas Mansion had been opened as the Jerome State Historic Park in 1965. It had been donated to the State of Arizona by James and Lewis Douglas in honor of their grandfather, father and uncle.

There are not anywhere near the number of clubs and organizations existing for the entertainment of people in Jerome now as there were in its more active, boomtown days. There is but a ghost of its former population on the streets today. The buildings have been decreased by almost half. Yet, there is a feeling, an essence if you will, of the old, unique Billion Dollar Copper Camp still around. You will find it, like a spook at night, when you least expect it. How could there not be, with so much having been done, by so many, for so long!

BIOGRAPHY

Nancy R. Smith, having been born, raised and educated on the East Coast, Nancy R. Smith followed an old dream to Arizona in 1970. Settling in historic Jerome in 1972, she became a part of the community bent on the preservation of Jerome and its colorful history. In 1981 Ms. Smith entered public life when she became a member of the Town's Design Review Board. She has continued to give volunteer time to the Town through this board, Planning and Zoning, and the Town Council.

Ms. Smith is employed as Archivist by the Jerome Historical Society, and as Archivist by the Camp Verde Historical Society. Her interests center on the history of the people and historic structures, using archives and records management and oral history to further the gathering and dissemination of area history.

Ms. Smith writes for and oversees the publication of the Jerome Historical Society's Quarterly THE JEROME CHRONICLE. She has presented papers at four of the Society's last annual symposia, which have been published by the Jerome Historical Society, and at the 1989 convention of the Arizona Historical Society in Yuma. Her Yuma paper was later published in Tucson Westerner's SMOKE SIGNALS. She also compiled a Jerome Design Review Guideline handbook, published by the Town of Jerome and the State Historic Preservation Office.

Ms. Smith is the mother of two daughters and spends her spare time with them or tinkering on her cars.

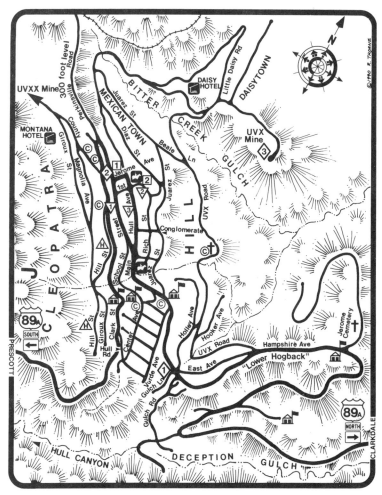

OLD JEROME

◇ Points of Interest: 1) Fred Hawkins House, 2) T.F. Miller Co. Bldg., 3) Douglas Mansion.

▽ Jailhouses in order 1, 2, and 3

© Major Churches ✝ Cemeteries

⚕ Hospitals ☐ Red Light Districts in Order 1 and 2

🏛 Schools 🐎 Livery Stables

267

BIBLIOGRAPHIES

Chapter One

The Starthrower by Loren Eiseley: Harcourt Brace Jovanovich, 1978.

Plateau Magazine of the Museum of Northern Arizona, volume 60, number 3. Copyright 1989

Roadside Geology of Arizona by Halka Chronic: Mountain Press Publishing Company, 1983.

A Guide to Exploring Oak Creek and the Sedona Area by Stewart Aitchison: RNM Press, 1989.

The U.S. Geological Survey, 1909 surveys of the Verde Valley.

The Ecological Conscience, Values for Survival edited by Robert Disch: Prentice Hall, Inc.

Ruins Along the River by Carle Hodge; copywright 1986 by Southwest Parks and Monuments Association.

Verde River Recreation Guide by Jim Slingluff; Golden West Publishers.

Interviews with: Joan Duke, *chief librarian, Sedona Public Library;* John Parsons, *Verde Valley eco-historian;* Warren Cremer, *co-owner of Time Expeditions;* Peter Pilles, *Forest Archeologist, Coconino National Forest;* Robert Gilles, *chief ranger, Sedona District, Coconino National Forest;* Dr. James Byrkit *on the faculty of Northern Arizona U. at Flagstaff.*

Chapter Two

AL SIEBER, Chief of Scouts by Dan L. Thrapp, University of Oklahoma Press, 1964

NORTHEASTERN AND WESTERN YAVAPAI by E. W. Gifford, U. of California Publications in American Archaeology and Ethnology, 1936, Vol. 34

THE YAVAPAI OF FORT MCDOWELL, U.S.Department of Housing and Urban Development, Sigrid Khera, editor, Washington, D.C. 1978

JOURNAL OF AMERICAN FOLKLORE, Northeastern and Western Yavapai Myths by E.W. Gifford, Vol. 36, 1933

VERDE TO SAN CARLOS by William Corbusier, Dale Stuart King, Publisher 1968

RED MAN'S AMERICA by Ruth M. Underhill, U. of Chicago Press, Chicago and London, 1953, 1971

CARLOS MONTEZUMA AND THE CHANGING WORLD OF THE AMERICAN INDIANS by Peter Iverson, U. of New Mexico Press, Albuquerque, 1982

HISTORICAL ATLAS OF ARIZONA by H.P. Walker and Don Bufkin, U. of Oklahoma Press, Norman and London, 1979, 1986

YAVAPAI INDIAN HISTORIC CALENDAR, Yavapai-Prescott Indian Tribe, Prescott, Arizona 1990

1877: ARIZONA AS IT WAS by Hiram C. Hodge, The Rio Grande Press 1877, 1965

ARIZONA CHARACTERS by Frank C. Lockwood, Los Angeles Times-Mirror Press, 1928, Pioneer letters on file at the Fort Verde Museum

ARIZONA REPUBLIC, "Massacre Of 'Apaches' Recalled By Yavapais" by James E. Cook, Tuesday, December 29, 1987

ARIZONA REPUBLIC, History From The Other Side, "White Historians Say Apaches Died In Skeleton Cave, But Yavapais Heard It Differently." by James E. Cook, 1970

THE PHOTOHISTORIC PERIOD IN THE NORTH AMERICAN SOUTHWEST, A D 1450 - 1700, A review of Yavapai Archaeology by Peter J. Pillis, Jr., Arizona State University, Anthropological Research Papers No. 24, 1981

THE SOCIAL ORGANIZATION OF THE WESTERN APACHE by Grenville Goodwin, U. of Arizona Press, Tucson, Arizona

PIONEER STORIES OF THE VERDE VALLEY, As told by themselves and compiled by the book committee, The Verde Valley pioneer's Association, 1954

YAVAPAI PRESCOTT INDIAN TRIBE, brochure, Yavapai-Prescott Indian Tribe, 1989

VIOLA JIMULLA: INDIAN CHIEFTESS by Franklin Barnett, Yavapai-Prescott Tribe, Prescott, AZ. 1965

ARIZONA HIGHWAYS, "The Man Who Captured Geronimo" The Story of John P. Clum by Bernard L. Fontana, September 1990

ARIZONA: A CAVALCADE OF HISTORY, Marshall Trimble, Treasure Chest Publications, Tucson Arizona 1989

THE PEOPLE OF THE VERDE VALLEY, Plateau Magazine, Vol. 53, No. 1, Museum of Northern Arizona

THE SMOKE SIGNAL, Fort Whipple in the Days of the

Empire by Andrew Wallace, Published by the Tucson Corral of the Westerners, Fall 1972

THE SMOKE SIGNAL, Camp Date Creek, Arizona Territory, Infantry Outpost in the Yavapai Wars 1867 -1873 by Sidney B. Brinckerhoff, Fall 1964, 1978

KING S WOOLSEY by John S. Goff, Black Mountain Press, Cave Creek, AZ. 1981

INTERVIEWS

David Sine - Yavapai-Apache, Camp Verde, AZ, 1989 - 90

Mabel Dogka, Yavapai-Apache, Kachina Point Nursing Home - Village of Oak Creek, Sedona, AZ. 1990

Louis Hood, Bernie Boyd, Sniffen Dickens, Fort McDowell Indian Reservation, Fountain Hills, AZ. 1990

The Elders of the Tribe, Yavapai-Apache Reservation, Clarkdale, AZ. 1989, 1990

Nancy Quaid, Yavapai-Prescott Tribe, Prescott, AZ. 1990

Vincent Randall, Tonto Apache historian and educator, Clarkdale, AZ. 1990

Chapter Three

ON THE BORDER WITH CROOK by John G. Bourke, U. of Nebraska Press, Lincoln and London 1891, 1976

FORTY MILES A DAY ON BEANS AND HAY by Don Rickey, Jr. U. of Oklahoma Press 1963, 1972

DEATH IN THE DESERT by Paul Wellman, U. of Nebraska Press, Lincoln and London 1935

FORT VERDE STATE PARK LIBRARY AND MUSEUM GENERAL CROOK IN INDIAN COUNTRY by John G. Bourke, The Filer Press, Colorado, 1891

BOARD OF ENGAGEMENTS WITH HOSTILE INDIANS 1868 - 1882, Washington Government Printing Office

SCOUT WITH BUFFALO SOLDIERS by Frederic Remington, The Filer Press, Colorado 1974

FIGHTING INDIANS OF THE WEST by Dee Brown with Martin Schmitt, Ballantine Books, New York, 1975

ARIZONA ADVENTURES by Marshall Trimble, Golden West Publishers, 1982

THE INDIAN WARS OF THE WEST by Paul Wellman, Double-day & Co., Inc. N.Y., 1934, 1947

THE TROOPERS by S.E. Whitman, Hasting House Publishers, N.Y. 1963

INDIAN WARS OF THE U.S. ARMY by Fairfax Downey Doubleday & Co., Inc. N.Y., 1963

FOLLOWING THE INDIAN WARS by Oliver Knight, U. of Okalahoma Press, Norman 1960

CAMPAIGNING WITH CROOK by Capt. Charles King, U. of Oklahoma Press, Norman 1964

VANISHED ARIZONA by Martha Summerhayes, U. of Nebraska Press, Lincoln and London, 1979

AL SIEBER, CHIEF OF SCOUTS by Dan Thrapp, U. of Oklahoma Press, Norman, 1964

DEPARTMENT OF ARIZONA CAMPAIGN REPORT TO ASSISTENT ADJUTANT GENERAL, Camp Verde, A.T., G.M. Brayton, Capt. 8th Infantry, 1877.

THE PAPERS OF THE ORDER OF INDIAN WARS by John M. Carroll, Old Army Press, Fort Collins, CO. 1975

SCOTTSDALE DAILY PROGRESS, "Cibicue Creek, Apache Battle Site Located," April 30, 1971

THE FIGHT AT CIBICUE, August 30, 1881 by Fred Coxens, Research Papers at Fort Verde State Park

THE TRUTH ABOUT GERONIMO by Britton Davis, Chapter II - "The Fight At Big Dry Wash"

HEADQUARTERS DEPT.OF ARIZONA, Whipple Barracks, Prescott, July 31, 1882, General Orders #37

COUNCIL OF ABANDONED MILITARY POSTS USA, "Battle of Big Dry Wash," Fort Verde State Park

ARIZONA REPUBLIC, "Big Dry Wash Battle Ended Apache Resistence" by James E. Cook, July 16, 1987

THE BATTLE OF CIBICUE AND ITS AFTERMATH, A White Mountain Apache's Account by William Kessel, U. of Arizona Ethnohistory, Spring 1974, Courtesy of Ruth Kessel, Sedona, AZ.

LETTERS OF CPL. CYRUS MILNER, Contributed to Fort Verde State Park Library by Catherine B. Bowen, 1978

Chapter Four

Ellison, Glenn R. "Slim". Cowboys under the Mogollon Rim, Tucson: University of Arizona Press, 1968.

Lightbourn, Til, & Lyons, Mary, By the Banks of Beaver Creek, Indiana: Evangel Press, 1989.

Pare, Madeline Ferrin, Arizona Pageant, Tempe, Arizona Historical Foundation, 1967.

Sedona Westerners, Those Early Days..., Arizona: 1968.

Taylor, Ezekiel B., Reflections of the Past As It Rolled Along, Arizona, 1987.

Verde Valley Pioneers, Pioneer Stories of Arizona's Verde Valley, Arizona, 1954.

Chapter Five

1. Barbarick, Rick, *Untitled Paper,* p. 1.
2. Miller, Ronald Dean, *Shady Ladies of the West.*
3. Trimble, Marshall, *Arizona.*
4. Brown, C.A., *History of Jerome, Arizona.*
5. Barbarick, Rick, *Untitiled Paper,* p. 1.
6. Barbarick, *Untitled Paper,* p. 1.
7. Barbarick, Rick, Interview with Laura Williams, May 8, 1972.
8. Brown, C.A. *History of Jerome, Arizona.*
9. Brown, C.A., *History of Jerome, Arizona.*
10. Smith, Nancy, *Women of the Half-World.*
11. Smith, Nancy, *Women of the Half-World.*

Chapter Six

ARIZONA, A SHORT HISTORY, by Odie B. Faulk

Prison Records from Yuma Territorial Prison

The Department of Library and Archives, Arizona

Arizona State University Library

The Yavapai County Board of Supervisors, Courtesy Ms. ???

Sedona, Arizona Library, courtesy Ms. Joan A.R. Duke, Mr. Gerry Garneau, and Ms. Patricia Stewart

"DYNAMITE AND SIX-SHOOTER," an Historical Report by Mr. Jeff Burton.

Tempe, Arizona Library

Mesa, Arizona Library

The Arizona Republican, various dates

The Copper Era, various dates

The Tombstone Epitaph, various dates

The Prescott Courier, various dates

The Arizona Daily Journal-Miner, various dates

The Daily Arizona Silver Belt, various dates

The Yuma Times, various dates

The Arizona Sentinel, various dates

Chapter Seven

Books:

Butler, Anne M. DAUGHTERS OF JOY, SISTERS OF MERCY: PROSTITUTES IN THE AMERICAN WEST, 1865-90. Urbana, Illinois: University of Illinois Press, 1985.

Dedera, Don. A LITTLE WAR OF OUR OWN. Flagstaff, Arizona: Northland Press, 1988.

Dial, Scott. SALOONS OF DENVER. Fort Collins, Colorado: The Old Army Press, 1973.

Eason, Nicholas J. FORT VERDE: AN ERA OF MEN AND COURAGE.

ECHOES OF THE PAST, VOL. II. Prescott, Arizona: The Yavapai Cowbelles, Inc.

ECHOES OF THE PAST, VOL. I. Prescott, Arizona: The Yavapai Cowbelles, Inc.

Erdoes, Richard. SALOONS OF THE OLD WEST. New York: Alfred A. Knopf, 1979.

Fireman, Bert M. ARIZONA: HISTORIC LAND. New York: Alfred A. Knopf, 1982.

Forrest, Earle R. ARIZONA'S DARK AND BLOODY GROUND. Caldwell, Idaho: the Caxton Printers, 1950.

Miller, Ronald Dean. SHADY LADIES OF THE WEST. Los Angeles: Westernlore Press, 1984.

Murbarger, Nell. GHOSTS OF THE ADOBE WALLS. Tucson, Arizona: Treasure Chest Publications, 1964.

PIONEER STORIES OF ARIZONA'S VERDE VALLEY. The Verde Valley Pioneers Assn., 1964.

THOSE EARLY DAYS. Sedona Westerners, 1975.

Trimble, Marshall. IN OLD ARIZONA. Phoenix, Arizona: Golden West Publishers, 1985.

Trimble, Marshall, ARIZONA. Garden City, New York: Doubleday & Company, 1977.

Walrod, Truman. THE ROLE OF SHERIFF: PAST-PRESENT-FUTURE. Washington, D.C.: National Sheriff's Association.

Willard, Don. AN OLD-TIMER'S SCRAPBOOK, 1984.

Williams, Sally Munds. HISTORY OF VALUABLE PIONEERS OF THE STATE OF ARIZONA.

Young, Herb. GHOSTS OF CLEOPATRA HILL. Jerome, Arizona: Jerome Historical Society, 1964.

NEWSPAPERS IN JEROME HISTORICAL SOCIETY:

ARIZONA REPUBLIC (Old issues)

JEROME MINING NEWS

JEROME TRAVELER, January, 1990

JEROME TRAVELER, June, 1990

TOMBSTONE EPITAPH

VERDE COPPER NEWS

INTERVIEWS:

Becker, Jack, Springerville, Arizona, by telephone, 8-27-90.

Broughton, Vera, at her home in Cottonwood, Arizona, 7-9-90.

Carlock, Bob, by telephone, 7-25-90.

Davisson, Lori, by telephone, 8-18-90.

Davisson, Lori, at the Arizona Historical Society, Tucson, Arizona, 8-22-90.

Dedera, Don, by telephone, 7-25-90.

Dickinson, Florence, by telephone, 7-12-90 and 7-26-90.

Fain, Norman, by telephone, 7-26-90.

Godard, Frank, at his home in Camp Verde, Arizona, 7-28-90.

Goddard, Jess, at his home in Camp Verde, Arizona, 1980.

Hallett, Margaret, by telephone, 7-13-90 and 10-14-90.

Hopkins, Dave, at his home in Camp Verde, Arizona, 7-28-90.

Leyel, Mattie, at Cottonwood, Arizona, November, 1981.

Loy, Sherman, by telephone, 7-8-90.

Martin, Ginger, Springerville Historical Society, by telephone, 8-27-90.

McDonald, Louis and Irene, at their home in Sedona, Arizona, June, 1990.

Munson, Robert, by telephone, 7-13-90.

Roberts, Bill, by telephone, 8-26-90.

Rudd, Eldon, at his home in Scottsdale, Arizona, 7-23-90.

MISCELLANEOUS:

Hawkins, Fred, File, Jerome Historical Society.

Hudgens, Johnny, File, Jerome Historical Society.

Microfilm: JEROME MINING NEWS, Jerome Historical Society.

Microfilm: VERDE COPPER NEWS, Jerome Historical Society.

Munds, Johnny, File, Jerome Historical Society.

Roberts, Jim, File, Jerome Historical Society.

ENDNOTES

1. Young, Herb, GHOSTS OF CLEOPATRA HILL.

2. Roberts File, Jerome Historical Society.

3. Roberts File, Jerome Historical Society.

4. Young, Herb, GHOSTS OF CLEOPATRA HILL.

5. Roberts File, Jerome Historical Society.

6. Trimble, Marshall, ARIZONA.

7. Trimble, Marshall, ARIZONA.

8. Roberts, Bill, THE JEROME TRAVELER, January, 1990.

9. Young, Herb, GHOSTS OF CLEOPATRA HILL.

10. Murbarger, Nell, GHOST OF THE ADOBE WALLS.

11. Young, Herb, GHOSTS OF CLEOPATRA HILL.

12. JEROME MINING NEWS, January 28, 1904.

13. JEROME MINING NEWS, January 28, 1904.

14. Young, Herb, GHOSTS OF CLEOPATRA HILL.

15. COCONINO SUN, Flagstaff, Arizona, July 21, 1918.

16. Young, Herb, Notes, Jerome Historical Society.

17. Hudgens File, Jerome Historical Society.

18. Young, Herb, GHOSTS OF CLEOPATRA HILL.

19. Hudgens, L. (wife of Johnny Hudgens), letter, Hudgens File, Jerome Historical Society.

20. Rudd, Eldon, Interview, July 23, 1990.

21. Rudd, Eldon, Interview, July 23, 1990.

22. Godard, Frank, Interview, July 28, 1990.

23. Hopkins, Dave, Interview, July 28, 1990.

24. Goddard, Jess, THE LION HUNT, a paper.
25. Godard, Frank, Interview, July 28, 1990.
26. Broughton, Vera Cruse, Interview, July 9, 1990.
27. Williams, Sally Munds, HISTORY OF VALUABLE PIONEERS OF THE STATE OF ARIZONA.
28. VERDE COPPER NEWS, July 17, 1918.
29. Walrod, Truman, THE ROLE OF SHERIFF, p. 10.
30. Buchanan, G.C. "Buck," Letter, October 15, 1990.
31. Walrod, Truman, THE ROLE OF SHERIFF, p. 11.

Chapter Eight

1. Barbarick, Rick, UNTITLED PAPER, p. 1
2. Miller, Ronald Dean, SHADY LADIES OF THE WEST
3. Trimble, Marshall, ARIZONA
4. Brown, C.A., HISTORY OF JEROME, ARIZONA
5. Barbarick, Rick, UNTITLED PAPER, p. 1
6. Barbarick, Rick, UNTITLED PAPER, p. 1
7. Barbarick, Rick, Interview with Laura Williams, May 8, 1972
8. Brown, C.A., HISTORY OF JEROME, ARIZONA
9. Brown, C.A., HISTORY OF JEROME, ARIZONA
10. Smith, Nancy, WOMEN OF THE HALF-WORLD
11. Smith, Nancy, WOMEN OF THE HALF-WORLD

Chapter Nine

Brown, Charlie, A HISTORY OF JEROME, Jerome Historical Society

Droubay, Helen, THOSE LIVELY OLD MINING CAMP DAYS, Salt Lake City, unpublished book, 1986

Hackmann, Mark, LIBERTY SILENT MOVIE THEATER, ASU paper

Hernandez, Lily, LOS PIONEROS MEXICANOS, 1990, Jerome Historical Society

Jerome Historical Society Archives & Research Center records, including but not limited to: Archives Document collection, Minty family collection, Gardner family collection, Ellen D. Hopkins collection, Helen Geary Quayle Oral History, Patrick Riordan family collection, Laura Williams Oral History, Herbert V. Young collection

Jerome newspapers: JEROME MINING NEWS, JEROME REPORTER, JEROME SUN, VERDE COPPER NEWS, VERDE DISTRICT SHOPPER

Jerome Town records, City Tax, and Common council minutes

McDonald, Lewis J., THE DEVELOPMENT OF JEROME - AN ARIZONA MINING TOWN, 1941, NAU paper

MINING CONGRESS JOURNAL, April 1930, "Recreation in the Verde District," by Noel Pegues

Shidler, Rosemary DeCamp, WIND 'EM UP, unpublished book

Smith, Nancy R. Personal Collection

Ward, Lois M., EARLY VERDE VALLEY AVIATION..., 1985, Jerome Historical Society

Young, Herbert V. newspaper notes, Jerome Historical Society

HOW TO ORDER

Experience Jerome and the . . . . **$12.95** Retail *$2.00 P & H*
Verde Valley Legends and Legacies

A true history of the Western frontier with chapters on the Yavapai Indians - before and after white contact; General Crook, the Pony Soldiers, Indian Scouts and the Indian Wars; Jerome's mining and social history; the outlaws and lawmen of the Verde Valley; Jerome's 'Ladies of the Night' and the valley's ranching and geological history.

288 pages with approximately 159 illustrations and five historic maps.

Experience Sedona Legends and Legacies . . . . **$8.95** Retail *$1.50 P & H*

An in-depth look at Sedona's early pioneers; how Sedona got its name; how Sedona became an arts community; Joe Beeler and the Cowboy Artists of America; Abe Miller and his creation of Tlaquepaque; Marguerite Staude and The Chapel of the Holy Cross; and a chapter on the Hollywood movies that were filmed in the Sedona area. Recommended reading by Elmer Dills - KABC-TV Channel 7 Eyewitness News - Los Angeles, California.

114 pages with over 100 illustrations and a historic site map. This book is in its second printing.

Experience Sedona Recreational Map . . . . **$4.95** *$1.25 P & H*

Includes 75 hiking trails in the Sedona-Oak Creek Canyon area; information on where to play golf, tennis, horseback ride, fish, off-road vehicle trails, mountain bike trails, special scenic locations for photographers, picnicking, geological and vortex information, where to stay, calendar of events and much more. Recommended by Judith Morgon, travel writer for the LOS ANGELES TIMES and by OFF-ROAD MAGAZINE. This map is now in its fourth printing.

From "THE EXPERIENCE PEOPLE"

Mail request with check
or money order to:

P.O. Box 2371
Sedona, AZ 86336
(602) 282-7508

Ship to: _____

Address: _____

City: _____ State: _____ Zip: _____

Indicate Amount Ordered:

Sedona Book _____   Sedona Map _____   Jerome Book _____

Amount Enclosed $ _____ with postage

There is a 40% discount for orders of 10 or more on all Thorne Enterprise publications.